The
Last
Viceroy

Peter Stursberg

and

Roland Michener

11/4/89

ROLAND MICHENER

The Last Viceroy

PETER STURSBERG

McGraw-Hill Ryerson
Toronto Montreal

ROLAND
MICHENER
The Last Viceroy

First published in 1989 by
McGraw-Hill Ryerson Limited
330 Progress Avenue
Scarborough, Ontario   M1P 2Z5

1 2 3 4 5 6 7 8 9 0 THB 8 7 6 5 4 3 2 1 0 9

CANADIAN CATALOGUING IN PUBLICATION DATA

Stursberg, Peter, date
    Roland Michener: the last viceroy

ISBN 0-07-549871-5

1. Michener, Roland, 1900-   . 2. Canada —
Politics and government — 1957-1963.*   3. Canada —
Politics and government — 1963-   .*
4. Governors general — Canada — Biography.
5. Politicians — Canada — Biography.   I. Title.

FC626.M52S88 1989   971.064'092'4   C89-094888-7
F1034.3.M52S88 1989

Printed and bound in Canada by
T.H. Best Printing Company Limited

❧ CONTENTS ❧

PREFACE *ix*

INTRODUCTION *xiii*

1
THE OXFORD
MEETING 1

2
ROAD TO
RED DEER 12

3
A POLITICAL
UPBRINGING 21

4

THEY

ALSO SERVE   33

5

LAW AND

MARRIAGE   43

6

IN FATHER'S

FOOTSTEPS   53

7

RECONSTRUCTING

ONTARIO   65

8

YEAR OF

TRANSITION   79

9

FRENCH AND THE

FEDERAL SCENE   91

10

T-TO-T,

BACKBENCH MP   103

11

SPEAKER AS

SECOND CHOICE   116

12

SPEAKER AND

PRIME MINISTER   128

13

PASSAGE

TO INDIA   142

14
TWENTIETH
GOVERNOR GENERAL   **156**

15
HOST TO
THE WORLD   **168**

16
EXTENDING THEIR
EXCELLENCIES   **182**

17
GOVERNOR
GENERALITIES   **195**

18
THE LAST
VICEROY   **207**

19
LIFE
AFTER   **219**

INDEX   **232**

❧ PREFACE ❧

I GOT TO KNOW the Right Honourable Roland Michener through that great social sport, tennis. We played at the Rockcliffe Tennis Club in Ottawa when he was Speaker of the House of Commons. In 1966 I visited India, where he was the Canadian High Commissioner, and we had a few games on a couple of occasions at the Delhi Gymkhana Club. I told him then that, before coming out, I had said in a broadcast that he was going to be the next Governor General. It was not meant as a question, but my remark drew no response whatsoever, not even a raised eyebrow.

One of Michener's first acts at Rideau Hall was to have the two lower courts resurfaced, the small clubhouse repainted, and a new refrigerator installed; these courts were across from the conservatory and the gardens and above the cricket grounds. The Governor General included me in the group that played there on weekends. Just before leaving Government House, Roly Michener presented us, the regular players, with badges in the royal colours of purple and gold, a crown above crossed tennis racquets, and underneath the letters, RHTSS, standing for "Rideau Hall Tennis and Shandy Society" — shandy (beer and ginger beer) being the very British beverage served by a footman in the clubhouse after two hours of doubles.

Although this biography has been done with Mr. Michener's co-operation and assistance — all his papers and records were made available to me — it is not an authorized work, which he did not want, and I have sought the views of his associates in business and in politics, of his supporters and critics, although the latter were difficult to find. I talked to the Right Honourable Pierre Trudeau, who was prime minister during most of Mr. Michener's term as Governor General; Honourable Mitchell Sharp, the External Affairs Minister at the time; Gordon Robertson, Clerk of the Privy Council; Dr. Eugene Forsey, the constitutional expert; Honourable Howard Green, the Diefenbaker Minister; Robert N. Thompson, former MP and Socred leader; Dr. Norman Keevil, the mining tycoon; E.W.S. Ted Kane and Howard T. Emery, boyhood friends; and Diana and Roy Schatz, his daughter and son-in-law.

I also recorded interviews with the following: Geoffrey Pearson, diplomat and son of Prime Minister Pearson; E.B. Ted Jolliffe, former member of the Lang Michener firm and CCF leader in Ontario; Robert A. Cranston, senior partner, Lang Michener; John W. Holmes, authority on international affairs; Erik Spicer, Parliamentary Librarian; Honourable Alvin Hamilton, Diefenbaker Minister; Honourable Paul Martin, External Affairs Minister; G.G.E. Ernie Steele, Under Secretary of State; Esmond Butler, secretary of Government House; Colonel (Naval Captain) Don McKinnon, comptroller of Government House; and R. H. Bob Hubbard, historian of Rideau Hall. The tapes and transcripts of these interviews, which varied in length from less than an hour to two or more hours, are in the National Archives in Ottawa and in the Simon Fraser University Archives in British Columbia.

My oral history material includes about thirty hours of interviews that I had with Roland Michener; some years ago I recorded his memoirs for the Joint Oral History Project of the Public Archives and the Parliamentary Library: there were four sessions lasting more than eight hours. However, I had interviewed him first for my books on Diefenbaker and Pearson, and, in a way, this biography concludes my oral or living history of the tenth decade of Confederation, which was such a fecund political period. These earlier interviews provided a framework for the book, and the further interviews filled in the gaps and made it a whole. (Copies of these tapes and transcripts are also in the sfu Archives.) I should also like to acknowledge my debt to interviews that Mr. Michener had with others on various aspects of his life, especially Professor Peter N. Oliver's interview on his early career in politics and with the Drew administration in Ontario; the interview by two House of Commons clerks, Charles Robert and Garnet Barlow, on his role as Speaker; and Sam Austman's interview, on behalf of Professor S. W. Jackman, on his term as Governor General.

Then there were his papers, his correspondance, the texts of his many speeches, the files and binders that filled several shelves in his Toronto home. First and foremost is the moving and vivid family history written by Roland's mother, Mary Edith Roland Michener, which was valuable source material for the early days in Alberta. I was aided greatly by David Raymont's research and his detailed account of Roland Michener's contribution to the Conservative Party from 1935 to 1957, as well as Raymont's summary of the political career of Roland's father, Senator Edward Michener. I want to thank Robert Marleau, the Clerk of the House of Commons, for letting me have Mr. Speaker Michener's most significant rulings as compiled by the Table Research Branch.

The bibliography included the autobiographies of John Diefenbaker, *One Canada* (three volumes), and L. B. Pearson, *Mike* (three volumes), as well as *The Power and the Tories* by Jonathan Manthorpe, *Maritain on the Nature of Man in a Christian Democracy* by Norah Michener, *Pipeline* by William Kilbourn, *Speakers of the House of Commons* by Gary Levy, *Memorandum for the Wives of Members of the Senate and the House of Commons* by Norah Michener, *Succession in India* by Michael Brecher, *Rideau Hall* by R. H. Hubbard, and *The Canadian Crown* by Jacques Monet. There were interesting references to Mr. Speaker Michener in *Renegade in Power* by Peter Newman, *Vision and Indecision* by Patrick Nicholson, *This Game of Politics* by Pierre Sevigny, and to Roland and Norah in Judy La Marsh's *Memoirs of a Bird in a Guilded Cage*. Mr. Michener wrote an introduction to Ellen Pettigrew's *Silent Enemy*, an account of the deadly 1918 flu epidemic in Canada.

Once again, I want to express my gratitude to Betty Jane Corson, whose publishing counsel and editing skill made this book possible, and I should also like to thank my wife, Jessamy, for her patience and support.

Peter Stursberg

❧ INTRODUCTION ❧

THE LIFE AND TIMES of Roland Michener match those of the twentieth century. He was born on April 19, 1900, at Lacombe in what was to become Alberta but was then the North West Territories. It was the last year of Queen Victoria's long reign but not the end of the Victorian era. Canada was proud to be part of the British Empire; "We hold a vaster empire than has been," a Canadian stamp of the period proclaimed — an empire that was more than a match for the overbearing republic to the south; Sir Wilfrid Laurier was prime minister and was as much a British subject as everyone else in the Dominion. Canadians were fighting in the Boer War — and, in Red Deer, Alberta, where Roland grew up, a hospital was built as a memorial to the three local soldier boys who were killed in that colonial war. Yet the winds of change were evident in the smoke billowing from the railway engines, the iron horses that were hauling thousands upon thousands of settlers to the prairies; the big empty land was beginning to fill up.

In 1911 Laurier and the Liberals were defeated over the issue of reciprocity, or free trade, with the United States; they were accused of disloyalty to the British by the Conservatives. Sir Robert Borden became prime minister, and eleven-year-old Roland remembered the rejoicing over the Tory triumph that took place at home in Red Deer. In 1917 Borden named Roland's father, Edward Michener, who was the Conservative leader in Alberta, to the Senate. When he was eighteen, Roland joined the Royal Air Force, but the Great War was almost over and he never got overseas, never even got to fly a plane. Not achieving his ambition to be a fighter pilot was his only early disappointment.

Two years later he went to Oxford University, thereby realizing another ambition: he had won the Rhodes scholarship for Alberta, only the second to be given since the war. The early twenties were a poignant time at Oxford. In the afterglow of the British Empire and the old imperialist world, it was as if the war had never happened, and the years he spent as a Rhodes Scholar shaped his life: it was an experience the young Roland Michener would never forget. Moreover, it was at Oxford that he met Mike Pearson and formed the friendship that would mean so much for him in the years to come.

Roland and Mike, or "Mitch and Mike" as they were known, were the prototype of the clean-cut Canadian youth of their day: both were handsome — Mitch with his curly blond hair, Mike with his boyish good looks, appearing younger than his friend, although he was three years older. Both loved sports and were athletic, but they were also serious students. Both came from the same nonconformist Protestant background, both were confident and carefree and, at the same time, conventional and the soul of propriety. In the twenties, it was a status symbol for well-to-do Canadian families to make a tour of Europe, and Mitch and Mike, as members of the unbeatable Oxford ice hockey team, visited Switzerland, Belgium, and France during the long winter holidays and spent a summer vacation in Germany. And like the Canadian families, they were tourists.

Neither of them spoke any language but English, and neither of them was concerned about this. Mitch did think that he should take advantage of being in Germany to learn German, so he hired a teacher, but Mike did not bother. Although he had taken German at college in Canada, he could not speak a word of it (he had done so, as he said in his memoirs, because he had to take a language and figured that German would be the easiest), and, in any case, he found that he did not need German or any other foreign language for sports, even team sports. Mitch and Mike were by no means bigots, although there was religious bigotry at the time they grew up and French was associated with Roman Catholics; they were enlightened, intelligent young men, but they were blissfully unaware of the importance of French in Canada, as were most other English Canadian students of their age.

It was not till thirty years later that they began to realize the error of their ways and, then, as so often happens, they went to the opposite extreme of asserting that French and English were equally important and were the official languages of the country. In this, there was an element of guilty conscience. Roland Michener felt uncomfortable that he could not speak French, especially since his wife Norah was fluently bilingual, and so in the 1950s he began immersion courses in the language. As a leading diplomat, Mike Pearson was embarrassed and almost ashamed that he knew no French, which was a language of diplomacy and of Canada, and when he became a politician, he eagerly accepted the advice of his Quebec colleagues that bilingualism was the answer to the country's woes.

As Canadian High Commissioner in New Delhi, Michener found that language could be as divisive an issue as any. In India it was the main problem: poverty, the caste system, and religious intolerance could be overcome, but there was no changing the fourteen major language groups. When he was there in 1965, the decision to replace English, which the Raj had left behind as the national language, with Hindi brought about language riots in which hundreds were killed; the non-Hindi speaking peoples of the south felt threatened, and the government of India had to back down and leave English as the country's lingua franca.

Although Roland Michener was a man of the twentieth century, his career was very little affected by the great events that occurred during that time. He was a married man with a family and was too old for the Second World War, just as he had been too young for the First World War. As an up-and-coming young lawyer in Toronto, he never really experienced the hard times of the Great Depression. There were, of course, setbacks, but with persistence and determination he overcame them. He could be said to have a charmed life, and one newspaper described him "as always one of fortune's favourites."

Michener was elected Speaker of the House of Commons in 1957 and was appointed Governor General of Canada in 1967. Thus, the two great offices that he held spanned what became known as the Tenth Decade of Confederation, which was an extraordinary period in Canadian history, a time of great celebration and change, encompassing, as it did, the Centennial. The decade — a term used loosely since it extended as far as the early 1970s — was also marked by political and social upheavals and terrorist violence in Quebec, culminating in the kidnapping and murder of the provincial minister Pierre La Porte and the proclamation of the authoritarian War Measures Act.

It was a time of youthful assertion and extravagance, when members of the postwar baby boom came of age, of the so-called Woodstock generation, of unwashed hippies dressed in unkempt clothes, of "flower power" and "love-ins," of social and political protest, of the Beatles, of rock musicals and *Jesus Christ Superstar*. The political role model was Jack Kennedy, whether he was alive or dead, the youngest president of the United States. Leaders had to be young; no one would vote for the old: it was an argument that was used to dump John Diefenbaker, who had turned seventy. Politicians fudged their age and dyed their hair, and Pierre Elliott Trudeau, the aspirant for the Liberal leadership, was found to be two years older than he was reported to be.

However, it was not just long hair and a laid-back communal lifestyle. There were the drug scenes and the student revolts in the universities and colleges, particularly at the Berkeley Campus of the University of California, Simon Fraser University in British Columbia, and Sir George Williams University in Montreal, where the computer centre was destroyed, and the love-in, or live-in, at Rochdale College in Toronto. An anti-Vietnam War riot in Chicago destroyed the Democrats' hopes of winning the 1968 election. The student revolt in Paris reached the proportions of an uprising against the government of President De Gaulle and led to a massive rightist counter-demonstration that spelled the beginning of the end of the hippie movement.

All of these happenings had their effect on the manners and mores of the nation as a whole. Even older men, including some of the country's leaders, aped the hippies with their long hair and beards — but not Roland Michener: as Governor General he insisted on proper attire for formal functions when members of elitist groups and the artistic and academic community were parading around in faded jeans and sandals. The subculture or counterculture of the beat generation with its underground newspapers had an influence on the public media and the general literature of the times; it released them from sexual inhibitions and allowed for greater freedom of expression, but Michener was disgusted to find that he had to present prizes for experimental prose that consisted of cards in a box and poetry that was little more than a string of obscenities.

The Centennial was a proud occasion for Canada, and during the year Roland Michener was host to scores of visiting world leaders. There was Expo 67, which was a magnificent showcase for the country. It was a joyful time when the separatist threat in Quebec was quietly subdued, and Canadians, from coast to coast, celebrated with the greatest enthusiasm the hundredth anniversary of Confederation.

Canada had come a long way since the colonial days of the nineteenth century and was counted as one of the leading industrial nations of the world; it was a fully independent country with paramount power exercised by Parliament, but there was one anomalous position: the head of state. The Governor General was the *pro-tem* head of state when Queen Elizabeth was not in Canada, which was most of the time, but Her Majesty was the head of state *de jure*, although she was not always recognized as such abroad. She was the Queen of England or the Queen of Britain when she travelled, not the Queen of Canada.

That was the constitutional dilemma, and in 1967, with the Centennial and Canada coming of age, so to speak, there was increased pressure to have it resolved. Prime Minister Trudeau brought in a bill to amend the constitution; he wanted the Governor General to assume more and more of the prerogatives of the Queen, but, aside from his being denounced by the monarchists, he ran into the opposition of his own External Affairs Minister Mitchell Sharp and the Ottawa bureaucrats. There were those who clamoured for a president and others who were vehemently opposed to any change whatsoever. Such were the contending forces, and Roland Michener, a traditionalist and a royalist, was caught in the middle. Yet he made the first official visits to foreign countries as Canadian head of state and was received with full honours. He did a lot to expand the role of the Governor General while at the same time remaining a loyal and true represenative of the Crown.

❧ 1 ❧

THE OXFORD
MEETING

To DANIEL ROLAND MICHENER, the young Rhodes Scholar from Red Deer, Alberta, Oxford was all that he had ever dreamed of or expected: the shining city of culture and civilization. The First World War was over but, in the euphoria of the times, Britannia still ruled the waves, and the British Empire had grown even larger and bestrode the Mercator projection so that fully half of it was coloured red. It might have been the last days of the Raj—although the Cassandras were derided or ignored—but the undergraduates in their college blazers and flapping, wide-bottomed flannel trousers, the "Oxford Bags," could expect to become viceroys or governors, ambassadors extraordinary or ministers plenipotentiary, if they were not sent down. Even if they were expelled, the cachet of the university was such that they would get lesser jobs ruling the lesser breeds in the colonial services or in the armed forces or in the paramilitary police.

Most of the students were callow youths from upper-class and aristocratic families who had just been relieved of the restraints and

discipline of Eton and Harrow and other elitist British schools; but
there was a leavening of older men, the survivors of the slaughter in
France and Flanders. Female students at such segregated colleges as
Lady Margaret Hall and St. Hilda's were not in the main stream of
Oxford undergraduate life, not in the 1920s.

One of the veterans was Lester Bowles Pearson, already
known as "Mike," the name given him by the recruiting officer when
he joined the Royal Flying Corps. He came to Oxford in 1921, the
year after Roland Michener, who could also be called a veteran since
he had joined the RAF in the last year of the war. However, Michener
had not gone overseas, and, aside from drilling and doing fatigues,
he had had the grim task of removing, from the base military hospital in Toronto, the dead, many of them his fellow cadets, victims of
the postwar Spanish flu epidemic. The toll during one day in
October was as many as twelve, Roland recalled.* He was three years
younger than Mike, but older than the average British public school-
boy undergraduate.

At the time, Canada and the other dominions, while self-
governing, were not fully independent and were still considered to be
colonies by the supremacists in Westminster. Furthermore, the young
Michener, although he was the scion of a distinguished Empire
Loyalist family, came from a pioneer part of the country—Alberta had
achieved provincial status only some fifteen years before — and his
alma mater, the University of Alberta, was no older, having been
founded in 1906. However, the brick buildings on the Edmonton
campus, where he studied and got his BA, were of a pleasing classical
design, but could not be compared with all the Gothic and Renais-
sance splendour of the Oxford colleges. Yet he was sophisticated
enough to steer a middle course between the opposite extremes of
Canadian behaviour at the university. At one end were those who
were more British than the British and wore the widest Oxford Bags,
twenty-six inches wide, and adopted a ripe English accent, while at
the other end were those who were suspicious and resentful of the
British and found their milieu among the Americans.

Michener enjoyed Hertford College, which was not Balliol or
Merton or All Souls, since it was one of the newest foundations (it

---

*It is estimated that between thirty thousand and fifty thousand Canadians died in
1918–19 from the flu epidemic. This compared with nearly sixty thousand killed in the
First World War. The worst hit were the native people: at Okak in Labrador only fifty-
nine survived out of a population of two hundred and sixty-six; in Hebron, seventy out
of a community of two hundred and twenty.

was refounded in 1874, since Hertford claimed descent from a small teaching hall). Nevertheless, it had its own peculiar customs and etiquettes, including the occasional club dinners in the senior club room, when everyone had to wear white tie and tails and a tremendous meal with wines and toasts was served. As Michener put it, "It was just a rag, a good time." But while these formalities appealed to him, he missed the easy camaraderie he had known back home. So he joined other Canadians and students from the other dominions in a group called, half in jest, the Colonial Club; its meetings were held in the Cadina Tea Rooms, which was town and not gown, since it was away from the colleges on Cornmarket Street.

"This was a welcome relief for the men from Canada who found the English a little slow to respond," Michener recalled, although, he said, "they [the English students] became good friends in time. We were all a little puzzled by the Englishmen," he went on, "their reserve and sort of indifference to such important people as Rhodes Scholars." The "secret agony" of the present-day Rhodes Scholars, according to a recent report in the press, was due partly to modesty and partly to the fact that certain British undergraduates resented their money and disdained them intellectually. However, Michener did not notice this when he was at Oxford, although he admitted that the "Scholars" at the university looked down on all Commoners, whether they were English or Colonial. The Rhodes Scholars and all who had won foreign scholarships, such as Pearson, who had a Massey Foundation Fellowship, were not recognized as Scholars at Oxford; they were lumped together with the Commoners and sat at their tables in the dining halls; whereas the Scholars, who had won Oxford scholarships, had their own tables, wore their own academic gowns, and relished their distinction.

It was at the Colonial Club that Michener and Pearson first met, and they took to each other immediately. In retrospect, Michener wondered whether it wasn't because they had similar backgrounds, that they were both sons of the manse: it was true that when Roland was born, his father was a Methodist parson, but the elder Michener had given up the ministry a year later and was a Senator when his son became a Rhodes Scholar, whereas Mike's father's life's work was with the church. Yet they did have similar backgrounds: they were from the same Protestant class of British ancestry that had built and ruled Canada and never thought of the country as anything but an English-speaking part of an English-speaking empire on which the sun never set.

Then, the young Roland Michener might have found Mike
Pearson to be the older brother he never had. He remembered him, in
those early days, as "a very delightful companion, informal, approach-
able, not aged by his war experience, sort of carefree, very sociable
and very intelligent, and interested both in his studies — although he
didn't talk much about them, he got a good degree — and other pur-
suits of the undergraduates of an intellectual kind, and, of course, very
much interested in sport." From then on, it was Mike and "Mitch," as
it was usually misspelled.

After the first meeting amid the familiar accents of the Colonial Club, in the cosy if plebian confines of the Cadina Tea Rooms,
they began to exchange visits between their colleges. Pearson was at a
much older college, St. John's (1555), where he was a member of the
venerable and famous Archery Club. Michener would be invited to
meetings of the club which always began with butts being set up in
the college's splendid walled gardens for an archery contest. However, the Archery Club, which might have been organized originally
to improve the students' skills in the use of bows and arrows, had,
with time and the advent of gunpowder, become a serious-minded
club where speeches were made and debates held in the convivial atmosphere of a dinner. In order to distinguish itself from the Raleigh
and so many other Oxford clubs, it opened its meetings with the ves-
tigial archery contest.

During the course of his visits to St. John's College, Mitch met
some of Mike's friends, and more than half a century later he could
remember them: Robert Graves, the poet and author of *I Claudius*;
Malcolm MacDonald, son of Ramsay MacDonald, who was to be British High Commissioner in Ottawa during much of the Second World
War; and Richard "Dick" Law, son of Bonar Law, the Canadian-born
wartime leader who served briefly as prime minister of Britain in
1922–23. Pearson made friends easily and his outgoing nature seemed
to melt British reserve.

"Another friend of his was old Sir William Holdsworth,"
Michener recalled. "He was professor of English law and a very
famous historian—he wrote a compendious history of English law. I
took tutorials with him for one term in the law of equity. He had
rooms in [St. John's] college. He was a bachelor and a good sport. His
friends who got locked out inadvertently could either climb the wall
of the college gardens, which was very hazardous as it was studded
with broken glass, or they could rap on Holdsworth's bedroom win-

dow and he would get up and let them in by his private door. So they'd get back into their beds and not be reported as absent, which was a rather serious offence."

The midnight curfew applied to all (male) colleges and was quite rigid. A minute after, even a few seconds after, and the student found himself locked out. The Canadians, who had been used to coming in whenever they saw fit at their universities, found the curfew oppressive and demeaning: it was, they said, "being treated like children." Mike and Mitch tried to keep to the rules; occasionally they did go to a dance in town, which was strictly out of bounds, but made sure of being back in good time. However, they did not escape the proctors, who would politely inquire, "Excuse me, sir, are you a member of this university?" If they tried to run — and the proctors could be easily recognized as they wore mortar boards — the bullers, who wore bowler hats and always accompanied the proctors, would give chase. Michener, who had an eye for the girls and liked to dance, was caught or "progged" four or five times; he was fined five shillings for each misdemeanor.

Once they were invited to a dance at one of the ladies' colleges. "It was such a dull affair we never went again," Michener said. "It began at seven-thirty and we had to leave at ten-thirty, and there was the watchful eye of the lady dons on you all the time. The poor women [students] in those days were guarded like the crown jewels. But today, Oxford has changed. There are women residents at my college and at Brasenose and other colleges. I suppose it's become, what do you call it, co-educational." (Since 1977 women have been considered for Rhodes scholarships and in 1986 five of Canada's eleven Rhodes Scholars were women.)

There was one time that Roland Michener did break the midnight curfew. He was taking jurisprudence at Oxford but was nevertheless registered as a law student at the Middle Temple in London, and he had to go there for three dinners a semester in order to qualify to write his exams. It was a process known as "eating dinners." He was given permission by the dean in charge of discipline at Hertford College, C.R.M.F. Cruttwell, a well-known historian, to go to London from Thursday to Saturday. Of course, Michener was delighted to be able to get away like that, but on one occasion it didn't suit him, as he put it, to go on Thursday; so he went on Friday and was away Friday night and Saturday night instead of Thursday night and Friday night. The scout—the manservant who looked after the students on his stair-

case — reported that Michener's bed had not been slept in on Saturday night. The following Monday morning the Rhodes Scholar was
called before the dean.

"Michener," Dean Cruttwell said, "you know, you Canadians
are an undisciplined lot. You set a bad example. We have these boys
fresh from the British public schools, where they have been disciplined and their lives regulated, and we can't leave them free to do as
they want. These rules are made to be obeyed. Now, you know this is
a serious matter. I could send you down for this. But, taking everything into consideration, I'll fine you five shillings. Don't do it again."

Although Hertford College was a modern building compared
to most of the other colleges in Oxford, it did not have central heating.
Roland's quarters (he had a bedroom as well as a living room) were
warmed by a single, small fireplace. The Canadians and Americans
found their accommodations to be freezing cold in winter, but their
blood soon thickened, as Michener said. His day was spent in attending two lectures in the morning and rowing or reading in his rooms
or in the library in the afternoon. Gowns were worn for dinner in the
great hall of Hertford College* and service club pranks were played.

"You could be sconced," Mitch said, "if you broke a rule such
as mentioning a lady's name, or quoting two or three words of a foreign language." The sconce was a two-handled silver mug holding
three quarts, and anyone found guilty of breaking a rule had to
pay for it to be filled with beer and then attempt to drink it down
without pausing; otherwise the sconce would be passed around
the assembled company.

It was ice hockey that really cemented the friendship of Roland
Michener and Mike Pearson. They were both on the Oxford University team, which was made up of Canadians, except for the American
captain, Mac Bacon, the former captain of the Harvard University
team. Others on the seven-man squad were Richard "Dick" Bonnycastle, who was to be named chairman of the Metropolitan Winnipeg
Council; E.B. Pitblado, another veteran who became a prominent
lawyer in Winnipeg; Ronnie McCaul of the Drummond McCaul family in Montreal; and Jack Farthing, the son of the Anglican Bishop of
Quebec. Mike played defence; he was a good stickhandler and would

---

*Charles Comfort's portrait of Roland as Governor General hangs in the great hall of
Hertford College with the paintings of famous dons and alumni such as the author,
Evelyn Waugh. Michener is an honourary fellow of the college and a vice-president
of the Hertford Society.

swerve back and forth across the rink, so that the Swiss sports writers called him "Herr Zig Zag." Mitch played left wing or "rover," the seventh man.

There were the team's wonderful ice hockey junkets during the long Christmas holidays, which culminated in a match against Cambridge in a swank Swiss winter resort. The Cambridge team was also made up of Canadians except for the goalkeeper, who was an Englishman. "I remember he couldn't skate," Michener said, "and when he got far out of the goal we had to stop the game and get him back in again. However, that wasn't a measure of the kind of hockey we played. It was pretty good intermediate hockey, at the level of university play [back home], because we'd all been on [Canadian or American] university teams."

On their way to Switzerland during the Christmas holidays of 1921, the first year that Michener and Pearson were on the Oxford University team, they stopped in Brussels to play the Belgian Olympic team (1920 Olympic Games). Although they had had no practice together, except for a team selection exercise in Manchester, on the only rink that they could find in England, they beat the Belgian team 6–0. Then they travelled to Murren in Switzerland for the Oxford–Cambridge match, but it turned out to be a very one-sided affair. "Mike says, in his book [Pearson *Memoirs*, Volume 1] that we beat Cambridge 27–0, but my recollection," Michener said, "is that it was more than that."

As a result, the Oxford University ice hockey team got the reputation in Europe of being world champions. They were ready to take on all comers, mostly Swiss teams, and they had no trouble winning. It was the winter season in Switzerland, and the hotels found that the Canadian hockey players were an attraction for their guests, so they were invited to stay on after the Oxford–Cambridge match was over. Actually, that year, there were two Oxford ice hockey teams, an A team and a B team, and when there were no opponents, the A team would play the B team, and often these were the best games. The students had a wonderful time: they spent three weeks living in luxury in the best hotels; they were lavishly entertained by the guests and were "the darlings of the girls from the finishing schools," and all they had to do was to play hockey on the resorts' outdoor rinks.

"We spent one Christmas in St. Moritz," Michener recalled. "We had a great party in Davos, a New Year's Eve party, which almost got us into trouble. You see, one of the Canadians dressed himself up as a girl and went to the ball; he was so convincing and was so beautiful that he attracted the attention of a French officer, who pursued him all through the dance until midnight when this fellow took off his wig. The Frenchman was so annoyed, so angry, and so humiliated that his judgment of women had been led so far astray, that he was ready to fight."

In the summer of 1922 Roland Michener, Mike Pearson and Dick Bonnycastle spent six weeks in Germany, mostly in Heidelberg, living very cheaply in a pension. They were supposed to be continuing their studies while on vacation, reading jurisprudence, as Michener did, or history and economics in Pearson's case since he was taking Modern Greats at Oxford; but that did not stop them enjoying themselves and going sightseeing. They took a tour of Wurttemberg, Nuremberg, and Munich; they sat through eight hours of the Passion Play at Oberammergau, which they found interesting if exhausting. Besides playing tennis on Heidelberg's public courts and swimming in the fast-flowing Neckar River, they went for long walks through the vineyards and woods of the hilly countryside.

However, this was not enough exercise for Pearson, who joined the local rugby football club; his lack of any German did not seem to be a hindrance because he was picked to play for the Heidelberg town team. He had played English rugby at Oxford, and while he was "given a varsity trial at fullback," he did not make the university fifteen, but was on his college team. He was also involved in lacrosse and was on a combined Oxford–Cambridge team that toured the United States in the Easter holidays of 1922. They played, "as was the custom in England," Pearson recalled in his memoirs, "without pads or protection against squads of well-trained hardhitting, heavily protected American athletes." It was so rough that their goalkeeper, Sherwood Lett, who was to become Chief Justice of British Columbia, got a fractured skull from a crack on the head. However, they returned to Britain, cheerful and triumphant, battered and bruised, having won most of their matches.

Michener admitted that he could not keep up with Pearson in sports; the only team on which they both played was the ice hockey team, although Michener went in for rowing, the most famous of the major sports at Oxford, while Pearson did not. "As an oarsman," Pearson said in his memoirs, "you could do little or nothing else in sports and I like variety." Michener found this to be only too true; he went rowing four times a week but he became "captain of boats" at

Hertford and, in the early spring of 1923, helped his college eight to five bumps, enough to be awarded a "bump supper." He did not make the Oxford eight that beat Cambridge that year, ending a long series of losses. Despite this, Michener overheard some light blue (Cambridge) supporters from the top of a taxi in Picadilly, boasting, "We don't have to have Rhodes Scholars to win the boat race."

Since ice hockey was regarded as a minor sport at Oxford, Mitch and Mike won only half-blues for playing on the unbeatable university team, but Roland was determined to get a full blue, if only for the "honour of Alberta." He did so by representing Oxford at a 1923 athletic meet with Cambridge in the newly introduced field event, the pole vault. He had had some experience in pole vaulting back home and won the event, clearing ten feet six inches, which was quite a feat in those days — and he reached that height, as he pointed out, with a bamboo pole. Oxford beat Cambridge in that meet by seven events to three, the three being the two sprints and the high hurdles that were all won by one athlete, H.M. Abrahams, later Olympic champion.

As serious students, Michener, Pearson and Bonnycastle did a certain amount of studying while on holiday in Germany, and besides law, Roland Michener took conversational lessons in German. Mike Pearson stuck to his economic and history books; he had no interest in languages at that time, and, in his previous experience in the armed forces and in school in Ontario, he had not met anyone who did not speak English. His ambitions, aside from sports, were in the realm of teaching history or other subjects for which no foreign language would be needed. Michener, on the other hand, had grown up in the West where most of the recent immigrants were from Central and Eastern Europe and many could speak little or no English. He had come to realize this when he was out campaigning with his father, who was the Conservative leader in Alberta before he was made a Senator, and Roland's ambition, even in his school days, was to get into politics, and law was the proper preparation for such a career.

Neither Mike nor Mitch, however, thought much about French, and, if it had been drawn to their attention that French was spoken in Canada by Canadians, they would have said that that was true but it was spoken by farm folk in Quebec, by the backward priest-ridden *habitants* there, and that all of the progressive French Canadians were bilingual and spoke English as well as they themselves did. Both of them would have been bemused and incredulous if they had been told that Canada was a bilingual country like Belgium, or would become one. They would have shaken their heads.

That summer of 1922 was the summer of discontent in Germany. Inflation was raging. When the Canadian students first exchanged money, they got twenty-five hundred marks to the pound sterling; six weeks later, just before they left, they received ten thousand marks to the pound. Soon, it would take a million marks to mail an ordinary letter. "It was rather an unusual opportunity," Michener said, "to live beyond one's means because prices didn't keep pace with the rapid increase in inflation."

So Roland Michener, Mike Pearson, and Dick Bonnycastle, who always met for dinner, could afford to dine at the Staatgarten in Heidelberg, where an orchestra played and a bottle of champagne could cost as little as twenty-five cents. Afterward, they would go to a coffeehouse for coffee and liqueurs. Sometimes they would visit a beer garden or a night club, but none of them had enough German to appreciate the entertainment or really understand what was going on. In that summer of 1922 they could not spend more than ten dollars a week without throwing money away.

They realized that the inflation, while it meant good times for them and others with foreign exchange, was a dreadful ordeal for the German people; in fact, it was doing untold damage to the German state. There was the case of the "ancient fraulein" who taught Roland German; after some years as owner and operator of a tea garden in the Orient, she had retired with what she considered a fortune of forty thousand marks, which was worth ten thousand pounds then, or some fifty thousand dollars. It had certainly seemed enough to look after herself in her old age, but during the past year she had seen it eaten up by inflation until it was worth nothing and she had to earn her own livelihood by teaching.

The Canadian students were sorry for the suffering that inflation caused individuals, especially those they knew, but they were not concerned with its overall effect. If they had been asked what they thought about the situation, they would have shrugged their shoulders and said that it was too bad but that the Germans had brought it on themselves by starting the war. They could not have foreseen that the inflation, by wiping out savings and pensions and reducing those on fixed incomes like the "ancient fraulein" to penury, would help to bring Adolf Hitler and the Nazis to power and inevitably lead to the Second World War.

Both Roland Michener and Mike Pearson returned home in the summer of 1923, and both of them went to Toronto. Michener's father, although a member of the Senate in Ottawa, had rented a house in Toronto while his son was in Oxford, and it was there that the family now lived. Pearson moved into the house that his mother and brother Vaughan had in the suburb of North Rosedale. Michener began to build his law practice, and Pearson became a professor of history at the University of Toronto and resident don at Burwash Hall, Victoria College. The two were able to continue their friendship. They played tennis regularly on the college courts and one year entered the Canadian Open Doubles Championship; after getting a bye into the second round, they were knocked out by a Davis Cup pair.

Mitch and Mike had birthdays within a few days of each other in April, Michener on April 19, 1900, and Pearson on April 23, 1897— and they often celebrated their birthdays together. It was a friendship that survived separation when Pearson joined the new Department of External Affairs in 1928 and moved to Ottawa and even farther away as a diplomat, while Michener remained in Toronto. The friendship also withstood the test of politics when they eventually found themselves on opposite sides of the Canadian Parliament.

Mitch and Mike were a modern-day Damon and Pythias, and while they did not face death as the inseparable friends of classical antiquity did,* they had their own tribulations to cope with. Michener, who became Speaker of the House of Commons in Ottawa, was to fall afoul of his leader and lose his seat in the 1962 federal election, and Pearson, who had himself risen from the ashes of a humiliating defeat to become prime minister in the year after, was to rescue his old friend from civilian life and make him a diplomat, High Commissioner to India, as a first step to having him appointed Governor General of Canada.

---

*Damon and Pythias were Syracusans of the first half of the fourth century BC. Pythias was condemned to death by Dionysius, the tyrant of Syracuse; he obtained leave to arrange his affairs on condition that Damon take his place and be executed should Pythias not return. Pythias was delayed and Damon was led to execution, but his friend arrived just in time to save him. Dionysius was so struck with this honourable friendship that he pardoned both of them.

❧ 2 ❧

ROAD TO
RED DEER

Iᴛ ᴡᴀꜱ, ᴘᴇʀʜᴀᴘꜱ, ᴀɴ ɪʀᴏɴʏ that the ancestors of Roland
Michener, who was to be the twentieth Governor General of Canada
and the representative of the Crown, should have come to the New
World of North America to escape from religious and political perse-
cution. They were Huguenots who were driven out of France by fire
and sword and the crusading zeal of Cardinal Richelieu, and Men-
nonites who fled from the wrath of both the Protestant and the
Catholic establishment in Central Europe, but mostly they were
Quakers. Among these Quakers seeking freedom of religion was John
Michener, the progenitor of all the Micheners in Canada and the
United States. He had been a husbandman, or farmer, on the estate of
the great William Penn in England, although Penn in a letter of introduction described him as his servant or bondsman; his wife Sarah
(Moore), who was also mentioned in the letter, had been a servant in
the household of the founder and first governor of Pennsylvania.

Although John Michener was born in the parish of Ash of
Normandy in Surrey, his Quaker family was probably of Anglo-Saxon

12

origin. *Minchin* is Anglo-Saxon for the "making of pastry or small cakes," and thus it is inferred that, just as *Kitchener* meant a cook in the kitchen, so Michener was a "pastry cook." In Anna Shaddinger's compendious work on the *Micheners in America*, and *More Micheners in America* there are various spellings of the name: Michner, Mitchener, and even Mitchenor.

John Michener did not accompany William Penn when he first set sail for America to claim the land granted him by Charles II; Penn's party of a hundred Friends or Quakers who left Deal with such high hopes on September 1, 1682, suffered grievously during the eight-week voyage, almost a third of them dying from smallpox. It was not until after their marriage in June 1686 that John and Sarah Michener ventured forth and by that time the colony of Pennsylvania was well established as a haven of religious freedom. Its reputation had spread so that many sought refuge there, among them the Mennonites who had come in great numbers and had settled in Germantown.

William Penn had drawn up a most liberal charter or "Frame of Government" for the colony; he dealt fairly with the Indians, always paying them for their property. He had a great city laid out which he named Philadelphia, the City of Brotherly Love. At the time that John Michener and his bride settled there, Philadelphia was not much more than a small country town with some three hundred houses and a population that numbered twenty-five hundred. The following year (1687) the birth of the Micheners' first child, Sarah, was recorded as having been in Phliladelphia, and their first son, William, a direct antecedent of Roland Michener, must have been born there, too, as there is no indication that the Micheners had to move until the early 1700s, and William was born in 1696

As a pioneer farmer in Pennsylvania, John Michener was not very successful and seemed to be constantly in debt. There are reports of the Quaker Monthly Meetings wrestling with his money problems and advising him "to give up what he hath to his creditors." Attempts were made to help him and Friends were asked to subscribe to a fund for the family's welfare. Finally a request was made for a certificate of removal and the Micheners left Philadelphia for Horsham (Township).

There were only eight generations of Micheners from the first arrival in North America to the twentieth Governor General of Canada, which is an indication of how long-lived a family they are. Joseph, Roland's great-grandfather and the first Michener to move to Canada, was ninety-three years old when he died in 1886. They were Pennsylvania country folk and Joseph served as a private in the

U.S. Army in the War of 1812; he came to Niagara around 1818 and settled on a farm near Campden, Lincoln County, Ontario, in 1822. There is a graphic account of travelling in those early days by a William Michener, who came to Canada about the same time as Joseph and would have been a close relative.

> "It is nigh onto seventy-three years sence we sot out [from Pennsylvania] for Canada," [the old man wrote in an article published in 1890, which faithfully reproduced his spelling]. "We travelled 400 miles, my mother and me, with a span of horses and a wagin. Theer w'a't no roads woth mentioning, and when we got to Buffalo the only means to cross the river was a scow manned by four hands. It took twenty-eight days to come here [Niagara Peninsula]. Buffalo w'a'nt of much account then. From Main Street to the lake was a marsh. I can Rec'lect only one store and one tavern, perhaps this was on account of the burning of the houses by the British during the war." *

As Anna Shaddinger's work shows, the Micheners are a large family who have spread out from their Quaker base in Pennsylvania across the United States and Canada and, like other large families who know their past and are proud of their heritage, they have yearly get-togethers. An annual picnic is held in June, at Doylestown, near Philadelphia, where the first Micheners settled and the greatest concentration of the clan still remains. When he was Speaker, Roland Michener went to one of these family reunions and met the famous author, James A. Michener.

Joseph Michener's son, Jacob, Roland's grandfather, married Eliza Catharine Patterson of Smithville; she came from a United Empire Loyalist family who settled in Louth Township near Lake Erie. His grandmother on his mother's side, Anna Margaret Roland, was descended from a prominent UEL officer of Butler's Rangers, Colonel Phillips Gregory, who also settled in Louth Township. So Roland Michener is of United Empire Loyalist stock on both side of his family.

While the Micheners came from Pennsylvania with the progenitor part of the William Penn entourage (John and Sarah were married at the Penn house, Worminghurst), so did the Rolands and the Dishers on his mother's side. The Rolands were probably of Huguenot descent while the Dishers were almost certainly Mennonites from Germany, the so-called Pennsylvania Dutch. Daniel C. Roland

---

*First published in *The Globe* in October 1890 and republished in *The Welland Tribune* in February 1928 and reprinted in *More Micheners in America*.

came to Canada in 1848 and six years later married Anna Margaret Disher, who was born on the Disher farm in Pelham Township, Lincoln County, Ontario.

It was on the same farm near Welland, Ontario, now known as the Roland farm, that Mary Edith, Roland Michener's mother, was born on July 22, 1872. As a teenage student at Pelham School, she fell in love with the new teacher, Edward Michener, who was five years older than she, having been born August 18, 1867, the second son of Jacob and Eliza Michener, whose farm was nearby at Tintern in Lincoln County. In fact, on her sixteenth birthday, Mary went on a school trip to Niagara Falls with the new teacher and she recorded "an understanding between us that we would wait for each other in the coming years."

Almost ten years were to pass before Edward and Mary married; they were formally engaged for five years. Edward Michener was never very strong (he weighed two and a half pounds at birth), and while he was a qualified teacher with a Second Class Certificate and preferred teaching to farming, he felt that he was not paid enough to support a wife. In fact, his heart was set on other occupations: on the law and, when that was beyond his means, on the Church. As a child Edward had been enthralled by stories about David Livingstone in Africa and he believed, as most of his countrymen did, in the civilizing mission of the Anglo-Saxon race. He became a student missionary with the Methodist Church and was sent to faraway British Columbia. In the meantime Mary went to Alma College, St. Thomas, and herself became a teacher. However, the idea of a wife working in those days was unthinkable. It was only when Edward was ordained as a minister that this honourable and upright young man decided that he could get married.

The wedding was on September 15, 1897, a clear and beautiful day, by Mary's account, in Southern Ontario. Two weeks later the bride and groom were on their way to Banff, where Edward had his first circuit as a Methodist minister. He had been back and forth on the newly built CPR so that the train trip was nothing new for him, but Mary was entranced, and he delighted in showing her the sights. She was so thrilled by the Rockies that she "just wanted to gaze and gaze." They found a log cabin of the kind that was rented to campers in the summer; it was close to the church and about the only accommodation they could afford, but it was difficult to heat and the stove they got proved "balky." The tiny cabin had a living room, two bedrooms, and a lean-to kitchen, but it was big enough to hold the piano that

Mr. Roland had given his daughter as a wedding present. Sometimes the cabin was almost buried by the blizzards that swept the mountains and Mary was often cold, but she loved it because it was their first home.

Edward had another church in Canmore where he had to go every second Sunday. Perhaps it was too much of a strain, ministering to two churches; in any case he found the preparation and delivery of sermons exhausting and he became incapacitated by headaches. Finally, a year after the young couple had taken up residence in the Rockies, a local doctor diagnosed his trouble as "congestion of the lower brain" and advised him to have a rest. He was granted a year's leave of absence by the Methodist Conference, and the Micheners left Banff and the mountains in the summer of 1898. They rented a farm on the plains near Lacombe, Alberta, where Edward hoped to recover his health and then return to his charge.

They had to sell the "beloved" piano to pay for the move, and Mary found their new house even smaller and more primitive than the log cabin in Banff; furthermore, it was in a very "smelly" condition: it reeked of tobacco from the incessant smoking of the previous occupants, a couple of bachelors. But scrubbing and a coat of paint soon made it "sweet and clean."

Old Mrs. Roland made the long journey West to be with her daughter for the birth of their first child, Anna Marie, in 1898. Farming and the outdoor life seemed to do Edward so much good that in the spring of the following year he was able to accept the invitation to become the Methodist minister in Lacombe, and in June 1899 the couple moved into the parsonage. For the first time since she was married, Mary was living in a house with white plastered walls. It was in the manse at Lacombe that a son was born on April 19, 1900; he was named after his grandfather, Daniel Roland Michener.

Edward began having the same headaches and fatigues that had afflicted him in Banff, and after talking it over with Mary, he decided to give up the ministry and take up farming full time. "Roly" was only six weeks old when they left the Lacombe manse and went East to visit the Michener and Roland families before settling on the land that they had bought some seven miles outside Red Deer, Alberta. They had to build a house and buy cattle and horses, and in order to keep down expenses Edward worked part time as a bookkeeper for a lumber company in town.

The first year a hailstorm wiped out their hay crop and the next year an epidemic of equine fever killed the horses, so they had to plow with oxen, and Edward faced the fact that he could make more money in Red Deer, particularly in the real estate business. A boom was beginning that was to last for more than a decade. Immigration was at its heights in the early 1900s and immigrants came by every train to the prairies looking for land. Red Deer was doubling in commerce and construction almost every year. Edward Michener went into the real estate and mortgage loan business. His timing could not have been better, and he prospered.

In 1901 he was joined by S.N. Carscallen and in 1903 by G.A. Love and the firm was known as Michener, Love and Carscallen. Subsequently, with the withdrawal of Mr. Love, it became Michener, Carscallen and Company, and life and fire insurance were added to the company business. The Micheners and Carscallens were great friends and for some time lived next door to each other in Red Deer and the Carscallens' boy, Allen, and the Micheners' third son, Charles, were buddies and played together as children.* Allen was best man at Charles's wedding in 1936.

As a leading businessman, Edward Michener took an interest in local politics and in 1904, when his old partner Mr. Love was unable to complete his term of office as mayor of Red Deer, he was persuaded to succeed him. Thus began Michener's political career. After being in municipal affairs for several years, he was elected as an Independent Conservative member to the Alberta Legislative Assembly, later becoming leader of the provincial Conservative Party; finally he was appointed to the Senate, where he served for thirty years until his death in 1947.

Quite obviously, as a municipal and provincial politician, and later as a Senator, Edward Michener had to make a great number of speeches both on the stump and in the House. How was it then that he was able to prepare and deliver these speeches without the splitting headaches and exhaustion that were the after effects of similar church work? His son, Roland Michener, said that his father had told him that he had to give up the ministry because of its effect on his health, that he found preaching sermons "too great a strain for his nervous system. However," he added, "I have since wondered whether growing personal doubts about Methodist doctrine were the real cause."

---

*Edward and Mary Edith Michener had nine children: Anna Marie, born July 29, 1898; Daniel Roland, born April 19, 1900; John Victor, born December 4, 1902; Marion Louise, born November 7, 1904; Charles Edward, born January 4, 1907; Margaret Ruth, born March 7, 1909; Grace Eileen, born March 28, 1911; Olive Rose, born June 4, 1913; and Joseph Stanley, born November 11, 1915. As of mid-1989, all but Anna Marie and John Victor are alive.

Edward Michener did not give up church work on leaving the ministry. When the Micheners were farming outside Red Deer, they helped to build the Methodist church there; Mary was the organist and said that the congregation surprised them one evening by presenting them with a china tea set. Edward threw himself into Sunday school work and became president of the Alberta Sunday School Association and superintendent of the Methodist Sunday School. He was also vice-president of the Lord's Day Alliance.* However, as he became more deeply involved in politics, he found that he had less time to spend on church work.

Once Edward was established in business in Red Deer, the family moved there and he turned the farm over to his sister Allie. He also traded the cattle for forty acres of land in town — an astute move considering the developing real estate boom. The Micheners lived first in an unfinished house that proved to be too large, so they built one on Hospital Hill. When that was sold, they moved into a brick house opposite the Armouries. Mary quoted Edward as saying that he would sell anything but his wife and children, and, indeed, it was not long before the brick house was sold and they moved into a white cottage. They lived there while they built a house on East Hill, now called Michener Hill, which turned out to be a more permanent home, and the place that Roland remembered best.

Mary took all the moving with good grace: she reckoned that she moved twenty-four times during her married life — a sign of how restless her husband was. She had a piano again, her second son, Victor, was born, and she revelled in their newfound prosperity. "Our youth was so blessed with peace and plenty," she wrote from the epochal distance of 1936, "We never knew fear or want or international unrest. What a different world today!" The times of the real estate boom and the opening of the West were certainly good for the Micheners and many Canadians. "When we look back now, over those prosperous years," Mary went on, "it seems like a dream."

However, with the sunshine, there was a black cloud. In December of 1903, during a visit to relatives in Southern Ontario, little Anne Marie took ill and within ten days was dead of scarlet fever.

*The Lord's Day Alliance of Canada was founded in 1888 by the Presbyterian Church to counteract the increasing secularization of the Sabbath. Supported by the hierarchy of the French-Canadian Catholic Church, the Alliance became a powerful lobby group and influenced Sir Wilfrid Laurier to introduce the Lord's Day Act, which became law in 1907. Its purpose was to restrict Sunday trade and recreation activities. Sunday shopping is still an issue in some provinces in Canada.

Mary was distraught. "Our hearts were broken," she said but she wished to testify that "all through this great first sorrow, the Saviour seemed very near and I could say, at last, 'Thy will be done.'" Shortly afterward Mary returned with her two sons to Red Deer and comforted herself by dwelling on Roly and his uncut yellow curls.

By the time Edward Michener became mayor, he had already done a lot for the city. He had donated land for the construction of a hospital as a memorial to the three Red Deer soldiers who lost their lives in the Boer War. He had subdivided the rest of the acreage that he owned into lots for housing and commercial purposes. He built a two storey, business block that bore his name, and when it burned down he had it rebuilt; it was on the site of the T. Eaton Company store in modern Red Deer. As mayor, he modernized the town, putting in waterworks and underground sewers. He was mayor for three successive terms and organized, and presided over, the Union of Municipalities of Alberta, a body that would speak for the mushrooming towns and cities in the province. His son said of Edward Michener's administration that it was businesslike and took a nonpartisan approach to issues and "established his career as a public man of note."

It was local concerns that drove Edward Michener into civic politics, and yet when he assumed the mayoralty, he found himself swept up in the wider movement for autonomy and provincial status. Although there was an administrative capital in Regina, the North West Territories, which included the vast stretch of the prairies from Manitoba to the Rockies, was run by Ottawa. Any request for assistance to improve municipal facilities or to upgrade the roads, which were often no better than winding buffalo trails, or to rebuild ramshackle bridges had to go to the capital, to an official who had never been West and had no understanding of its problems. It was a frustrating situation that drove responsible, law-abiding citizens to talk of civil disobedience and even of rebellion.

Finally, as a result of the pressure of politics and population,* Ottawa agreed to the division of the North West Territories below the sixtieth parallel into two new self-governing areas. It was on September 1, 1905, more than a year after Edward Michener had become mayor of Red Deer, that the provinces of Alberta and Saskatchewan came into being. Their creation was not without contro-

---

*In the decade between 1901 and 1911, more than three hundred thousand people poured into Alberta, increasing its population from 73,022 to 373,943.

versy. Alberta wanted the boundary with Saskatchewan to be much farther east but had to settle for the 110th meridian. Then there were the rights of the Roman Catholic minority to publicly funded separate schools, which, it was felt, was imposed by Sir Wilfrid Laurier and the Liberal government in Ottawa. And Edmonton was named the provincial capital over the claims of Calgary; although this did not worry the Micheners since Red Deer was halfway between the two cities, it infuriated the Calgarians. It added to a legacy of bitterness over what was perceived to be federal interference in local matters.

The most contentious issue and the one that left an abiding suspicion and antagonism of Ottawa was the federal government's decision to retain control of the Crown lands and natural resources. Despite constant protests, this discriminatory treatment of the new Western provinces was maintained for a quarter of a century. It was not till 1930, when Edward Michener was a Senator, that Ottawa agreed to return the control of the land and resources to Alberta and Saskatchewan.

❧ 3 ❧

A POLITICAL
UPBRINGING

Roland WAS HARDLY NINE YEARS OLD when his father became involved in provincial politics. His mother recorded the fact that her husband attended his first political meeting on the night that their sixth child, Margaret, was born; it was the night of March 9, 1909. As the active nonpartisan mayor of Red Deer, Edward Michener had become increasingly disenchanted with the new Liberal government of Premier Alex Rutherford in Edmonton. It was already embroiled in patronage, with jobs in the embryo provincial civil service going exclusively to party supporters. Like the old Territorial administration in Ottawa, it was doing nothing about the urgent requests of the municipalities for railway connections and improved roads and bridges. There was also a demand for public ownership of the telephone system to break the monopoly of the American Bell Telephone Company, but the Rutherford government ignored it.

When Premier Rutherford called a provincial election for the spring of 1909, Edward Michener decided to contest the Red Deer riding, and succeeded in defeating the incumbent, John T. Moore,* a fellow businessman who had held the seat for the Liberals during the first legislature of the Alberta House. Edward ran as an Independent Conservative, and according to Roland, it was "no easy decision" for his father to join the Conservatives since he came from a fairly Liberal part of Southern Ontario and the Micheners and the Rolands had always been supporters of the Liberal Party. He made his decision as a matter of principle and, to assure his broadminded, nonpartisan approach to politics, he insisted on being called an Independent Conservative.

Roland recalled that there was much talk of politics around the family dinner table, especially after his father became an MLA; there was great excitement about the new transcontinental railways, the Canadian Northern and the Grand Trunk Pacific, and speculation as to where they would go: would the new lines pass through Red Deer? (In the end neither did.) Then there were discussions about the weak and disorganized state of the Conservative Party. Only two other members besides Edward Michener had been elected in the 1909 general election, George Hoadley from nearby Okotoks, and R.B. Bennett in Calgary. There were charges that the Liberals were bribing the immigrants with all sorts of promises. The Conservatives had lost because they had no organization compared to the Liberals' well-oiled machine. They were the political underdogs all right.

It was inevitable that Roland should be influenced by his father's progressive attitude toward politics and the political parties— so much so that he was to say, "It's a curious fact of Canadian political life that the two major parties are each divided into right and left wings. I have always seen myself as a liberal in the Conservative Party, and the fact that I am a Conservative is because I was raised in my father's house."

After being shuffled around from one temporary residence to another, the Micheners had now got a permanent home, the House on the Hill that became known as Michener Hill. It was ideal, according to Mary, so near the town yet practically in the country. There were three acres of grounds and the house had a "grand and glorious" view of the foothills and of the valley of the Red Deer River. The hillsides were covered with shrubs and trees and, in the autumn, there were wild saskatoons and other berries to pick. The whole countryside was

---

*John T. Moore brought electricity to Red Deer; he built the first electric power plant. He had been a Toronto real estate developer and Moore Park in that city was named after him.

at their disposal, and Roland used to go hunting in the fall and shoot all manner of prairie chickens and partridges, rabbits, ducks, and other game.

The boys had their own ponies. "I got my first pony when I was seven," Michener recalled, "and the pony— it was a Shetland— was [also] seven. It had been in a circus and was quite a gentle creature but it had been taught to buck the clown off, so we had great bucking matches on our lawn. If you sat on its rump, it would buck you off. Then the pony would come around to see that you were all right." The ponies were harnessed to a small buggy in the summertime and in the winter pulled a grey cutter, built by McLaughlin Carriage Works (which became McLaughlin Buick), that had doors like an automobile's with a latch to open them. The Shetlands were a great attraction, and children came to Michener Hill in droves to play with them. Roland built a bobsleigh, twelve feet long with a big square box, and the kids would pile on the box and he would give them a sleigh-ride down the main street and through the town.

Beside the bobsleigh and the ponies, the boys had a tree house that they reached by means of a rope and pulley. When they got tired of that, there were caves that the youngsters dug into the hillside and where they pretended to live. Bits of old furniture kept disappearing and Mary knew that they would be found in the "secret cave." Then there was the "old swimming hole" at the bottom of the hill in Waskasoo Creek. It was a wonderful way to grow up, and Roland often wished that he had been able to give his own children "that sort of upbringing— of the early West."

When it was first built, the house on Michener Hill was not large but, as Mary said, "very compact and cosy." However, it was soon not big enough, the family had grown, there were now five children, Roland, Victor, Marion, Charles, and Margaret, and in the fall of 1909 an English architect was employed to plan an addition. The work began in September and went on all winter, and Mary was almost distracted by such noise and confusion. When completed, the house was double the size of the original; there were six bedrooms, a sleeping porch, and a sunroom, as well as hot-water heating and three fireplaces. Two rooms had been turned into a large and handsome dining room.

The house was the right size for entertaining, and there were musical evenings and masquerades and, in summer, parties outdoors on the lawn. There was scarcely a Sunday without some friends joining them for dinner. But Mary was fortunate in having "splendid" servants, maids who were "strong and reliable," and a succession of

nannies for the children; then she found an English couple, Edward
and Minnie Glasson, to run the house, Minnie as housekeeper and
Edward as gardener and coachman. The House on the Hill had become the finest residence in Red Deer, a home worthy of the former
mayor and new member of the Alberta Legislature.

Although Roland Michener remembered little of his father's
election in 1909, he did recall going to Edmonton later on to hear him
speak in the Alberta House. He said that his father was quite an ora-
tor and would have made a good preacher if it had not been for the
headaches. Edward Michener spoke for four hours on the Alberta and
Great Waterways Railway scandal and his young son found it to be
"quite a strain on my patience to listen."

This scandal had a long life because it happened to be the
main issue of debate when Edward was first elected to the provincial legislature. A contract had been awarded the Alberta and Great
Waterways Railway to build a line north from Edmonton to Fort
McMurray; it was to be a major undertaking, designed to open up the
northern regions of the province for settlement, and it called for the
expenditure of large sums of money. But there was mismanagement
and soon mounting evidence of political corruption. R.B. Bennett
had made a telling and detailed attack on Premier Rutherford's handling of the railway question, and Edward Michener followed him
with what was described as a moderate and straightforward address
critical of the government's unbusinesslike attitude. "The government," he said, "pledged its credit to a company of which they knew
practically nothing."

Rutherford was forced to resign, but in order to keep the Liberals in power, his place was taken by Arthur Sifton, the chief justice
of the province and the elder brother of the former federal Cabinet
minister, Sir Clifford Sifton. The new premier immediately asked for
and got prorogation before the Conservatives could bring in a nonconfidence motion, and thus gained time to recoup his forces. In retrospect, Roland Michener asserted, "Had an election been called on this
issue, I am sure that Sifton would have been thrown out of power."

The Alberta Conservatives had also to find a new leader.
R.B. Bennett had the best claim; he had been the party's leader at
the time of the first provincial election in 1905, but he had resigned
after failing to win a seat.* Now that he had been elected, he was not

*Only two Conservatives were elected in 1905, Cornelius Hiebert of Rosebud and
A.J. Robertson from High River, and both lost their seats in the 1909 provincial
election.

interested in the leadership; his law partnership with Senator James Lougheed and his varied business interests were of greater concern than provincial politics. The other elected Conservative, George Hoadley, was not considered strong enough for the leadership. "That left my father, who had been elected as an Independent," Roland said. "His background in municipal affairs impressed many and his reputation was clean. Reluctantly, and only after much persuasion, my father accepted the job of leading the Conservative opposition in Alberta." Thus, in only a few months, Edward Michener had gone from the back benches of the Assembly to the forefront of provincial politics.

One of Edward's first tasks as leader was to assist the federal Conservatives in the 1911 election. The party's national leader, Robert Borden, toured the West in the early summer and spoke in Red Deer; he attacked Sir Wilfrid Laurier's proposed reciprocity treaty, and his words were greeted with cheers even by the recent American settlers in the region. In fact, one of these settlers was quoted by the *Montreal Star* as saying that reciprocity would lead to Canadian affairs being dominated by the United States. Yet, in spite of Borden's enthusiastic reception, only one Conservative was elected to Alberta's seven seats: R.B. Bennett, who had resigned as a provincial member to run federally, won Calgary and thus began a political career that was to end with his becoming prime minister. However, the Conservatives swept Ontario and much of English Canada and did sufficiently well in Quebec to oust Laurier from power; it was the Liberals' first defeat in fifteen years.

Unlike the 1909 provincial election of which he had only a hazy memory, Roland Michener did have some recollections of the 1911 federal election. While the Conservatives had not done so well in Alberta, he remembered that there was "great rejoicing at the announcement of Borden's victory." Later he was to hear the Conservative leader speak; he found him to be "a stolid and uninspiring man" but went on to assert that he admired Sir Robert Borden very much for the honesty and courage he showed in governing the country during peace and war. "His victory in 1911," Roland said, "boosted the morale of the Alberta Conservatives and encouraged my father and his colleagues in the legislature to work even harder to unseat the Sifton government."

However, Edward Michener was exhausted by the events of the year and decided to take his family to California for a winter holiday. This was not the first time that he had sought to escape from Alberta's cold weather. Some years before, there had been a disastrous trip to Victoria; they could not find suitable accommodation and it was rainy and foggy. Edward could not abide the "murky climate." They tried the Okanagan but it was just as wet. They could not return to Red Deer since their house was rented, so they made the long journey east to visit their relatives in Ontario, only to have the children come down with scarlet fever; everyone recovered but they were quarantined for six weeks. Mary was never so glad to get home.

By contrast, the trip to California was so successful that the Micheners stayed on and on. They spent a month by the sea at Long Beach; then they went to the town of Ontario, between Los Angeles and San Bernardino, where they found a "dear little bungalow." Edward bought it and furnished it, and they settled down, with the children attending the local public school. They spent Christmas, 1912, in California, and it was "warm and lovely," Mary recalled. An orange tree served as a Christmas tree, and the four oldest children got bicycles as presents.

"We were very cosy in our little home," Mary said, "but father saw an orange grove that pleased him. He made a trade and we went to live in the [orange grove's] larger but older house." This acquisition forced a decision on Edward: should he stay year round with his family in California, "that enchanted land of perpetual summer," or should he return to Alberta and continue his political career? The Legislature in Edmonton would be meeting soon, and he was Leader of the Opposition. He paced the floor trying to make up his mind, according to Mary's account, and finally decided that duty called him to Canada.

So he headed north in May, leaving Mary behind with six children to look after in a strange place. "It took all the courage I could muster to go through those months," she said, "I was alright in the daytime but, as soon as night began to fall, I wanted all the family inside, and doors locked." Edward would return for visits, but he was away many months at a time. Finally, in the spring of 1913 he decided to take his family back to Alberta. He arrived at their California home on June 4, 1913, the day the Micheners' "American" child, Olive Rose, was born at Upland Hospital, just outside Ontario, exactly a month before they left for the journey north to Red Deer.

The California school was the second school that Roland attended. Although he did well as a student, always finishing near the top if not the top of his class, he did not begin school until he was seven years old. This was not due to a lack of educational facilities in the North West Territories; Red Deer was a progressive little town with an elementary and high school when Alberta was founded. It was because his mother had suffered so grievously with the death of her eldest child, Anna Marie, and wanted to keep her remaining children beside her at home. "She enjoyed teaching me," Roland said. "She was of a literary turn of mind, she played the piano well, she painted and wrote a little poetry. She was a romantic young mother."

When he entered school, Roland could read and write and was immediately advanced to second grade. It was no little red schoolhouse that Red Deer had at the turn of the century but a good-sized eight-room elementary school and, nearby, a four-room high school. All the teachers in the elementary school were women, including the principal, a kind-hearted, motherly person, Mrs. Wanless, whose duty was to maintain discipline. "She had to strap five or six of us for carving our names in the desks," Michener recalled. "She got us lined up in her room and with a leather strap she whacked us all on the hand in turn and she wept copious tears all through the punishment. We took it lightly."

It was a good all-round education in the Red Deer public school system and Roland enjoyed it. He moved rapidly through the lower grades into high school, where there were good teachers and everything was taught except foreign languages. Although he had no opportunity to learn French, he was thrilled by the adventures of the French in New France.

He remembered one teacher, Miss Goudie, who had taught in South Africa. She talked about diamonds in the blue clay of Kimberley, and Cecil Rhodes and the scholarships that he had established. "From then on," Michener said, "I was interested in applying eventually for one of the Alberta Rhodes scholarships."

Roland's best friend in Red Deer was Edward William Scott Kane, known as Ted Kane. They grew up together, went to university in Edmonton together, and joined the air force at the end of the First World War together. Usually they got along very well—Ted liked to play practical jokes and tell tall tales— but if they disagreed they would fight it out. They would wrestle rather than punch each other. Roland recalled that they were wrestling one day over the question of whether a Hudson Super 6, Ted's champion, was superior to a McLaughlin Buick, Roly's favourite, "a very serious issue in those days among us fourteen-year-olds." Ted got a stranglehold on Roly's neck and the McLaughlin Buick had to yield to the Hudson Super 6.

The election of the Borden government spurred the provincial Conservatives to greater efforts, and in May 1912, after their leader,

Edward Michener, returned to Alberta, they held a policy conference
in Calgary. A new platform was drawn up calling for the construction
of a publicly owned railroad to unsettled regions, the establishment of
a public telephone system, state-operated grain elevators, state administered hail insurance, low-interest loans for new settlers, and a
plebiscite on the prohibition of liquor. The degree of state involvement in the 1912 Tory platform was noted by Roland Michener years
later; he felt that it reflected the political thinking of the times: the
prairie provinces were much readier to have the state correct and
supplement private enterprise than they were in the East.

It was a bold platform and it caught the attention of the public, including Arthur Sifton's, and the Liberal premier proceeded to
make the Conservative policy his own. However, this slick manoeuvre did not prevent the Conservatives picking up four seats in a
sweep of the 1912 by-elections. But by the time an election was called
in 1913, Premier Sifton had stolen so much of the Conservative program that "there was little that my father and his followers could do
but complain about the manner in which their proposals had been
enacted."

The 1913 election was the first time that the voters of Alberta
could choose between the leadership of Sifton or Michener. The Liberals campaigned on their achievements as a government and tried to
bury the Alberta and Great Waterways scandal. The Conservatives
attacked the call for a "snap" election and ran an advertisement
signed by "E. Michener" that asked a series of questions, among them:
"Why did the Sifton Government not bring before this [past] session
of the Legislature any proposal for a settlement of the A. & G.W.
[Alberta and Great Waterways Railway] entanglement? Why is the
Province paying over one million dollars in interest while the Province only has a departmental revenue of less than two million dollars
a year? Why is the Provincial credit being impaired to such an extent
that the Province was required to pay 5 3/4 percent on their money?"
Edward expressed his political credo in the following terms:

"What we need is an honest business administration. I would
like to see every district elect its best businessman; then there should
be chosen from those businessmen a business administration to conduct the business of the province."

Edward Michener won handily in Red Deer, defeating Robert
Welliver, the mayor and president of the local Liberal Association, but
elsewhere in the province his party did not do so well. A redistri-

bution bill had heavily weighted the vote in favour of the northern agricultural areas where the Liberals were popular, and at the expense of the cities and towns. (The Rutherford and Sifton governments had increased the number of seats in the Alberta Legislature from twenty-five in 1905 to fifty-six in 1913.) Besides this gerrymandering, there were widespread cases of ballot-box stuffing and fraud. The Conservatives filed protests over twenty of the election results, but all were rejected by Liberal-appointed judges. As an example, there was Clearwater, where the returning officer recorded one hundred and three votes in a community with a population of seventy-four. It was the sort of political corruption that might have occurred below the border but not in the Canadian West; Edward Michener had been robbed and the only consolation he had was that the Conservatives had won more seats than ever before; their strength in the Legislature had risen from seven to seventeen members.

It was only after the 1913 election that Roland returned to Red Deer, but his interest in politics was aroused on the journey home by his father's accounts of the provincial campaign. He was determined to become involved and there were soon by-elections for which he could put up signs and distribute flyers, and drive his father and other speakers around in the family car, a two-cylinder Maxwell that was built like a buggy "and had a hood you could put up like a buggy's and I'm not sure it didn't have a whip holder in the dash." There were no driver's licences in those days, and at thirteen or fourteen, Roland could drive and, what was more important, he could repair the tires. The roads were so rough and the tires so vulnerable that almost every day, and sometimes twice a day, he would have to jack up the car, lever off the outer tube, and patch the inner tube. Off they would go again, chug-chug-chugging along in the old Maxwell.

One day, when he was driving a speaker to a meeting in the country, he got stuck in gumbo; in trying to get out, he spun a tire off. The speaker thumbed a ride in a passing buggy. Since it was getting dark, Roland trudged some distance to the nearest house where a friendly Scandinavian farmer put him up for the night. The next day the farmer's team of horses pulled the Maxwell out of the gumbo. Roland repaired the tire, and was off electioneering again. "The excitement of campaigning got into my blood," Roland said. "From that time on, I wanted to take part in public affairs."

On August 4, 1914, the British Empire entered the "Great War," and when Sir Wilfrid Laurier heard the news, he called for a political truce. Prime Minister Borden was only too happy to accept the offer since he had been considering a fall election despite the poor harvests in the West and the increase in unemployment in the Eastern cities. There were reports of families in Southern Alberta living on a soup made from gophers and Russian thistle; Bennett had warned that the coming winter could be the worst in memory. The life of Parliament was extended by an annual agreement between the two party leaders to avoid a wartime election.

In many provinces there were similar truces, but not in Alberta. Sifton continued to play hard politics and was confident that he could outmanoeuvre Michener as he had done in the past. A cartoon in the *Calgary Eye Opener** illustrated the differing styles of the two leaders. It showed them playing poker, with Sifton having the better cards, each one inscribed with a Conservative policy plank. The caption read, "Oh well, Michener will deal himself a good hand some day."

By 1917 the situation on the Western Front was becoming desperate. There were not enough reinforcements for the Canadian troops who had suffered heavy casualties in the bitter trench warfare of the previous year, and conscription was being touted as the only honourable and patriotic solution. However, this did not go down well with the farmers who did not want to lose any more agricultural labour to the war effort. Sifton knew of the opposition to conscription in the rural areas and shrewdly guessed that this was a good time to consolidate his hold on the farm vote. He called an election for June of 1917.

It was the first time that women could vote in Alberta and many of them took part in the campaign. The Manitoba suffragette leader Nellie McClung appeared on the same platform with Sifton since it was his Liberal government that had framed the legislation giving women the vote. Although Michener had supported this initiative and was wholeheartedly in favour of women's suffrage, he was unable to turn the issue to his advantage.

Mary was proud that Alberta was the first province to give women the franchise and that it was the first province to have a sit-

---

*The *Eye Opener* was a lively broadsheet published spasmodically at the turn of the century by Bob Edwards, who was called the "most extraordinary Canadian man of this century." Actually, Edwards was a well-educated Englishman who had settled in Calgary when it was a wide-open frontier town; he wrote most of the *Eye Opener* himself.

ting woman member, Mrs. Louise McKinney, who, Mary said, was the first woman elected to a legislature in the British Empire.* However, she was not blind to the behaviour of women when they got the vote. "Words fail me to describe that election campaign," she wrote in her family history, "I do not wish to dwell on it— I wish to hurry over it, as I blush with shame when I think how petty and mean my own sex can be at such times." Apparently the participation of women for the first time in an election campaign made for "a bitterness of feeling," according to Mary, that surpassed all others. Although she did record the fact that she had "the proud honour to cast my first vote for my dear husband," Mary was too busy looking after the family and the house to take much part in the election campaign. Her last child, Joseph Stanley, was born on November 11, 1915.

Once again, Michener criticized Sifton's management of the provincial government and his continued expropriation of Conservative policy proposals; he promised a nonpartisan administration, an independent civil service commission, extension of the telephone system, expanded rural hospital services, and improved roads. While Sifton campaigned on his government's record, as he had done in the previous election, he was not averse to gutter politics: Liberal canvassers went around the ridings telling farmers that Michener and the Conservatives represented the "war Party" and that a vote for them would bring in conscription and a loss of their sons and all farm labour. Edward could not deny that he had certainly done a lot of voluntary work for the war effort and had helped to raise the 187th Battalion, and as a result of this scurrilous campaign, Edward Michener almost lost his Red Deer seat in the Alberta House.

Roland remembered that election night; just out of high school and ready to enter college in the fall, he had acted as a chauffeur for his father during the election campaign and had driven voters to the polls that day. "Ostensibly, the Liberal candidate, who was again Robert Welliver, had won," he said. "All of the returns were in, except for one polling subdivision, which was out at Rocky Mountain House, and Welliver had a small majority but it seemed to be solid enough. So a great celebration began at the Liberal committee rooms in town."

---

*Actually, there were two women elected to the Alberta Legislature in 1917. Lieutenant Roberta MacAdams of Calgary, a nurse, was an armed forces representative. Louise McKinney was a member of the Non-Partisan League and elected on the Prohibition ticket; she was president of the WCTU. Both Roberta MacAdams and Louise McKinney had the the honour of being the first women elected to a legislative assembly in the British Empire.

The Conservatives were dejected. However, Edward had a good friend at Rocky Mountain House, G. A. Love, whose retirement had led to him becoming mayor of Red Deer, and Mr. Love had helped rally the vote. The next morning when the ballot boxes were brought in and the votes counted, Michener was shown to be the winner by a scant forty votes. Roland remembered that there was quite a celebration, and Mary said that the Conservatives rallied their men and held a big parade that ended with Edward's addressing them in Red Deer's public square.

Despite the attempts to link the party to the issue of conscription, the Conservatives did well in the 1917 Alberta election, picking up a couple more seats for a total of nineteen, but not well enough for Edward Michener to become premier. The tallying of the soldiers' vote was popularly blamed for preventing the party from winning the half-dozen more seats that would have made them the government. "After the smoke of election battle had rolled away," Mary wrote, "Father and I entertained at a garden party for his supporters. It was a glorious evening and we had arranged tables on the lawn, and the front verandah was fitted up as a stage for the program." However, just as it was about to begin, a "terrible wind" came up with some rain, and they had to have the party indoors.

The following spring, as he was preparing as Leader of the Opposition to meet the Liberals in the new Assembly, Edward Michener was surprised to receive a letter from Ottawa informing him that he had been "summoned to the Senate." It was greeted throughout the province of Alberta as a popular and well-deserved appointment by Sir Robert Borden's new Union government; congratulations poured in to the house on Michener Hill, but many of his Conservative followers were loath to see him leave the provincial arena.

❧ 4 ❧

THEY
ALSO SERVE

As a PROVINCIAL POLITICIAN and party leader, Edward Michener had been away from home for days and weeks when campaigning or when the legislature was meeting in Edmonton, and Mary had grown accustomed to this; the house on Michener Hill could hardly be called a lonely place with all the children racketing around and the servants. However, when Edward became a Senator, she did not realize that "this new honour was going to mean such long yearly absence from home." Then, in the fall of 1917, Roland, who had, as he was expected to do in those days, assumed the role of head of the household in the absence of his father, left for Edmonton to attend the University of Alberta. It was not so pleasant, being left on her own, but Mary was long-suffering and, as she said, tended to her flock and "kept the home fires burning."

When he went to university, the young master of Michener Hill was a local hero in Red Deer. Not only did he finish at or near the top of his class, but he alternated as champion athlete with a fellow student of his age, Jonas Jonasson. "We were great rivals," Michener said. "We did hop, skip, and jump and the high jump, and we ran the hundred yards, the two-twenty and the four-forty, and the one who got the most prizes was the leader for the year. One year I won it and another year he won it." Roland might have mentioned the new field sport of pole vaulting which was to help him win the "Victor Ludorum"—and he would have known what that meant because he took private tuition in Latin in order to pass the entrance exam to the University of Alberta. It was his experience in pole vaulting that gained him a "Blue" at Oxford.

Then there was tennis, and at twelve years old he was knocking a ball around on the bumpy lawn at Michener Hill. Later his father had a cinder court built with chicken wire netting around it so that the ball would not end up in Waskasoo Creek. There he learned to play tennis. It was the game of his life, the game that he enjoyed most.

Roland Michener was gifted with a quick learning ability that made schooling seem easy; he was a conscientious student and showed at the earliest age an obsession with the Protestant work ethic; he never stopped working, as his colleagues in later life were to say, and as a boy he hated to be idle. He was always busy: in Sunday School where he was awarded the Raikes diploma for fifty-two weeks' continuous attendance, in the Boy Scouts where his proficiency gained him most if not all the badges, as the "furnace man" at home who kept the soft-coal fires burning all night, and as entrepreneur in developing his own milk route. The family had a couple of Jersey cows at Michener Hill and, in return for feeding and milking them and supplying his mother with all she needed, he could sell the rest. So he would go the rounds of the neighbours before breakfast, delivering milk at twelve and a half cents a quart; on most days, he sold eight quarts, thereby earning a dollar, which was four times as much as the weekly allowance of twenty-five cents from his father.

He played the piano at home for family parties and singsongs and when he was sixteen, the year before he went to the University of Alberta, he played the cornet in the Red Deer Citizens' Band and earned five dollars a day for the three days that the band was engaged at the Red Deer Fair. He counted himself as well-to-do.

Scouting came to Red Deer in 1910, only a couple of years after Robert Baden-Powell founded the movement. "We had a very good troop," Michener said. "I think we preceded Calgary, which was one of the earliest troops—as I found out when as Governor General

I became Chief Scout of Canada. The Calgary troop celebrated its six-tieth anniversary [in 1971]." The Red Deer scouts had their camp at Sylvan Lake, a nearby summer resort. Roland belonged to the Wolf troop and, before he left to go to college, became a scout leader and head of patrol.

One extraordinary experience he had as a young scout was when the boys of his troop were asked to leave school and help a posse round up a man who had shot and wounded the town's only policeman. It was not known who he was but it was believed that he was hiding in the bushes on the outskirts of Red Deer. "Here I was, at the age of eleven," Michener said, "without even a staff in my hand, going in open formation with the other Boy Scouts across the scrubby, vacant land between the Exhibition Grounds to the south and the nearest house. We were about twenty-five feet apart as we advanced and finally we flushed him out from behind a bush where he had been sleeping. He jumped up, gun in hand, and ran down into a swamp. There were a couple of shots fired but nobody was hurt." The men in the posse, who had guns, captured the man and took him off to jail. It could not have been more exciting and the boys were almost beside themselves as they blurted the story out to their parents, who were not in the least pleased at the use of scouts as auxiliary policemen. Still, it was such a stirring event in the placid life of Red Deer that the citizens subscribed enough money to send two scouts to the Great Jamboree in Britain that year (1911).

Although the University of Alberta was only a few years old in 1917, it was well established, with substantial brick buildings on a large campus in Edmonton. There were some fifteen hundred stu-dents, more than half of whom were women. Roland had a room to himself in one of the residences; there were no services, no frills, but there was a bathroom on the same floor, and he was to find that his room there was much more comfortable than the much grander quarters he occupied in Oxford. As a graduate of twelfth grade, he was an instant sophomore, starting in the second year of his Arts course, and finishing that before enlisting in the RAF. After a brief stint in the armed forces, he completed his third year in the first four months of 1919 but had a full fourth year, graduating with a first class honours BA in May 1920. He made a special effort to take French at the university, and by the time he became a lawyer he was able to read French novels and "who-dun-its."

His principal sport at the University of Alberta was hockey and during his last year he was on the university team. Roland also played football, the old Canadian game before the forward pass. The star of the Alberta team was George Langford, later professor of geology and mining at the University of Toronto; he was a big man, six-feet six-inches tall and over two hundred pounds. "Big Six, he was called," Michener said, "and we would gather behind him and push and he was bound to make a couple of yards before he fell down." This was known as bucking the line. There were three downs, but without the forward pass, they consisted of two bucks and, if ten yards were not made, then the team had to kick. So it was two bucks and a kick, and, in Michener's opinion, not much of a game.

Meanwhile the war went on, and there seemed to be no end to the carnage. Although there was some good news in 1917, with the Canadians taking Vimy Ridge and the United States declaring war on Germany, which made Mary say, "We seemed to breathe easier after that," it was nevertheless a year of disruption and of discontent. The casualties kept mounting and the demands for reinforcements were such that Prime Minister Borden decided there had to be conscription. A large number of Liberal members agreed with him and crossed the floor of the House of Commons to join the Conservatives in forming the Union Government. An election was called for December 17 and the country divided, with English Canada giving the Borden Unionist government an overwhelming majority of one hundred and fifty-three seats and French Canada, with some help from the Maritimes, providing the Laurier Liberals with the rest, eighty-two seats.

Roland took no part in the 1917 federal election but there was no doubt where his sympathies lay. He was all in favour of conscription and a strong supporter of the Union government, as were most of his fellow students. He and his friends were "champing at the bit," as he put it, to join up; they wanted to be fighter pilots and they were afraid that the war would be over before they could follow in the flight paths of Billy Bishop or Billy Barker or Edmonton's Punch Dickens. They never thought of being shot down, and certainly not of dying of the flu. However, Roland had promised his father that he would not enlist before he reached the legal age to do so, but on April 19, 1918, he was eighteen, and, as Mary admitted, "We could not say no."

Shortly after his birthday and completion of the second year of his Arts course, he joined the Royal Air Force* with three of his pals

---

*The Royal Air Force was formed early in 1918 as a merger of the Royal Flying Corps and the Royal Naval Air Service. The Royal Canadian Air Force was not formed until 1924.

from university, Ted Kane, who was from Red Deer and was to become a judge of the Supreme Court of Alberta, and Howard T. Emery
and Alan Burnside Harvey of Edmonton. The four would-be aces set
off together, but the air force had all the cadets they needed and told
them to go home and wait to be called up. So Roland spent the summer at Michener Hill, much to his mother's delight, and in September
reported for duty at the RAF recruits' depot in the Jesse Ketchum
School on Davenport Road in Toronto.

He was separated from his three pals, who had been sent to
flying camps at places like Beamsville, Ontario, which had its pluses
and minuses as far as achieving their ambitions of becoming pilots
was concerned. At least they were among aircraft and could persuade
friendly instructors to give them the odd flight, and so they had more
fun than Roland, who was taking basic training, "square bashing" at
Long Branch on the outskirts of Toronto. Since there were too many
recruits, they were not being taught to fly but were being used to do
such fatigues as oiling and servicing the planes — all of which was so
demeaning and ignoble for officer cadets in their natty uniforms with
the distinctive white band around their wedge caps.

It was cold in Toronto that fall, and the RAF depot was un-
heated, and Roland was glad to put on the heavy issue underwear,
however scratchy; at night he wrapped himself in the thick grey blankets, not only to keep warm, but to cushion the boards of his wooden
bunk, which had no mattress. The air force did not pamper its recruits,
and he was glad to escape on a Saturday or Sunday to the warm, comfortable house of Miss Mabel Christie, a well-to-do spinster teacher
and friend of a friend of the family whose contribution to the war effort was to entertain young cadets and provide them with a home
away from home. There, Roland would be served a good breakfast of
bacon and eggs and fried tomatoes, and he would feel better about
facing basic training and the bleak barracks.

Meanwhile the influenza epidemic that was sweeping a war-
devastated world was spreading across Canada. Roland and other
recruits were taken off basic training to work as orderlies at the base
military hospital, a wooden structure in the centre of Toronto that was
built to accommodate three hundred patients but by then was over-
crowded with nine hundred or more. They removed used blankets for
fumigation, acted as stretcher-bearers for the sick, and carried out the
dead. As might be expected, Roland came down with the flu and he
was shipped off to the hospital and a bed in the corridor.

"Of the next two or three days," he said, "I have almost no recollection. I must have slept continuously until the fever subsided. I was soon sufficiently over the crisis to be sent for convalescence to the East House of the residences of University College [University of Toronto]. For ten peaceful days I enjoyed a life of ease, until I was well enough to go on happily with my routine training at Long Branch."

He was there when the first false news of the armistice was reported. It was not difficult to get a pass and he spent a day with his friends at the Beamsville camp where he had the thrill of a flight; he ended the day in Hamilton, "which was delirious with peace celebrations." The real armistice of November 11 came the next weekend and he got leave to go downtown in Toronto, where "the outburst of joy and relief was almost beyond expression." Soon afterward he was demobilized and discharged as an "honourary pilot officer." He had had all the basic training, had learned the Morse Code, and had been taught aeronautics — but he had received no flying instruction.

By the time Roland had recovered from the flu, the epidemic had reached the West. Schools, churches, and places of entertainment were closed, and a law was passed in Alberta compelling people to wear mouth-and-nose masks in public places. No nurses were to be had, the doctors were overworked, and it looked "pretty blue," according to Mary Michener. One by one her children took sick, despite the fact that they had been inoculated in school. Apparently nothing could stop this virulent virus.

> Fortunately, [she wrote] neither father nor I took the disease, but we were nursing night and day, and we brought them safely through. One symptom was the terrific bleeding from the nose. We were so thankful that we were spared to nurse our children. I never had any fear of the flu, and right here I wish to express the opinion, that fear was one thing that made the epidemic worse. If you are not afraid of disease you are not apt to take it.
>
> *'After a day of cloud and wind and rain,*
> *Sometimes the setting sun breaks forth again.'*

On November 11, Armistice Day, which was their youngest son's, little Joe's, third birthday, the Micheners—and it was now Senator and Mrs. Michener — could not go down to the town square to help celebrate, as they would have been expected to do, because their children were too sick. "But," Mary said, "we watched from our hill, and saw the crowds and heard the shouts, and bells ringing. The war was over! Yes, the World War was over!"

Roland got home for Christmas, and, according to Mary, it was for them "the happiest Christmas ever." His war experience, while not the glory he had envisioned earlier, had matured him. Howard Emery, who was a year older, remembered him as "a very fine young man, very popular. He never threw his weight around," Emery said "He had a good personality, and everybody liked him and respected him." Roland was able to resume his studies at the University of Alberta in January of 1919, and he completed the third year of his Arts course in the four months before the long summer vacation. It was a general course with no specialization; among the subjects he studied were economics, constitutional history, English literature, and geology. This last course proved to be of immediate value because he got a job with a geologist who was prospecting for Imperial Oil.

It was probably his father who found him this summer employment: Senator Michener had developed a keen interest in the oil industry, which was in its infancy in Alberta at the time, and he was to drill a number of wells, but he did not have much success in finding a commercial quantity of oil. Roland worked as an assistant to a Mr. Shepherd, an English geologist whom he described as "an able and delightful fellow." They made their headquarters in a hotel at Pincher Creek, and Roland would drive him around in a Model-T Ford to various sites in the foothills of the Rockies where Shepherd tested the rocks and tried to find formations that contained oil.

Some Doukhobors had a place nearby, and Roland remembered seeing Peter Verigin, the charismatic leader of the dissenting Russian sect, come to town. "He drove into Pincher Creek in great style, in a buggy with a galloping team of horses and four outriders, two on each side. It created quite a sensation. That was why we called him the King of the Doukhobors."

When Roland returned to the University of Alberta for the fourth year of his Arts course in the fall of 1919, he found that the college had changed: the veterans were there in force and they gave the institution a much more serious tone. The appointment of Rhodes Scholars had resumed and Roland was a candidate for the 1918 scholarship competition that was held in the autumn of 1919, but it was won by his friend, Alan Harvey. The 1919 scholarship came up in February of 1920 and Roland tried again; this time he was successful.

In applying, he had to write a three-hundred word précis of his life and his ambitions and objectives; he said that ultimately he wanted to be in the public administration of the country, and with that

goal in view he was going to study law. He also had to submit his
academic record and an account of his athletic achievements, as well
as the names of six people who would vouch for him. Then there was
the interview with the selection committee, and its members asked all
kinds of questions about his ambitions. "I told them," Michener said,
"that I didn't think there was enough honesty in public life—which
was pretty bumptious of me—but I was thinking of my father's experience at the hands of the corrupt Liberal government in Alberta."

A month later he was officially informed that he had been
awarded a Rhodes scholarship and should choose a college; he opted
for New College or Balliol but they were full and the only one with
room was Hertford, which he had never considerd. At that time the
scholarship was worth 250 pounds a year, plus a bonus of 50 pounds;
his father added to that amount because Roland was not only taking
jurisprudence at Oxford but was entered as a student at the Middle
Temple in London. By doing so, he could qualify as a barrister and
therefore would have to write the bar exams there.

"It wasn't a lavish life, but it was comfortable and cheap,"
Michener said. "Clothes were cheap, food was cheap, Britain was one
of the cheapest places in the world to live in those days."

Roland still had to finish his Arts course at the University of
Alberta, and he did not rest on the laurels of the Rhodes scholarship;
in fact, he worked even harder to win the gold medal for finishing first
in his class. The university's annual, *The Gateway*, said of him:

> Whilst at the university he has taken an active interest in all of the af-
> fairs of the institution, being a member of the dramatic society, presi-
> dent of the University YMCA and secretary of the Students' Union. Roly
> played hockey on both the first and second teams, while many lost
> hearts are the direct result of his efforts from the dramat. This curly
> headed youth goes to Oxford this year, having gained the Rhodes Schol-
> arship for 1919, an honour which he well deserves."

That summer of 1920 was a time of splendid expectation for
young Michener: he spent part of it at home, but when he learned that
he had been accepted at Hertford College and had communicated
with Carlton Alan, who was to be his tutor in jurisprudence at Oxford,
he left Red Deer to visit his relatives in Ontario. There he earned some
money by house painting. Knowing that his father was not as well off
as he had been, Roland did not want to ask him for any extra funds.
He knew that law could be expensive, and then, too, he wanted to
have a little loose cash on his first transatlantic crossing. He travelled
cabin class on a Canadian Pacific liner to England in September 1920.

Edward Michener had left his real estate firm when he became seriously involved in party politics, which was well before he was appointed a Senator. However, the business was carried on by his partners — for too long, as it proved: they had operated as if the land boom, which had gone on for a decade, would not stop and they had got into debt when the bust came, as it did in the year before the outbreak of the First World War. Edward had been the guarantor of their bank loans, which amounted to fifty thousand dollars — a considerable sum in those days — and it fell on him to pay them off, which, according to his son, took him a number of years to do.

This indebtedness meant that Senator Michener had to sell his interest in Commonwealth Petroleum, which was the most successful of the companies he had formed, and so he never really benefited from his active interest in oil exploration and production. He drilled a large number of wells not only in Alberta but in Manitoba and across Lake Ontario near Smithsville, where there was shallow gas, and even down on the banks of the St. Lawrence River in Quebec. Most were dry holes, while some showed gas or oil but not in commercial quantities. He was successful in the Turner Valley where he had a profitable well, but he was never able to make a new strike and bring in a new oil field. "That ambition of his was never realized," his son said. "He was fifteen years ahead of the game."

Whenever he could, Edward Michener retained the mineral rights to any land he owned. He did so with regard to a quarter-section near Red Deer; after paying taxes on it for years he sold the "surface" to a friend for two dollars an acre (altogether three hundred and twenty dollars). He bought a nine-hundred-acre farm in Manitoba because he thought that beneath the fields there was oil or gas, but it turned out to be a good farm. "When my father died [in 1947]," Roland said, "the tenant gave my mother half the profits from the crop, which came to a couple of thousand a year."

Then there was the 350-acre tract that the Senator acquired in the San Joaquim Valley, California; he bought it in conjunction with a partner, Ernest Wilson, a friend and associate in Red Deer. Where irrigation was available, the Valley was a wonderful fruit-growing area and Edward wanted to cultivate the property and live there and escape from the cold Canadian winters, but there were mineral rights and "he always had oil at the back of his mind in his later years." So he sold Michener Hill in Red Deer shortly after Roland became a Rhodes Scholar and moved his family to the ranch in a little place called Clovis, near Fresno. They lived there for three years; Edward

Michener would make the long journey to Ottawa for every session of the Senate and the children went to school in the San Joaquim Valley. They were there all the time that Roland was at Oxford.

When Senator Michener died, the mineral rights were inherited by his widow. "They're not really good prospects, but the family does have the oil rights in California, the oil rights of a quarter-section in Red Deer, and the oil rights for nine hundred acres in Manitoba," Michener said and added with a wry smile, "If any of my father's dreams come true, it will be after my time."

By the time that Roland returned home in 1923, Senator Michener had moved the family once more, this time to Toronto. The dairy farming he had tried to do in the San Joaquim Valley had proved to be too much work for him and was not really a paying proposition; he should have been in fruit, in such cash crops as oranges and papayas, which did so well there. So he sold the property, retaining, of course, the mineral rights. His partner, Ernest Wilson, stayed and the younger Melville Wilson, Ernest's son, known as "Mivvie," became a wealthy trader in the produce of the Valley, with his own private plane.

To read jurisprudence at Oxford was, in Roland Michener's view, the best possible way to become a lawyer. There was the Moot Club, where mock trials were staged; the bewigged judges who presided included Mr. Justice Darling and other famous British magistrates. Roland worked hard at Oxford and got the prestigious degree of BCL, Bachelor of Civil Law, and he qualified as a barrister of Middle Temple, Uter Bar. "I remember," Michener said, "I was called to the Bar by Sir Edward Carson, who was the head of the Middle Temple, the treasurer, as we called him, of the Middle Temple." Roland Michener was now a barrister and could practise in Britain but not in Canada, and he was soon to find that it was difficult to become a member of the Ontario Bar.

❧ 5 ❧

LAW AND
MARRIAGE

WHEN ROLAND MICHENER RETURNED to Canada and went to
Toronto to live with his family in a large house on Grenadier Road,
he was carrying some heavy baggage: there was his oar from the
Hertford College eight which was to be proudly displayed in his
home, and the dark blue blazer which he could wear as a "full blue"
for winning the pole vault, and the striped blazer of the "half blue"
for playing on the championship ice hockey team. But there were
also the intangible and weighty effects of an Oxford education, of
three years of the Rhodes scholarship, of the gentlemanly and clois-
tered academic life, and of the cultural high-jinks, the rags, and eating
dinners in the Middle Temple. He knew that Rhodes Scholars were
sometimes derided as being too perfect boys but he regarded this as a
compliment, and he realized the success that he had had at an early
age could be self-destructive.

Still, he came back full of enthusiasm and great expectations
and would have rejected any wisecrack to the effect that Rhodes

Scholars were people with a brilliant future behind them. He felt sure that his Oxford degree would open doors for him and Rhodes Scholars were welcomed to the higher seats in the universities and to the upper echelons of the public service and, later, to diplomatic posts in the Department of External Affairs. But when he applied immediately to the Law Society of Upper Canada, he was turned down.

He was told that the society's rules allowed them to take a barrister from another Commonwealth Bar if that Bar granted equal privileges to an Ontario barrister, and, in the case of the Middle Temple in London, none had been granted. However, it came out that no Ontario barrister had applied, and Michener argued that if one did go to London and ask to be admitted to the English Bar, he would be taken in. *No, no;* the old lawyer who headed the Law Society of Upper Canada was polite but adamant. Despite his education and the fact that he was a barrister in the Middle Temple, he could not be called to the Ontario Bar.

At the same time Roland wanted to work as a devil, or student, in the law office of Newton Wesley Rowell, who was at the height of his fame as a counsel; furthermore, Rowell was a close friend of his father, both of them being good Western Methodists, and young Michener felt fairly certain that he would be accepted. It would be the best possible experience. But it turned out that Rowell had all the students he needed and could not take on another. Roland was disappointed again. Any youthful arrogance that he had as a result of Oxford and the Rhodes scholarship was now subdued by the harsh realities of the legal profession in Toronto.

By contrast, his good friend, Mike Pearson, who had come home at the same time, had no trouble finding his niche. While he was still at Oxford, Mike had been approached by Professor G. M. Wrong, the head of the history department at the University of Toronto, and offered a job. So that in September of 1923 Pearson, who, it should be said, had a Massey Foundation Fellowship and not a Rhodes scholarship, took up the position of lecturer in modern history at what he described in volume one of his autobiography as "an awe-inspiring salary of $2,000 a year."

There were a couple of others in the same predicament as Roland Michener over the restrictions of the Law Society of Upper Canada. Alan Harvey, the old friend from Edmonton days, who had been the 1918 Alberta Rhodes Scholar, was in the same fix. Terry Sheard, who had been at Magdalen College, had got around the rules by going to Manitoba and being called to the Bar there. Then he came to Toronto and as a Manitoba barrister had no difficulty in being called to the Bar in Ontario. The only trouble with this manoeuvre was that it was costly: there was an admission fee of fifteen hundred dollars, which was much more than Roland could afford.

Alan and Roland put their heads together and found that a person could be called to the Bar of Ontario by an Act of the Legislature. This had occurred in the case of a notary public who evidently had considerable pull with his party and had been made a lawyer by legislation. "Why can't we do that?" they asked themselves. "We're Canadians, we've had a good legal training, we're entitled to be barristers." Furthermore, they figured that they had a good cause and that the Rhodes scholarship would count for a lot more with the legislature than with the law society. So they sought out an MPP who was a farmer and was duly impressed by their educational qualifications, and he said, "Sure, I'll introduce two private bills, one for each of you, to make you barristers."

In due course the private bills were written and published in the *Gazette*, and thus came to the attention of the law society. The benchers were horrified; they had visions of being ordered to appear before a committee of the legislature—a committee composed mainly of farmers who had no love for lawyers in any event—and being asked to explain why they were preventing these two young, well-educated Canadians, Rhodes Scholars no less, from being called to the Bar. They would be made to look foolish; the adverse publicity would be terrible. The only way out was to accept the two young men.

"You're articled as students for six months," the Law Society told them, "after which there will be an examination on the statute and practise of the province, and then we'll admit you to the Bar."

In six months' time, early in 1924, both Roland and Alan came to Osgoode Hall for the examination. Michener remembered his. One of the benchers said to him, "You're Roland Michener, aren't you?" "Yes." "You've been educated in England and want to practise here?" "Yes." "Are you enjoying yourself?" "Yes, I've got a good job," Roland replied, "I'm making a living, and I'm looking forward to practising law here." The bencher said, "All right, you've passed." That was the examination.

After being turned down by Rowell, Michener became articled as a student to Goldwyn Gregory of the firm of Gregory and Gregory, whose practice consisted almost entirely of the lending of money on mortgages. Gregory and Gregory were Quakers and the senior Gregory, W.R. Gregory, was a prominent practising Quaker with very good contacts among his fellow religionists in England and among the wealthy Quaker companies there. The firm had about twenty million dollars on loan which kept it going, but there was some litigation by troublesome clients, and Goldwyn, who was a self-indulgent but intelligent man as well as a lately returned war veteran, got Roland to look after the legal business.

Michener started with Gregory and Gregory in the summer of 1923; he was paid $125 a month, which, after a short time, was increased to $175 a month. This was a princely salary for a young fellow in the 1920s, but there was just not enough work and he was not earning his pay. Goldwyn had been too optimistic about the development of the firm's legal business, and it fell on the senior partner, W. R. Gregory, to tell Roland that his fees were not enough to pay his share of the office expenses and his salary.

By this time Michener had been called to the Ontario Bar, and he decided to strike out on his own. He opened an office in an empty shop on upper Yonge Street and put his shingle in the window. He was to say later that he had no expenses because he had no clients; fortunately he was living at home and could walk to his office, which was near Glencairn Avenue, to which the family had moved.

To pass the time away, he wrote for the *Canadian Encyclopedic Digest* (Ontario Edition). He was paid the most miserable space rate of a dollar a page; it was a miserly time for free-lance writers. His first article was on motor vehicle law and Roland spent hours reading all the cases that came to court; then he summarized them in a general statement and footnoted each case. It was a big subject and he finished up with some sixty pages of motor vehicle case law, all neatly and systematically digested. He did some other subjects for the same encyclopaedia, and he estimated that he never earned more than a dollar a day. However, it kept him busy and, as he said, he became well acquainted with the case law of Ontario.

Still, it wasn't enough for a man-about-town, even if the man-about-town lived at home. So Michener looked around and remembered that there was a lawyer, Daniel Webster Lang, who shared the top floor of a downtown office building with the Gregorys and who seemed to have more work than he could handle. In fact, he had said that he was looking for assistance, and Roland, who was tired of writing for an encyclopaedic pittance, was only too happy to take up his offer. Lang had been briefly a law student in Northern Ontario and then had worked for ten years with the Union Trust Company in Toronto; he had become very well known and very highly regarded as a trust officer, so it was easy for him to start his own practice. Since he had more clients than he could look after and, as Michener said, "I had none," it turned out to be a perfect match.

Once he was established with Daniel Lang and had a regular income with the likelihood of substantial increments, Roland found himself a large apartment on the second floor of a house and he shared it with a couple of other people, including his sister Marion. In any case, the house on Glencairn Avenue was only rented and when the lease ran out, his father decided to move back to Alberta; he had to attend the Senate in Ottawa and left Roly's mother to find a house in Calgary. "This may have had some bearing on my mother's displeasure at having to move so often," Michener said.

For a couple of years Roland worked as a junior for Daniel Lang; his office was next door to his old office with Gregory and Gregory, and they even acted as counsel for the Quakers. While Michener had degrees from two universities, Lang, who was ten years older, had never been to a university; he had become a lawyer in the old way of being articled as a student for five years with an established lawyer and passing the exams to be called to the Bar. While Michener was an Oxford "Blue," Lang had played semi-professional baseball. Despite these differences, the two men got along very well together and in many ways they had an ideal working relationship; so it was not long before they decided to form a partnership. On January 1, 1927, the firm of Lang Michener came into being, with new offices located on the fourteenth floor of the Sterling Tower on Bay Street.

The times were prosperous, there was a mining boom, and Michener's first clients in the newly formed partnership were mostly mining people. This was because Lang had cut his legal teeth on the prospectors in Northern Ontario. Among those first clients were such earthy characters as Robert S. Potter, the "Old Man of the North" as he was called, who was a lumberman but with a genius for mining ventures. Michener incorporated a number of companies including a gold mining company near Timmins, which was called Broulan, after Brousseau and Lang, the two promoters and prospectors who put their properties together to form the company. He acted as secretary of Broulan, which was a profitable enterprise and paid dividends for quite a time. He visited Northern Ontario to look over mining claims and even had a miner's licence to help him in his work. (He was to admit later that he had enough certificates of failed mining claims to "wallpaper a room or two" and gave up accepting shares in payment of fees because "you couldn't pay the rent with them.")

Although Michener was barrister, solicitor, and notary public, he did little court work. He acted as defence counsel in the case of a counterfeiter, a young engraver who was caught making five-dollar bills; he was obviously guilty but Michener tried to get him off because he felt that he was under the influence of an older man. However, the attorney general did not agree and his client was sent to jail, although not to the penitentiary. Michener found that he did not enjoy being a defence counsel. His emotions were involved: "I felt sorry that I couldn't have done more for him because I saw him more as a victim than a wrongdoer." Also, he found that he could never be sure of when he'd be called into court and this interfered with his other work.

Lang had some very good clients, large companies such as Kimberley Clark, the paper manufacturer, but what impressed Michener most about his partner was that he was so well known and had so many contacts. Roland had the disadvantage of being a newcomer to Toronto: he knew few of its citizens and he had not been to school or university there. So in the first year of the partnership he joined the Toronto Board of Trade as well as the social side of the organization, the Board of Trade Club, and through them he met many of the city's businessmen. At the same time he joined the Toronto Lawyers' Club, which was a young men's foundation then, and thereby got to know his fellow lawyers. "It's much more civilized practising law," Michener said, "when you're dealing with friends because you're fair and you trust each other." He took an active part in community life, serving on charity boards, and also became a member of the Canadian Institute of International Affairs and of the Ontario Selection Committee of the Rhodes Trust.

It was in his latter role—and he had by then become the selection committee's secretary—that Roland Michener got to know E.B. "Ted" Jolliffe* and Harold Day, both of whom won the 1931 Ontario Rhodes scholarships. They took law at Oxford and were called to the English Bar (Ted Jolliffe was a member of Gray's Inn) and both of them later joined the firm of Lang Michener. Jolliffe was the first to be recruited; when he returned to Canada in 1934, he went to see Michener to ask his advice about job prospects and Michener said:

---

*E.B. "Ted" Jolliffe was born at Luchow, China of Canadian missionary parents in 1909; he came to Canada when he was seventeen and took an honours course in modern history at the University of Toronto. He had a remarkable political career as leader of the CCF in Ontario and almost became premier of the province. (For further details, see following chapters.)

"Well, why not join us?" It was still a very small law firm seven years after its formation: just the two partners, Daniel Lang and Roland Michener. Harold Day entered the fold sometime later that year and a young Toronto barrister, Charles Moore Rickets, was the third man in the 1934 expansion of the firm. Lang Michener had suddenly shot up and the staff had more than doubled, but it was to remain the same size for some years to come. "The story of the firm," Michener was to say in reflecting on the tremendous expansion that occurred in later years, "is rather like the story of Toronto itself. From very small beginnings, it has progressed, it has grown, it has changed."

As Rhodes Scholars, Ted Jolliffe and Harold Day would not have been admitted to the Ontario Bar had it not been for Roly Michener. He interceded with the then-treasurer of the law society, W. N. Tilley, a "fearsome figure," according to Jolliffe, "the leading lawyer of his day, who thought that you didn't learn any law from textbooks or schools, you learned it all by hard work in a law office; therefore, he had no patience with the idea that anyone could transfer from anyplace to Ontario unless they had experience in Ontario." Michener, however, was able to persuade Tilley that special consideration should be given Ontario scholars who had taken law at Oxford and been called to the English Bar, and a special rule was passed making this possible. In doing this, Michener had shown considerable diplomatic skill. He got to know Tilley quite well and found that his only interest was the law, he took his briefs home at night and never went out, and while Michener admired him and considered him to be a "magnificent counsel," he had no ambition, as he said, to be another Tilley.

The year 1927 was a momentous one in the life of Daniel Roland Michener, for it was not only the year that the law firm of Lang Michener was formed, but it was the year that he got married. The two events were, of course, related: Roland was the model of middle-class morality and respectability and he would have considered it totally irresponsible to take a wife without the security of an established legal practice. "My two main partnerships were formed in the same year," he said. "Both lasted and both were happy."

Roly met Norah Evangeline Willis in 1924, at the home of Miss Mabel Christie, the kindly spinster who had been a "fairy godmother" to him and offered him the comforts of home when he was an RAF recruit. They had kept in touch and when he returned from Oxford, she had invited him to the occasional tea parties that she

gave for the bright and eligible young men and women of her acquaintance. In fact, Miss Christie took a personal interest in Roly's
welfare; she wanted to find him a good wife and had someone in
mind but Roly considered her to be too old and, as he said, "not
pretty enough." However, he was attracted to a good-looking girl
with beautiful red hair at one of these tea parties; he noticed Norah
Willis because she was asked to play the piano; but aside from
making a mental note, he did nothing about it. (At the time he was
interested in another girl, Margaret Thomas, whom he met while visiting Mike Pearson at Burwash Hall, University of Toronto; she later
married N.A.M. "Larry" Mackenzie, the international lawyer and
university president.)

It was Norah who made the first approach. She was studying
music at the University of Toronto and she invited him to a masked
ball at the Art Gallery. The ball had a Florentine theme and they were
to go dressed as mediaeval Florentines, and she said she would see
to it that he was properly outfitted. So he saw her every day for seven
days while the costume was being made for him: it consisted of a gold-
coloured jacket with a belt, waist-high green stocking trousers, slip-
pers, and a small sword. Norah was dressed as a Florentine lady, and
she conducted the orchestra for the entertainment she had devised
which was called "The Masque of the Dead Florentines." "There were
people impersonating famous Florentines of the period," Roly said. "I
don't know who I was supposed to be."

The daily costume fittings brought them close together and
in that short time they grew fond of each other. In fact, Roly made
up his mind then that he was going to ask her to be his wife. He
did so at the costume ball which was held in the old Goldwyn Smith
mansion that was part of the Art Gallery of Ontario. "At midnight,"
Michener recalled, "I took her up the stairs a bit. We sat down and I
asked her if she would be interested in marrying me. To my surprise,
she accepted."

The masked ball was in the spring of 1925, but they did not get
married until after the formation of the Lang Michener partnership in
1927. "We were very much suited to each other," Michener said. "She
was a beautiful girl and she danced exquisitely and I loved dancing.
She was so light on her feet that I couldn't make any mistakes."

They were married in the High Anglican church St. Mary
Magdalene in Toronto on February 26, 1927. However, St. Paul's became their family church when Roland joined and was confirmed by
the Bishop of Toronto (he said he didn't find that being an Anglican,

and not a Methodist, made a great deal of difference to his outlook on religion or life); the reason for this switch in churches was because Norah was a chorister at St. Mary Magdalene. She studied with Healey Willan, the great musician and leading composer of church music in the country, at the Toronto Conservatory of Music. When he came to Canada, Willan had become organist at St. Paul's, but he wanted to play the higher church liturgy which the rector, Canon H.J. Cody, would not countenance, so he went to St. Mary Magdalene at what was purported to be half the salary. Norah sang in the loft choir, which was a mixed choir that Healey Willan had at the rear of the church and opposite his main male choir. The wedding was conducted with great oratorical and liturgical ceremony.

The young couple went to live in an apartment on the ground floor of a house owned by Miss Mabel Christie's brother on Classic Avenue. It was large enough to accommodate their parents if they came to visit and it was, according to Michener, very cheap. Miss Christie helped to make the arrangements for housekeeping; continuing the role of fairy godmother to Norah, whose elderly parents, Mr. and Mrs. Robert Willis, lived in Vancouver. (Norah's first cousin was Eric Willis, the Conservative leader in Manitoba who was deputy premier of the province in the 1943–48 Liberal Conservative coalition government and later lieutenant-governor.)

When their first child, Joan, was born on October 3, 1927 (she was a premature baby), the Micheners moved into the upstairs flat, which occupied the whole of the second and third floors. They were within easy walking distance of 12 Admiral Road where the Pearsons had the top-floor apartment. Mike had married Maryon Moody about a year and a half before the Micheners' wedding. Maryon had been one of Professor Pearson's history students, and Roland had met her on his many visits to Burwash Hall for tea and tennis with Mike and remembered her as a pretty, dark-haired girl with a lively interest in all that was going on. He had taken Norah around to meet them when they were going out together, and Norah and Maryon had become friends. Both of them had children about the same time (the Pearsons' son, Geoffrey, was born on December 25, 1927) and, in the good weather, they would wheel them around in prams to each other's apartments.

Mitch and Mike's friendship was not lessened in any way by marriage. They had some hilarious times together, not the least of which was a diaper-changing contest. At least this is what Mike Pearson, who had recently retired as prime minister, told a black-tie dinner honouring Governor General Michener at the Rideau Club in Ottawa. He said that they were alone in the old Admiral Road flat with his little son and Roland's little daughter—they were probably baby-sitting while Norah and Maryon were at the movies or out somewhere. At any rate, they had a competition to see who could change diapers more quickly and, according to Pearson, Michener was a little faster than he was. The dinner party was amused and the Governor General surprised: he did not remember the event, although he was to say that there was "some semblance of truth to it" because the two families were very close and visited each other often until Mike won the External Affairs competition a few months later and the Pearsons moved to Ottawa.

Norah gave up studying music; she had decided that, while she played the piano quite well, she would never make a mark as an instrumentalist. She was more interested in teaching but she gave that up when her first child was born. After her children were old enough to go to school, she went back to the University of Toronto to study philosophy and eventually got a doctorate in philosophy.

Roland continued to practise law. He had a prodigious capacity for hard work, according to Ted Jolliffe, and he could get through a great deal of work in a short time. He always tried to identify the positive and constructive aspect of any situation. "He had the ability not only to do a job well but to maintain the appropriate connections to do the job," Jolliffe said. "Now in this I must say that his late wife was a great help to him because she was good at that, too." However, Michener was not tied to law as the great counsel W.N. Tilley was; he had never given up his interest in politics and, as he said, he had taken up law as a means to politics. It was not long before that happened.

❧ 6 ❧

IN FATHER'S
FOOTSTEPS

ALTHOUGH MOST OF LANG MICHENER'S clients were in natural resources and the mining or lumber industries, there was, from the beginning, a political side to the firm's work. Daniel Lang was a bag man for the Liberal Party of Ontario and became its treasurer and Premier Mitchell Hepburn would often visit the office. As a perquisite or reward for his money-raising, Lang was made a trustee of the Dionne quintuplets, helped to negotiate some of the lucrative advertising contracts for them, and acted as a banker for the babies. Roland Michener was not involved in any way with the quintuplets, but when he was up at North Bay he did visit Callendar and was welcomed as a partner of the trustee and met the parents and the famous children. He himself was to say that he spent most of the twenties and thirties consolidating his law practice and making sure that his family would not suffer for lack of a secure income.

However, there was his father, Senator Edward Michener, who became a government supporter and spokesman in the Upper

House when the Conservatives came to power in 1930. Yet he was *persona non grata* with the prime minister: R.B. Bennett had always resented the fact that Michener had been made a Senator; he thought that he should have had the appointment in recognition of his work as Director General of National Services in the First World War. He had protested loudly and long to Sir Robert Borden. Bennett had neither forgotten nor forgiven and did not hide his dislike of Senator Michener,* although he was always cordial to the son whenever they met in Ottawa. "We couldn't understand it," Roland said. "If he had got the Senate appointment instead of my father, he would never have become prime minister. Yet here he was still bearing this grudge." Despite all this, the younger Michener joined the Conservative Albany Club in the mid-thirties; he was tiptoeing in his father's footsteps.

At about the same time the newly returned Rhodes Scholar Ted Jolliffe started with the Lang Michener firm. He had become a socialist at Oxford and was a member of the university's very large Labour Club. He was at the crowded Oxford Union meeting at which the celebrated anti-war resolution was adopted; it states, in so many words, they "would not fight for king or country." Jolliffe and fellow Rhodes Scholar David Lewis held an organizational conference in Oxford for the newly formed socialist party, the Co-operative Commonwealth Federation (CCF), which was attended by some fifty Canadian university students. As might be expected, shortly after his return, Jolliffe joined the St. Paul's CCF Club in central Toronto, and was the CCF candidate for St. Paul's riding in the 1935 federal election (he got five thousand votes, which was more than he expected).

It was in the early forties that the full extent of the law firm's political involvement became apparent and was the subject of some ribbing by colleagues and derisory comments in the press. In the spring of 1942 Ted Jolliffe was made leader of the Ontario CCF Party;

---

*While in Ottawa, Senator Edward Michener became interested in the occult. His son never shared this interest. Spiritualism was popular after the First World War because so many people longed to communicate with departed loved ones. The Senator (and his wife) visited mediums, particularly one in Toledo, Ohio, who purported to be in touch with his first-born child, Anna Marie, who had died in infancy. A "spirit" picture was taken and the poltergeist behind him bore an uncanny resemblance to his father-in-law. The Senator went to England to attend meetings of the British Psychic Society. His behaviour was similar to that of Mackenzie King, although he hardly knew him; however, Senator Michener was different from the Liberal prime minister in that he eventually became disillusioned with the occult. He came to the conclusion that there were as likely to be evil spirits as good spirits, and in his last years he went to no séances. Edward also believed in divining for oil; he made up a metal wand that he used without success. Roland and another son, Charles, who was a geologist, pooh-poohed the idea.

in the following year, Roland Michener became the Conservative candidate for the St. David's riding in the 1943 provincial election; and Daniel Lang continued to be treasurer of the Ontario Liberal Party. Lang Michener, according to the newspapers, had every political party covered; it was taking no chances and would get government business, whoever won. But Michener saw it differently: "We were like a ship with an anchor in every direction," he said, "and consequently there was no possibility of movement."

The Liberal–Conservative–CCF troika did not last for long. By becoming the Ontario CCF leader, Jolliffe lost a major client, the Canadian Press, the cooperative news agency, which, not unreasonably but reluctantly, agreed that it could not have a party leader as its counsel, and while he was getting some trade union and professional association work, he soon realized that he could not spend enough time on his practice. Michener felt that Jolliffe's position as CCF leader was "not an association that was conducive to business." However, it was by mutual consent that they parted company; Jolliffe left the Lang Michener firm at the time of the 1943 election to campaign as a full-time party leader; in any case, he would have had to leave after the election because he became Leader of the Opposition at Queen's Park.

On joining the Albany Club, which had a certain stuffy reputation, Michener found a lively discussion group of younger members who called themselves "The Drones"; they adopted the slogan "Above All No Zeal," and affected the role of dilettantes, although they were essentially realists who were committed to making the Conservative Party more modern in its outlook. The group, which was described by Michener as a Tory "ginger group," was organized by Beverly Matthews, a young corporation lawyer, and included, beside Michener, such people as Leslie Blackwell, Dana Porter, Fred Gardiner, Donald Fleming, and David Walker, all of whom were to make their mark in public life. Most of them also belonged to another discussion group that had no particular name and whose mentor was an older member, James M. Macdonnell, president of the National Trust Company. Although a prominent businessman himself, Macdonnell was an advocate of greater state control of the economy as a way of overcoming the Depression. Michener never knew a more dedicated Tory than Macdonnell, who took early retirement in order to devote the rest of his life to the party.

As a result of Daniel Lang's connection with the Ontario Liberals, Roland Michener got to know Mitchell Hepburn and even went to one or two of his meetings. He found the premier to be an engaging platform speaker who had a way of getting an audience on his side, although Michener said, "I don't think his speeches made a lasting impression." Hepburn had a well-developed sense of humour and Michener recalled a joke he played on the Albany Club. It was after an annual meeting and some of the younger members stayed on to celebrate; they decided that the bust of Sir John A. Macdonald, the founder of the club, needed cleaning. So they took it from its place of honour in the dining room to an upstairs bathroom where they proceeded to wash it, only to find that the bust was made of plaster and was rapidly disintegrating.

This was a very serious matter for the Albany Club but, as Michener said, one fellow remembered there was a bust of Macdonald at the Ontario Legislature, and he was able to get the premier on the telephone to ask if they could borrow it. Mitch Hepburn was most understanding and said that he would arrange with the night watchman to have the bust ready for them to pick up. A delegation of members in a joyful, much relieved mood set out for Queen's Park, picked up the bust, and quickly returned to the Albany Club and put it in its proper place before any of the older members knew what had happened. Two weeks were to pass before someone noticed that the bust was that of Sir Wilfrid Laurier.

It was not till January 1940 that Roland Michener took part in practical politics. Prime Minister Mackenzie King had called a snap election for March 26 (his pretext was a motion censuring his government for its war effort which had been passed by the Ontario Legislature with the full support of Premier Hepburn). Michener was behind the effort of H.R. Jackman, a Toronto financier, to wrest the nomination for the Rosedale riding from H.G. Clarke, the unpopular incumbent. There was an uproar at the meeting when the chairman, who was described as "a dainty, middle-aged woman," tried to push Clarke off the platform. Jackman won the nomination and with the full support of the Rosedale Conservatives went on to win the seat. However, while the Tories were a great success in Toronto, they failed dismally across the country, ending up with only forty Members of Parliament and the loss of their leader, Robert Manion.

Most members of the Albany Club had not been greatly impressed with Manion before the election and afterward blamed him for its disastrous outcome. The leadership had become an issue that was to plague the Conservatives for years to come, and it was never worse than in the early forties when the party was at its lowest ebb. The Tories decided to do without a convention and managed to per-

suade the former prime minister, Arthur Meighen, to leave his comfortable seat in the Senate and resume the leadership. R.B. Hanson,
a former Bennett cabinet minister, led the party in the House of
Commons, but Meighen was really in charge and issued directives
from the public gallery. The situation was too awkward to last for
long, and so, in February of 1942, Arthur Meighen tried to get elected in the constituency of York South which had been opened up for
him by the resignation of the Conservative MP Lieutenant Colonel
Alan Cockeram.

In an astute political move, Prime Minister Mackenzie King
decided that the Liberals would not contest the by-election, leaving
Meighen to face the little-known CCF candidate, J. W. Noseworthy. At
the time there was a rising demand for conscription, and Meighen
based his campaign on conscription and criticism of the Liberal war
effort. (Roland Michener was in favour of conscription, and felt that
the least he could do was to join up, and so, after Pearl Harbor, he
enlisted as a gunner in a reserve battery of the Royal Canadian
Artillery in Toronto and shortly afterward was commissioned as a
lieutenant.) It might have been better if Meighen had listened to the
advice of one of The Drones, Fred Gardiner, who recommended campaigning on postwar policies, because the old Tory leader was
swamped at the polls by Noseworthy who won by more than four
thousand votes.

While he was no great fan of Meighen, Jim Macdonnell was
nevertheless disturbed by the outcome of the York South by-election.
He had been studying public opinion polls and had noticed that
the CCF was gaining strength at the expense of the Conservatives, and
he was afraid that a polarization in Canadian politics could occur
with the Tories being all but wiped out. Macdonnell wrote to R.B.
Hanson, the acting Conservative leader, about his concerns for the
future and recommended a serious examination of the party's policies
on welfare and postwar reconstruction. Hanson agreed, and thus the
idea of a "thinkers' conference" grew out of the debacle of the York
South by-election.

Macdonnell recruited the organizers of the conference from
The Drones but he brought in a Winnipeg lawyer, Rod Finlayson, a
former executive assistant to Prime Minister R.B. Bennett, to help
frame the policy resolutions. They decided that the conference would
be held on the Labour Day weekend of 1942 at Trinity College in
Port Hope, Ontario, and that, instead of involving elected politicians,
delegates be chosen from the party's membership lists on the basis

of their prominence and influence in business and the professions. Macdonnell and Finlayson worked all summer preparing an agenda and outlining programs for the conference.

Roland Michener remembered Macdonnell speaking to the Toronto Conservative Businessmen's Club and posing the rhetorical question: "Would you rather adopt a policy which will retain the largest amount of free enterprise or hand over to the CCF?" That seemed to sum up the whole purpose of the coming Port Hope Conference. The organizers' efforts were successful. Despite wartime restrictions on travel, 159 delegates attended, according to the official count; the majority (94) were from Ontario, but there were 10 French-speaking Canadians from Quebec, and all regions were represented. Among the delegates were Charlotte Whitton, the pioneering social scientist, Sidney Smith, president of the University of Manitoba, Floyd Chalmers, editor of the *Financial Post*; and Harry Hopper, a representative of the Trades and Labour Council.

Port Hope was the first national political meeting that Michener ever attended, and he was impressed by both the high calibre of the delegates and the tone of the debate. The conference was divided into five committees dealing with the five main problems: war, labour, agriculture, education, and reconstruction. Michener was on the reconstruction committee, which was chaired by Donald Fleming and which was, in many ways, the most important committee since it dealt with postwar Canada. The committee recommended the creation of a federal ministry of social security and reconstruction to administer unemployment insurance and various welfare programs. It also endorsed a national low-cost housing program, the provision of adequate health services for all Canadians, equality of the sexes in the workplace, and increased old age pensions. The resolutions of each committee had to be adopted unanimously by all delegates before they could be accepted by the conference.

After almost four days of intense discussion and negotiation, the Port Hope Conference ended with congratulations all around. Michener found the experience exciting: his interest in policymaking had been aroused and he felt that the attention that the conference and the Conservative Party had received in the press had made it "all quite worthwhile."

The departure of the delegates did not mean that the work of the conference was over since the party had called for a leadership convention to be held in Winnipeg on December 9–11, 1942, and Macdonnell was determined that the resolutions passed at Port Hope would be the basis for the party's new "National Policy." Therefore he got Michener to help him and Finlayson to edit and summarize the committees' reports and resolutions, and he had them published as the main policy papers for the Winnipeg leadership convention.

The old Tory, Arthur Meighen, had apparently accepted his critics' claim that he was too reactionary and had gone to the other extreme of wanting John Bracken, the Premier of Manitoba, who was a Progressive, to succeed him as leader of the Conservative Party. This wish and Meighen's belief that the prairies were the last bastion of true Conservatism in Canada despite the rejection of the Tories in every election simply baffled Michener and other members of the Albany Club. In the weeks leading up to the Winnipeg convention, there were also reports that during trips to the prairies Jim Macdonnell was lining up delegates for Murdoch MacPherson, the former attorney general of Saskatchewan and farmers' advocate. MacPherson had made a great impression at the 1938 Conservative leadership convention in Toronto when his popularity and oratory almost upset the carefully organized effort to make Dr. Robert Manion the leader.

However, Roland Michener denied these reports and said that Macdonnell was mainly interested in policy and had told him that, as far as the leadership was concerned, he favoured Bracken. The day before the convention began, Michener and Macdonnell and others from the Albany Club went to Winnipeg in order to drum up support for the Port Hope program. He was part of a "policy team" organized by Rod Finlayson that included Cecil Frost,* Fred Gardiner, Donald Fleming, and Dick Bell, at the time Hanson's secretary. Bell's task was to assist Frost, who headed the main resolutions committee at the convention. They were entirely successful "without too much effort," as Michener said, and the whole Port Hope program was adopted by the Conservative Party under the slogan: "Freedom—Security—Opportunity and the British Partnership." It was a slogan that summed up the aims of the new policy and captured the spirit of the times, and it was devised by Michener.

---

*Cecil Frost was the younger brother of Leslie Frost, who became premier of Ontario. Both were First World War veterans, and when the war ended both returned to study law and set up a practice together in Lindsay, Ontario. Both wanted political careers but they realized that one of them had to manage their law firm. They decided to flip a coin, with the result that Leslie became the politician and Cecil remained the lawyer although he did take an active part in Conservative Party organization; he was president of the Ontario Conservatives from 1938 to 1943. Cecil died in 1947, a couple of years before his brother, Leslie, became premier.

"We were no longer 'True Blue' Tories who were sentimental over the British connection and opposed state involvement in the economy," Michener said in commenting on the new platform adopted at the Winnipeg convention, "but we still firmly believed that wealth could not be effectively created without the free play of capitalism and that world peace and security were best assured by an active alliance between the British Commonwealth and the United States." While Michener was actively involved in the party's policy decisions, he took no part in the leadership race. Yet it was the Tories' "new look" that made Bracken finally agree at the last moment to be drafted for the leadership. An advance copy of the policy resolutions was shown him and he was particularly impressed by the agricultural proposals, which promised marketing boards and price stabilization. They were what his Progressives wanted, and Bracken's condition for leading the party was that it be renamed the Progressive Conservative Party.

Although Roland Michener stayed aloof from the leadership race and left "king making" to others, he was intrigued by the whole process. He felt that he was too much of a newcomer to campaign actively for one or other of the candidates, as his colleague from the Albany Club, David Walker, was doing in the case of John Diefenbaker. It was the first time that he had ever seen Diefenbaker, the prairie lawyer, who was considered to be an upstart since he had been a member of Parliament for a mere twenty-one months. Then he was introduced with the German pronunciation of his name, "Diefenbarker," which must have upset him as he rattled off the words of his speech at a machine gun rate. Michener was not impressed and, as he said, "few would have predicted that he was to make such a mark on our nation's affairs from his performance at the Winnipeg convention."

Another candidate whom Michener noted was Howard Green, who later became External Affairs Minister in the Diefenbaker government; Green must have been overwhelmed by the whole affair as he fainted part way through his speech. He was revived and was allowed to finish his remarks the following day. Both Green and Diefenbaker were among the also-rans at the convention, with Green getting eighty-eight votes and Diefenbaker one hundred and twenty on the first ballot. Michener recalled that Lieutenant-Colonel George Drew, Conservative leader in Ontario, was under a great deal of pressure to run, "but he had the sense not to be tempted onto the federal scene at that time." When it came to the vote, Michener, who had been a fascinated observer, cast his ballot for Murdoch MacPherson, the runner-up to John Bracken for the leadership of the Progressive Conservative Party.

Meanwhile there were ructions at Queen's Park. For no apparent reason, Premier Mitchell Hepburn had suddenly resigned and turned over his office to his attorney general, Gordon Conant. The scuttlebut was that he had quit in order to rally Ontario behind him in his fight with Prime Minister Mackenzie King, but Michener believed that if he had not resigned, his party would have kicked him out. Even though Hepburn's erratic behaviour redounded to the credit of the Conservatives, Michener frowned on it: he felt that no provincial leader should go around criticizing his federal leader in the way Hepburn did. Shortly afterward, Conant, who was a colourless personality and proved to be inept as premier, bowed to demands that there should be a leadership convention and one was held in April 1943. Harry Nixon, a Brant County farmer and veteran Liberal cabinet minister, was elected leader; Nixon was not an enthusiastic politician and had said that a herd of Holsteins was a lot more dependable for a living than a fickle electorate. Nevertheless he put his fate in the latter's hands by calling a provincial election for August 4, 1943.

Although Roland Michener had got to know George Drew when he was the first Securities Commissioner for the province and had played squash with him at the University Club, he was not close to him because he was interested primarily in federal politics. Michener knew that Drew was concerned with postwar reconstruction and had shown a great interest in the results of the Port Hope Conference that had been adopted as the party's platform at the Winnipeg convention and, in fact, had urged local riding associations to study the new policy, and so he wrote the Ontario Conservative leader recommending that a provincial policy convention be held.

I feel that the similar procedure in the federal area was a great stimulus to the party, and also had very considerable publicity value, [Michener said in his letter]. Both of these benefits might be obtained in the provincial area by similar tactics. There appears to be no need in the province for a laymen's movement such as Port Hope. As I see it the whole matter might be done officially by the Ontario Conservative Association. Roughly, the procedure would be for the Association to appoint a general policy committee, with authority to name preconvention sub-committees on each of the important issues, and to organize these sub-committees and set them to work six weeks or two months in advance of the date for the provincial meeting. I feel that the provincial meeting ought to be held in July, and as much earlier as is possible depending on how well the preconvention work is advanced.

What I suggest is not intended to be a reflection in any way on the provincial leader of the Party.

The convention may be able to do very little other than to endorse the sub-committee's conclusions. However, the participation and co-operation of many people is certainly a benefit to them and may very well produce some new and useful ideas on provincial affairs.

George Drew liked Michener's idea, and Cecil Frost, the Tories' workhorse, was able to organize all the details of the committee's and subcommittees' work in time for holding a convention in Toronto on July 3, 1943. At the meeting the Ontario Party accepted the name "Progressive Conservative" and discussed and approved the policy platform that Drew had drawn up with the assistance of the provincial party stalwarts, Ed Bickle and Alex Mackenzie, and which became famous as the "Twenty-two Points." In Michener's view, there was nothing to match the foresight and broadmindedness and popular appeal of the Twenty-two Points; they were in keeping with the Port Hope proposals, with which Drew did not want to be associated, but focused more clearly on the needs of mining and agriculture and on the issues of dominion-provincial relations and of social security legislation for the postwar period. (Drew, who was always conscious of his authority, had felt that the calling of the Port Hope Conference undermined his leadership.)

During the days leading up to the July policy conference, the joint Rosedale–St. David's–Ward 2 Conservative Association approached Michener, who was making his mark as a Tory activist, and asked him if he would be interested in contesting the St. David's provincial seat. The Conservative candidate for the riding from the previous campaign was on active service and wanted to step down in favour of whomever the party chose. Although his chief interest was in federal politics, Roland Michener decided that he should accept the nomination out of a sense of duty to the party; and then dangling before him was the ultimate political experience of being a candidate and taking part in an election campaign.

The nomination meeting was held on the evening of June 17, 1943. The former candidate for St. David's, Wilfrid Heighington, was able to attend and gave his blessing to the proceedings, and the meeting elected Roland Michener by acclamation to be the Conservative candidate in the next provincial election, which was expected to be called at any time. Following the meeting, Michener wrote Drew offering his "undivided support" and saying that he was afraid that he would be "awkward at the game at first and shall appreciate your assistance and advice."

However, there was little time for advice or preparation of any kind because it was on July 1 that the new Liberal Premier of Ontario, Harry Nixon, called for the election on August 4. While the Liberals might have been confident that they would be returned to power on the basis of their record and promises of reform, it was soon apparent that they were losing ground to the Progressive Conservatives and the CCF. The election had become a showdown between those supporting a free marketplace and those advocating a socialist system of a controlled economy. The CCF, under their new leader and former Michener associate, Ted Jolliffe, were not beyond crying alarm: their election pamphlets claimed that if either the Liberals or the Progressive Conservatives were in power after the war ended, there would be disastrous unemployment and the Depression would return.

In St. David's, Roland Michener campaigned vigourously on the Twenty-two Points and on the PC slogan "Make Ontario Strong," but it was a difficult fight. His opponents were two seasoned campaigners, Allan Lamport, the encumbent Liberal member, and the CCF candidate, William Dennison, who had been active in muncipal politics since 1935 (he was to become mayor of Toronto). Michener asserted that Dennison "knew everybody south of Bloor Street by his first name, and called on everyone regularly." As a result of this thorough door-to-door canvassing, which was already an important part of a CCF campaign, Dennison won with 5,668 votes to Michener's 5,059, with Lamport well behind in third place.

St. David's reflected the Ontario electoral scene only in the closeness of the result. Provincially, George Drew's Progressive Conservatives won thirty-eight seats, the CCF thirty-four, the Liberals fifteen and the Communists two. Michener expressed himself as being "very alarmed at the close call that the province had from being immersed in a socialist regime, being subjected to socialist policies and programs—there was only four seats difference [between the PCs and the CCF] and Mr. Jolliffe was almost the premier."

Roland Michener had his political baptism at forty-three years of age. Despite his having said that it was his boyhood dream to follow in his father's footsteps, he had not joined a student Conservative club as there was none at the University of Alberta, and, at Oxford, he had been a guest and felt that any interest in politics would be out of place. However, when he returned home, he had not become a member of the Young Conservative Association, perhaps because he was too busy with his law practice and his young family. It was not till his late thirties when he joined the Albany Club that he became involved in any way with the Tories, and he was in his fifties when he achieved his real ambition of becoming a Member of Parliament. Michener came late into politics but, because of his capacity for work and his concentration rather than charisma, that tardiness did not seem to hinder his progress.

∞ 7 ∞

RECONSTRUCTING
ONTARIO

S⊤. DAVID'S RESULT WAS a disappointment for Roland Michener. It was a close call, just a little over six hundred votes: he thought that if he had spent more time in the riding, in door-to-door canvassing, as Bill Dennison had done, instead of going around the province helping his leader, George Drew, and preparing position papers for him, he might have won. At any rate, he had made a good showing for a first time, and that was what his supporters said. It was disappointing yet thrilling and he would never forget the excitement of election night as the polls reported; it reminded him of the tense election night atmosphere long ago in Alberta when his father was the candidate. Michener went back to work in his law office but he knew that it would never be the same. He had succumbed to the political bug, and within weeks of the provincial election he was talking to people in the riding, telling them where he stood on the issues of the day and that he would be running again.

It was obvious that the minority Drew government could not last long and that another election could occur at any time. The Progressive Conservative Party began making immediate preparations for the hustings; it had no difficulty replenishing its treasury since businessmen were having nightmares about Red Revolution and saw the party as the only bulwark against socialism. The Liberals, whose leadership had reverted to Mitch Hepburn, were regarded as a lost cause. Michener denied charges that the Tories had more money than they knew what to do with, although he admitted that they did not lack for funds. However, he pointed out that he had nothing to do with this part of the organization. At the same time W.E. Gladstone Murray, the former general manager of the Canadian Broadcasting Corporation, began an anti-socialist campaign that was said to have been financed by Bay Street. Some characterized it as a "witch hunt," but Michener thought that "on the whole it was helpful" and said that "he presented his case very well."

Meanwhile George Drew behaved as if he had a majority, and, as often happens when there has been a change of government but without a majority, a lot of good legislation was passed. Even the CCF admitted as much. Although Michener was outside the legislature, on occasion the new premier called on him for research assignments. He said that Drew felt that he should wait a couple of years before he could decently "complete the circuit," but once that period of grace was up, he was ready and willing to have a provincial election. And Michener believed that Drew had been able to manoeuvre the Liberals and the CCF into bringing down his government, but he was not in the House at the time and did not know the full story.

However, his erstwhile colleague, Ted Jolliffe, was a leading participant. Jolliffe spoke of the great pressure exerted on the CCF by "certain unions, particularly those under Communist influence" to "get rid of Drew at all costs." There were two Communist members of the Ontario Legislature, J. B. Salsberg and Alex A. MacLeod, and they were cronies of Mitch Hepburn, who had resumed the leadership of the Liberals, and they kept goading him to throw the Tories out. MacLeod, according to Jolliffe, had a "sinister influence" on the former premier. At any rate, Hepburn came to see the CCF leader and proposed that "we unite to defeat Drew and then advise the lieutenant-governor that we could form a government—and his proposal was that I should be prime minister, and his only stipulation was that he [Hepburn] should be provincial treasurer." Harry Nixon, the former Liberal leader, who was also at this clandestine meeting, seemed doubtful that the lieutenant-governor would comply, but nevertheless he wanted to give it a try. "I didn't buy it," Jolliffe asserted; "I knew the CCF would not buy it and I didn't think it would work with anybody as volatile and unpredictable as Hepburn."

The upshot of these conspiratorial comings and goings at Queen's Park was that Ted Jolliffe, as Opposition Leader, moved the conventional nonconfidence amendment to the Speech from the Throne, in the expectation that it would not pass. However, Mitch Hepburn, as leader of the third party, moved an amendment to the amendment which was voted on first and was couched in terms that the CCF could not but support. "The government was defeated," Jolliffe said, "which was exactly what Drew wanted. He wanted an election and, at that point, he was sure he could win." The nonconfidence vote was on March 22, 1945, and Drew immediately and gleefully called an election for June 4.

It was a debacle. There was, of course, no attempt on the part of the CCF and the Liberals to call on the lieutenant-governor and say that they had a coalition and could carry on government because there had been no agreement. Jolliffe had refused to go along with Hepburn's wild scheme. Roland Michener wondered what kind of a premier Ted Jolliffe would have made; he did not regard his former associate as a dangerous radical but "just a sincere reformer who had thrown in his lot with the socialist party," and he thought that "with the responsibility of power, he would be a perfectly acceptable head of government." (Jolliffe would probably have agreed with that description of himself; he disliked the term "right-wing socialist" and said that he was always "in the middle of the road, the left road.")

The 1945 provincial election was very different from the 1943 election. The tide was running in favour of the Tories and Michener could sense this, and that "it was a very different wicket," as he put it, from the last time. "But," he said, "I've never been confident of being elected, and for very good reason: I was elected four times and defeated four times and I couldn't see any reason for the change. It was there and it occurred. The pendulum swings back and forth regardless of what you do."

However, Michener was more experienced and better organized and prepared for this second try. He concentrated on the St. David's riding this time, and he and his PC supporters canvassed every home in an all-out effort to unseat the CCF member, Bill Dennison. The 1945 provincial election was a head-on struggle between the Progressive Conservatives and the Co-operative Commonwealth

Federation, with the Liberals virtually ignored; it was a clear-cut confrontation between capitalism and socialism. The participants recognized it as such, and the Tories shovelled out reams of anti-socialist literature, some of it written by Gladstone Murray, as well as pamphlets praising the Twenty-two Points and the achievements of the minority Drew government. Michener, on his part, distributed condensed versions of the economist Freiderich Hayek's attack on socialism entitled *The Road to Serfdom*; and his campaign organizers ran a newspaper advertisement with the heading in large type: Asks Labour Support for Free Enterprise.

Although the CCF had been caught on a confidence vote and was very much on the defensive, it had on its side the *Toronto Star* with the biggest daily circulation in Canada. Ted Jolliffe struck back toward the end of the election campaign with the charge of "Gestapo" tactics against George Drew. This referred to security measures taken during the war when thousands of people were investigated for sub-versive activities; the records were kept in filing cabinets at Queen's Park. Michener described it as "a sort-of mare's nest"; a leftover of wartime espionage in charge of a couple of policemen. There were probably names of CCFers in the files, but there might have been files on a lot of Conservatives and Liberals too, and Michener said, "They were collected not for political purposes but because of the war and it was just accidental that they were there; they were not being kept up or augmented." However, Jolliffe asserted that George Drew, as premier, had given his approval to these spying activities and that there were files on "all sorts of people, trade unionists, doctors, lawyers, the principal of Queen's University, anybody and everybody who had ever contributed to or encouraged the Aid-to-Russia cam-paign during the war."

The CCF leader made the Gestapo charge only two weeks be-fore the election although he had known about the secret service work at Queen's Park for fully a year and a half. His explanation was that he had done so to protect his source, one of the agents, who was pro-viding him with carbon copies of his reports, but he might have felt that he could not attack the Tories on this matter until the war in Europe was over (VE Day was May 8, 1945). At any rate, Roland Michener dismissed it as an "extravagant charge, baseless," and said that he paid practically no attention to it, and "if it had any effect on the election, I think it was helpful to the Conservatives."

Ted Jolliffe had to agree, although he was ambivalent about its effect on his own party; during the campaign he sensed that support for the CCF had dwindled, and said the Gestapo charge "did not greatly reduce our total vote but it did hurt us because it tended to bring out large numbers of Conservatively minded voters who hadn't bothered to vote in 1943. They came out in droves—there was a heavy vote—because they were alarmed." However, Jolliffe felt that, as a matter of principle, he had to expose the secret police operations at Queen's Park and point out the danger that they represented to a free society, and after the election, which proved disastrous for the CCF, he was given a vote of confidence on the Gestapo issue at the party's provincial convention.

As expected, the election resulted in a triumph for the Progressive Conservatives: eleven of Toronto's thirteen seats went to the Tories, with Roland Michener winning St. David's by a decisive plurality of almost three thousand votes; the two other Toronto seats were held by encumbent Labour Progressive or Communist members Salsberg and MacLeod (the CCF lost all four city seats). Premier George Drew had a handsome majority of sixty-six in a legislature of only ninety members, but that was not as good an indication of his sweeping victory as the fact that his party got 79 1/2 percent of the vote, which must be the highest percentage that the Tories ever won in Ontario, certainly since the First World War. The landslide was such that the leaders of both opposition parties, the CCF's Ted Jolliffe and the Liberals' Mitch Hepburn,* were defeated. (The CCF finished up with eight seats and was no longer the official opposition because the Liberals won eleven seat and with the Liberal Labour could count fourteen members.)

Almost immediately following the election, Premier George Drew asked Roland Michener to join the Ontario delegation to the first meeting of the Dominion-Provincial Conference on Post-War Reconstruction; Drew had been impressed with the research work that Michener had done for him in the days of his minority Conservative government and was sure that he would be able to gather together precedents to support his stand for provincial rights and a decentral-

---

*Mitchell Hepburn, the popular and affable onion farmer from St. Thomas, Ontario, was a political phenomenon when he led the Liberals to power at Queen's Park in 1934. He had the same huge majority as Drew's in 1945, sixty-six out of the Legislature's ninety seats. He had had almost as big a victory in 1937 with sixty-three members. However, his increasingly erratic behaviour and his bitter clash with the federal Liberal leader, Mackenzie King, brought about his downfall and that of his party. After his personal defeat in the 1945 provincial election, he did not run again and was fifty-seven years old when he died at St. Thomas in 1953.

ized authority. Michener enjoyed the work and felt that his services were appreciated. "I had the right kind of training," he said, "and I used to find him ammunition and prepare it for the firing line. We worked well together."

The provinces had come to the conference in the hope that the federal government would return to them some if not all the taxing powers that they had given up for the duration of the war. The provincial view as expressed by Michener was that Ottawa had given a firm undertaking that they would do so as soon as the conflict was over. However, the flood of preconference proposals and position papers aroused the suspicion that the federal government would not keep its word. There were the so-called "Red Books," which were based on the Rowell-Sirois Commission report on the Canadian economy and said that federal sponsorship of welfare programs and unemployment insurance was needed to see the country through the anticipated postwar recession.

It was known that the Ottawa bureaucrats wanted to hang on to their wartime powers but, from the opening of the conference, the federal representatives, the prime minister, Mackenzie King, the finance minister, J.L. Illsley, the justice minister, Louis St. Laurent, and the minister of reconstruction, C.D. Howe, made it clear that they considered welfare to be their responsibility. In fact, Ottawa had released its proposals for the establishment of a welfare system to the newspapers before the provincial delegations had received them. The atmosphere of the conference was poisoned by the federal action, which put the provinces on the defensive and left them little to propose. George Drew was furious and so was the Quebec premier, Maurice Duplessis. There was no love lost between Duplessis and St. Laurent who sat next to each other. The Quebec premier baited the federal minister over the defeat of his nephew in a by-election. "I speak for Quebec," Duplessis said. "You couldn't even get your nephew elected." The meeting went on for three days but, as Michener said, it got nowhere.

As a private member of the provincial legislature, Michener acted as an advisor to the Ontario delegation and sat behind Premier Drew in the chamber of the House of Commons, Ottawa, where the conference was held early in August 1945. His main memory of this abortive meeting was that Mackenzie King told the delegates at one of the sessions that he had just learned that the atomic bomb had been dropped on Hiroshima. A pall of silence fell on the meeting as everyone realized the awful importance of the news, although no one understood it fully. The prime minister could give no further information but said gravely that they were at the beginning of a new era.

There was a further dominion-provincial conference the following year and Roland Michener was again a member of the Ontario delegation. He recalled that this time they were ready to reach a fiscal agreement whereby Ottawa would retain much of the taxation field it had taken over during the war, as long as it gave back what were called the "six minor taxes." These included such things as corporation stock transfer taxes, theatre and amusement taxes, the gasoline tax, and so on, and Michener believed that they yielded seventy or eighty million dollars a year. "That doesn't sound like much," he said, "and even Mr. Duplessis had agreed with Mr. Drew that he would accept the proposal and they would enter into a fiscal agreement if that one concession were made."

The argument went on that night and the next morning and Finance Minister Illsley, whom, Michener felt, was worn out from the war effort and "perhaps a bit rigid on that account," said "No." Duplessis did not wait for the end of the day's conference; he walked out and got on the train at about two o'clock in the afternoon and left Ottawa. "The rest of us stayed on," Michener said, "but it was the end of bargaining and attempts to reach an agreement." The federal government had failed to get consent for its fiscal policies, which included transfer or equalization payments from the rich provinces, and especially Ontario, to the poorer provinces, but Ottawa found a way around to get what it wanted by legislation. It offered welfare agreements to individual provinces, thus inaugurating a patchwork system of social services across Canada that remained in effect until 1961, when the Diefenbaker government, with the cooperation of the provinces, was able to create a more comprehensive national welfare program.

On April 15, 1946, Roland Michener was officially sworn into the Ontario government as provincial secretary. Premier Drew conceived of the provincial secretary's office as the connecting link for all the departments of government but, first of all, he asked Michener to organize the business of the provincial cabinet which was conducted in a haphazard, nineteenth century manner, without an agenda and with no real secretary. The clerk of the Privy Council, or Executive Council as it was called in Ontario, kept track of the orders-in-council that were passed, but he did not attend cabinet meetings: no civil servant was allowed in the *sanctum sanctorum* of government.

Fortunately for Michener, there were two effective precedents: in 1916 the British prime minister, David Lloyd George, found that he had to improve the government's conduct of the war and introduced a secretariat that sat in on cabinet meetings. This was the first precedent and it was followed in Canada when Arnold Heeney advised Prime Minister Mackenzie King in 1938 on the establishment of a cabinet secretariat similar to that in Westminster. Michener consulted Heeney, who was junior to him in years but also a Rhodes Scholar. "We went over the whole program that he had established and I adapted it as far as I could to Ontario needs."

As a result, a cabinet office was formed in the Department of the Provincial Secretary; it was put in charge of a deputy minister who was also to be Secretary of the Cabinet. All business to come before the Executive Council was to be sent first to that office. A confidential agenda and memorandum were then prepared and sent to each minister at least the day before a cabinet meeting. Thus the ministers came to the Council fully briefed on what was to be considered, and were able to take part in discussions. The Secretary of the Cabinet would attend all regular meetings and would record the decisions; he would also advise any ministers who were absent of decisions that affected them and their departments.

The first difficulty that the new organization faced was that the veteran agriculture minister, Tom Kennedy, whom Michener described as a "true Conservative in that sense," could not accustom himself to the idea of bringing a stranger into the cabinet meetings; he would not agree to an official coming in to take the minutes. "So," Michener said, "for the first year of the new regime, which I had established with all its agenda and its confidential papers and its follow-up, I had to do it myself. I had to take the minutes of the meetings as well as participate as a minister. This lasted until we finally got Tom Kennedy mollified. Then I introduced Lorne Macdonald, a civil servant, to the cabinet as its secretary. From there on, the Secretariat developed and it became a much more workable system."

It was Premier Drew who pressed for the introduction of efficient business methods to the cabinet and also to the government as a whole. For that reason he saw the need to lift the provincial civil service out of the political pork barrel and put it on a merit basis. When Mitch Hepburn came to power in the thirties, he swept out most officials — Michener put the number at eleven thousand — and replaced them with Liberal Party stalwarts. Drew wanted a public service commission, similar to the one in Ottawa, that would be responsible for hiring all government employees below the rank of deputy minister. By the time Roland Michener became provincial secretary, legislation had been passed setting up such a commission and he found himself in charge.

He had become boss of the bureaucracy, and it was not an enviable job, as he was to say years later. He had to hear complaints and deal with personnel problems. There had to be a complete revision of wage scales and he was able to negotiate satisfactory cost-of-living adjustments to meet the postwar inflation, but all was not as easygoing as that. He remembered one Christmas when the civil servants were expecting an increase in pay as a Christmas present and, as the minister responsible, he had applied for such an increase, but it had not been approved by the government. Premier Drew should have met with them and told them, and he had agreed to do so, but when the time came he backed out. "So," Michener said, "I had to go and wish them a Merry Christmas and tell them that there would be no pay increase, no Christmas present."

The Ontario Public Service Commission was one of the crown agencies for which Roland Michener, as provincial secretary, was responsible and for which he was to be the "connecting link" if Premier Drew and the Conservative government's wishes were to be carried out. "Nobody knew how many agencies there were," Michener said. "I got one of my staff to make a list of all the government corporations and councils and commissions and so on, and I was surprised to find how many there were. They ranged from the Ontario Hydro-Electric Power Commission and the Ontario Northland Railway to the smallest kind of subcommittee or organization that functioned with government authority." These various crown agencies were under many ministries but the order was that they should all report through the provincial secretary.

"We tried to do it," Michener said. "It meant that I and the minister responsible for the agency were both involved and, while it didn't always lead to clashes, it did result in a blurring of responsibility and some confusion. So we tried to set up an interdepartmental committee, which was to be chaired by me and was to comprise all the deputy ministers; it was to meet every two weeks to go over what had occurred in each department during that period so that every department would know what the other one was doing and they wouldn't be working at cross-purposes."

However, he could not get the deputies to meet and it was soon apparent that his fellow ministers were not in favour of an interdepartmental committee, and certainly not one chaired by the provincial secretary. Michener complained to Premier Drew, who did not seem to understand that, if such a committee was to work, he would have to chair it himself — or, if he did understand, he did not want to add to his already onerous duties. This was a pioneer attempt to make government more efficient and to prevent overlapping by bureaucratic empire builders and wasteful duplication, and subsequent experience with a coordinating body such as an interdepartmental committee showed that it would be successful only if it were chaired by someone with the supreme authority of a prime minister or premier. At any rate, it was a failure and Michener tended to blame himself and his administration more than the premier's, although he felt there was a "lack of a follow-up" on the part of Drew since, after all, it was his idea.

This was a minus in his work with the crown agencies, but Michener felt there were many pluses. He was especially interested in the work of the Ontario Research Commission, which was attempting to provide some coordination to the practical scientific research being conducted by business, industry, universities, and government. As a result of the commission's investigations and report, Michener introduced a bill in the spring of 1948 to establish the Research Council of Ontario: the purposes of the Council, as spelled out in the legislation, were to encourage private research, to circulate scientific and technical information, and to provide scholarships and bursaries.

Another important commission was Major General Howard Kennedy's examination of the forestry industry in Ontario. The Kennedy report was critical of the way that previous governments had squandered the province's heritage. The general proposed a new system of leasing land to timber companies; these leases would be on a long-term or "sustaining" basis to encourage companies to crop trees and replant cut-over areas. Although the Kennedy report was rational and far-sighted, it proved difficult to implement, but there were definite improvements in forest management as a result of its recommendations.

So many commissions had been set up by the Progressive Conservatives since 1943 that the opposition Liberal and CCF parties began calling Drew's administration "government by commission." Some of them did serve to streamline operations, such as the Ontario Northland Transportation Commission, which allowed for the expansion of the Ontario Northland Railway to include related services such as hotels and shipping as well as buses and planes. Just before

Michener took office, the name of the railway was changed from the Temiskaming and Northern Ontario Railway; the latter's initials were constantly being confused with those of the Tennessee and Ohio Railway with the result that provincially owned boxcars often ended up far to the south of the Temiskaming and Cochrane districts through which the railway's lines ran. Substantial changes were made in the way the railway operated and Michener found that they were spending too much money on the shipping, which was on the decline. He also saw to it that there was much greater participation of local people in the work of the commission, and thus made it better able to serve the needs of Northern Ontario.

One of the smaller commissions was the Niagara Falls Bridge Commission, which was ready to install its carillon when Michener took over the provincial secretary's portfolio. Although the bells had been ordered before the war, they were not cast till after the war and they had just arrived. The commission asked to be relieved of the customs duty of ten thousand dollars. James J. McCann, the Minister of National Revenue, went to Niagara Falls to see the bells that the federal government was being asked to let in free. On the largest bell were inscribed the words: TO THE GLORY OF GOD AND OF OUR NATIONS' LEADERS, FRANKLIN DELANO ROOSEVELT AND WINSTON SPENCER CHURCHILL.

When Jim McCann read the inscription he was incensed that there was no mention of William Lyon Mackenzie King. He went back to Ottawa and told the prime minister and others, and soon the matter was raised in the House of Commons and there was a great to-do about "this insult to the Prime Minister of Canada." It became a public issue, and the commission, which consisted of four Americans appointed by New York State and four Canadians appointed by the Province of Ontario, decided that it had to do something. But what? Should the names be erased? It was said that this could ruin the bell and would arouse the ire of George Drew, who had let it be known that he would never tolerate the removal of Churchill's name. Nevertheless, the commission met and agreed to do just that. Premier Drew acted immediately: he fired the four Ontario commissioners, appointed Michener in their place, and told him to go there and see that no names were removed from the bell.

"I met the Americans in Buffalo," Michener said. "One new Canadian commissioner and four Americans, and I spent two hours with them, exercising all the diplomacy and persuasion that I could devise to get them to rescind their decision. I said that it was an unfortunate controversy politically and that we had better let this blow over. Just rescind your decision. Just do nothing. And they agreed. Then they said, 'But what are we going to do with the bells?' When feelings had cooled, I proposed that the bells be put up without any ceremony. And that was done."

The bells hang in the Niagara Falls carillon just as they were cast. The political tempest was caused by the animosity that Thomas Baker McQuesten, the provincial highways minister at the time the bells were ordered, felt toward the person of Mackenzie King. He and his leader, Mitch Hepburn, were determined that they were not going to have the wartime prime minister's name on the bell, Michener said, but did not add that their veto was confirmed by George Drew, who was as contemptuous of Mackenzie King as they were.

Of all Premier Drew's projects, the most spectacular was his plan to bring one hundred thousand British immigrants to Ontario, and Roland Michener played a crucial role in making this a reality. It began with the re-opening of Ontario House in London which Premier Hepburn had closed as an economy measure in the thirties; Hepburn also closed the lieutenant-governor's residence in Toronto. The Ontario House re-opening was one of Drew's 1943 election promises: besides its wartime use as a centre in London where Ontario servicemen and women could meet, it would provide a postwar base for the promotion of the province. (Neither Drew nor any of his successors as premier of Ontario did anything about reversing Hepburn's other closure of the lieutenant-governor's residence.) An energetic former soldier, Major James Armstrong, was appointed agent general and set to work immediately drumming up immigrants for Ontario.

By the time that Roland Michener became provincial secretary, and Ontario House was one of the many agencies under his jurisdiction, there was a huge backlog of would-be immigrants and no way to move them to their new homes because of the shortage of shipping. The immigration office at Ontario House worked cooperatively with the federal authorities, and, as Michener said, all these applicants had had medical examinations and had been properly vetted and were ready to go.

The only way was to fly them over, but there were no Canadian planes available. However, Premier Drew found a group of former American air force pilots who were using converted military aircraft to provide a charter service under the name of Trans-Ocean Airways, and he was able to work out a contract with them. The plan was for them to fly as many British immigrants as were needed from

London to Toronto that summer of 1947. However, there was a holdup. Air Canada, or Trans-Canada Airlines as it was called then, objected. Apparently the contract with the American charter group violated a bilateral agreement between the British and Canadian governments on trans-Atlantic air travel. This was unknown at Queen's Park until the federal minister of reconstruction, C.D. Howe, made public the terms of the agreement. There were negotiations but no resolution was reached and the time came for the first four or five planes to take off.

Premier Drew and Dana Porter, the provincial minister of planning and development, whose department was in charge of the airlift, set off for London to see the first immigrants off and left Roland Michener to make a deal with the federal government on their landing in Canada. The best that could be done was to fly the immigrants to Buffalo and bus them to Toronto, and nobody wanted that. Michener wondered what he should do; then he remembered that his old friend, Mike Pearson, had recently left Washington where he had been the Canadian ambassador and was now in Ottawa as undersecretary of state for external affairs.

"So I went to see Pearson," Michener said, "and he was sympathetic. I explained to him that this was all to the good of the country and couldn't he find a way out. He [Pearson] spoke to Howe and Howe was tractable. And that way [through Howe] we arranged a meeting with the president of Trans-Canada Airlines [H.J. Symington] and we worked out a deal which was sensible enough. It gave Trans-Canada control of the operations; they accepted the charter arrangement as theirs and made a subcontract with Trans-Ocean. And the thing went on [the immigrants could land in Canada]."

It was a job well done and Drew was delighted. Michener felt that he had stepped in at the right time. The Ontario government was determined to go ahead with the airlift and, he said, "I don't think the federal government would have liked to have made us land there [in Buffalo]. When it came down to that point, things were going for us." This was why there was such a quick settlement, but it was only just in time. The agreement between Trans-Canada Airlines, which had the only right, under treaty, to fly between Britain and Canada, and Trans-Ocean was reached on July 25, 1947, just twenty-four hours before the first flight was due to take off from London. Altogether, ten thousand British immigrants, rather than the originally planned for seven thousand, took advantage of the inexpensive airfare (eighty pounds) to come to Ontario; there were hundreds of flights because the converted military planes could not carry many passengers. The trans-Atlantic immigrant airlift proved to be a landmark in the history of Canada and of aviation.

As premier of Ontario, George Drew was often charged with being an authoritarian and running a one-man show, but Roland Michener denied this and said that most of the government's decisions were arrived at by consensus. There were regular weekly cabinet meetings and special meetings on occasion and Drew would chair these meetings; he was a good chairman, Michener said, who gave full rein to his ministers. He did not always stick to the agenda and did not always get through all the items on it, and sometimes he allowed discussions to go on too long but, generally speaking, his conduct of cabinet meetings was reasonably effective.

"Of course, we never voted," Michener asserted. The discussions would reach a stage where a consensus was evident and Drew would say, "Well, I think this is what we should do." However, it was always recognized that the decision was his. At times there might be some ministers who would have preferred another course but they accepted his view and Michener knew of no heated disagreement or serious split in the Drew cabinet. He did feel frustrated on occasion when he could not get everything done that was on the agenda and that affected his department because the premier was off on a political tangent, and politics and the necessity of staying in power always took priority.

Michener's experience with George Drew—and, as his coordinator of government agencies and departments, he saw a lot of him—was that he was full of ideas and projects but that he was not a very systematic administrator. "He started more than he could keep track of," Michener said. "I would do, to the best of my ability, what he wanted me to do, but he might not think of it again and I would be wasting my time. I sympathized with him because he was carrying a big load, and I remember one day I went in to talk to him about something. He sat in his chair and I was standing talking to him and he went to sleep. He was so tired — that illustrates how he overworked himself, exhausted himself."

Yet George Drew was, in Michener's view, one of the best premiers that Ontario ever had; he started the dynasty that was to keep the Tories in power for more than forty years. The Progressive Conservative government, under his leadership, "certainly got a great deal done" in the three years of majority government between 1945 and 1948.

1812 VETERAN. Great-grandfather Joseph Michener (1792 – 1886) was born in Pennsylvania, fought in the War of 1812, and immigrated to Canada in 1818 or 1819. He married Margaret Hipple (1803 – 1890?) in 1821 and they settled on a farm near Campden, Ontario, in 1822. (Courtesy Roland Michener.)

PATERNAL GRANDPARENTS. Eliza Catharine Patterson and Jacob Michener (1839 – 1921). (Courtesy Roland Michener.)

MATERNAL GRANDPARENTS. Pennsylvania-born Daniel C. Roland (1828 – 1904) and Canadian Anna Margaret Disher (1831 – 1920). (Courtesy Roland Michener.)

ROLAND AT FOUR. Edward and Mary Edith Michener with sons Roland and Victor in 1904. (Courtesy Roland Michener.)

FAMILY PORTRAIT I, 1915. Edward and Mary Michener and their children. Left to right, back row: Roland, Charles, Victor; middle row: Marion, Margaret, Grace; in front, Olive and Joseph. (Courtesy Marion Michener Macdonald.)

FAMILY HOME. The house on Michener Hill, Red Deer, circa 1910. (Courtesy Roland Michener.)

DREAMS OF GLORY. Michener as Cadet, 1918. (Courtesy Roland Michener.)

CORNET PLAYER. Michener played in the University of Alberta Band (back row, middle). (Courtesy Roland Michener.)

HIGH JINKS. Rhodes Scholar Michener, leapfrogging over teammate Mac Bacon. (Courtesy Roland Michener.)

UNBEATABLE. The Oxford Ice Hockey Team, 1921 – 22. Left to right: G.A Nanton, R.H.G. (Dick) Bonnycastle, Mike Pearson, Ed Pitblado, Kenneth Taylor, J.C. Farthing, Roland Michener, G.R. McCall, F.M. Bacon. Taken at Hôtel des Alpes, Murren, Switzerland. (Courtesy Roland Michener.)

ONTARIO MINISTER.
Michener being sworn in
as Provincial Secretary,
with Ontario Premier
George E. Drew at left,
September 16, 1946.
(Courtesy Roland
Michener.)

MR. SPEAKER.
Prime Minister Diefen-
baker and wife Olive
greet Speaker Roland
Michener and wife
Norah. (Canapress Photo
Service.)

INDIAN CAB RIDE. The Micheners in an Indian gharry in Delhi. (Photo by Baldev, New Delhi, courtesy Roland Michener.)

ENVOY TO INDIA. Michener presenting letter of credence as Canadian High Commissioner to President S. Radhakrishnan, 1964. (Punjab Photo Service photo, courtesy Roland Michener.)

DEDICATION. The High Commisioner lays a cornerstone at the University of Rajasthan, 1965. (Courtesy Roland Michener.)

FAMILY PORTRAIT II, 1964.
Left to right: Grace Amos;
Marion Macdonald; Olive
Brown; Margaret Lasher;
Roland, Joseph, and
Charles Michener.
(Courtesy Roland
Michener.)

GOVERNOR GENERAL. Roland and Norah Michener arriving in a coach at the Parliament Buildings for his installation, April 1967. (*The Globe and Mail*, Toronto.)

∾ 8 ∾

YEAR OF
TRANSITION

THE BIGGEST BY FAR of the crown corporations that came under the aegis of Roland Michener as provincial secretary was the Hydro-Electric Power Commission of Ontario, to give its full legal name, or Ontario Hydro as it was generally known. It was a vast undertaking, employing thousands of people, and providing millions of kilowatt-hours of energy that made the province the workshop of the country and, during the war, the arsenal of the Canadian forces. Ontario Hydro had enormous prestige and, as the first provincially owned utility in Canada (it was established by an act of the legislature in 1906), it was held up as a model of public enterprise, which sheltered its often arbitrary and high-handed measures from the sort of virulent criticism that socialists and their kind would have heaped on private enterprise in similar circumstances. Its engineers were considered the best and its chairman was counted among the province's leaders. In fact, Robert Saunders, who headed Hydro during Michener's time in office, was even spoken of as a possible premier.

Yet the electricity that the commission was transmitting to much of the province, including Toronto, was of the old, flickering twenty-five cycle frequency; in other places it was fifty cycles and in some areas the standard sixty-cycle. The probable explanation of this hodge-podge of frequencies was that Ontario Hydro had been too busy trying to keep up with the province's ever-increasing demand for energy to worry about standardization, although Michener did say that they "had marked time during the war" and had not kept up with the growth in industrial and domestic consumption. So much so that there was rationing of power in Toronto during 1946 and 1947 because of shortages.

At any rate, at the end of the war a firm of American engineers was commissioned by Ontario Hydro to look into the whole matter of the production and transmission of electricity and Bob Saunders put their report on Michener's desk in the early spring of 1948. This thoroughgoing examination of the situation urged the immediate standardization of electricity in the province. This would not only allow Ontario to retain its primary position in manufacturing but would make possible the sale of electrical power to the United States and other provinces.

It was a most important report, and Michener recognized this, and that it had to be implemented. There was no doubt that, if Ontario was to keep pace with modern industrial development, the out-of-date twenty-five cycle frequency and the oddball fifty-cycle had to be up-graded and made compatible with the standard sixty-cycle frequency across the border. However, it would be an extremely expensive and disruptive business, and the report put the cost at six hundred million dollars—a staggering amount in those days, it almost equalled the budget of the federal government prior to the Second World War. Standardization would also be a lengthy process and the money would not be spent in one lump sum but would be spread over years. Even at that, Premier George Drew felt that such a large project required the sanction of the Ontario voters, and Roland Michener and other members of the cabinet agreed.

Did Drew really believe that the initiation of such a necessary measure as the standardization of electrical frequencies should be approved by the people? Or did he seize on the Hydro report as a pretext to have an election after three years in power? It was more likely the latter for, as Michener said, "Ontario politicians [of all parties] believe that in three years you can be re-elected, in five years you can't." Drew had a large majority and could have stayed in power for four years or the full five years, but he chose to go in three years. There might have been another reason: Michener thought that the premier was looking toward the next federal leadership convention of the Progressive Conservative Party. If he had such an ambition, it would obiously be much better to retire in triumph after getting his provincial government re-elected with a solid majority. This might have been at the back of his mind, since he had resisted pressure to be a candidate at the 1942 national convention and Bracken, as Michener said, "was not filling the bill," but it would not have been a major factor. Drew was merely following the provincial political equation of three plus and all else minus.

The election was called for June 7, 1948. Roland Michener was confident that he, individually, and the government, collectively, would be returned to power. He felt that he had established a record of competence and efficiency as provincial secretary, and he believed that the newspapers and radio had kept the good constituents of St. David's informed of his hard work on their behalf. His campaign literature stated: "In asking for you to support me again, I do so with a sense of my own limitations but with the knowledge that you have had an honest and businesslike administration from the Drew government, combined with a vision of the needs of our people and faith in the future."

However, the CCF candidate, who was once again William Dennison, launched a strong attack on Michener as a lackey of George Drew, "the Bay Street Colonel," who represented big business and had no understanding of the needs of the common citizens. At an all-candidates meeting in Rose Avenue School on June 1, Michener was frequently heckled and his remarks interrupted by the Socialist candidate's supporters. The CCF concentrated its efforts on the rows of apartments and rooming houses in the south end of the riding where a great deal of the party's strength was concentrated.

On election night the results showed that Roland Michener swept the polls in the north end of St. David's where the single-family homes were; but this was not enough to stem the tide of Socialist votes from the south end of the riding. It was a close race with Dennison being elected with a plurality of 676 votes. Nevertheless, the Progressive Conservatives won the 1948 election and ended up with fifty-three of the ninety seats and a comfortable majority at Queen's Park. "It was a rural majority," Michener said. "The cities were against us." And the Tories lost eleven seats in Toronto and its environs, all to the CCF. Two cabinet ministers were defeated: Michener in St. David's and Premier Drew in High Park. Of the latter, Michener said that he had lost because of the liquor legislation. It was a strong temperance riding and "the church people were against George and wouldn't vote for him."

The CCF had done a very successful job of rebuilding the party after its demise in the 1945 election, and Ted Jolliffe had run a brilliant campaign, concentrating on Drew and his alleged indifference to the claims of working people and reviving fears that the Tories would bring about hard times, if not a depression. As a result he rose phoenix-like from the ashes of his personal defeat in 1945 to take his place once again in the legislature as Leader of the Opposition. The CCF had tripled its representation at Queen's Park from seven members at dissolution to twenty-one, while the Liberals had stood still with thirteen members; the two veteran Toronto Communists, Salsberg and McLeod, were re-elected.

Jolliffe's was an extraordinary achievement: he had only two terms in the Ontario Legislature, from 1943 to 1945, and 1948 to 1951, and both times he was Leader of the Opposition, a feat never equalled by anyone else in the party, whether it was called the CCF or NDP. He was the beneficiary and the victim of the enormous swings in public opinion at the time, as he lost his seat in the 1951 election when Leslie Frost, who had become premier and Conservative leader, reduced the CCF to a minuscule faction of two members. Jolliffe had a relatively brief political career; he retired as Ontario leader of the CCF in 1953 and returned to the anonymity of being a labour lawyer. Roland Michener called his old legal associate and fellow Rhodes Scholar "Canada's forgotten Socialist leader."

Michener himself was shocked by his defeat in St. David's. He wondered whether he had paid enough attention to his constituents, but then he lived in the riding and took it for granted that they knew that he was hard at work as a minister. He blamed it all on the sweeping changes that occurred in the city. On the morning after the election, Michener offered his resignation as provincial secretary to Premier Drew, but it was refused. His government had been returned with a good majority, Drew said, and Michener should continue as minister, just as he would continue as premier, and they would both seek re-election in other ridings at the same time.

However, within a few weeks, circumstances had changed. On July 17, 1948, John Bracken announced his resignation as leader of the federal Progressive Conservative Party. He had lost the support of the Tory establishment in the 1945 election when he won sixty-seven

seats, which was much more than the Conservatives had had before but was nothing compared with George Drew's smashing victory
in Ontario—and the Ontario election occurred just a week before
the federal election. Then there was the drop in the Tory vote in by-
elections, especially the one in Halifax, and the loss of the Yale seat
to the CCF. Roland Michener said of Bracken, "He was a good con-
ciliator of farmers — that's about all he could do." The party executive
met and decided to hold a leadership convention in Ottawa from
September 30 to October 2, 1948. During the Ontario election campaign there had been speculation that the premier would leave provincial politics for the federal stage, and with Bracken quitting, Drew
became the potential front-runner for the leadership, in the estimation
of political analysts.

Meanwhile Roland Michener continued to attend to his duties
as provincial secretary, with nothing being done about his finding a
seat in the legislature. As planning for the federal convention proceeded, he was granted delegate-at-large status and appointed to the
policy committee, which was chaired by an old colleague from the
Albany Club, Fred Gardiner. The committee increased rapidly in size
and soon had over 190 members, but Gardiner was able to keep a firm
hand on the development of policy by appointing an inner council of
some thirty members, including Michener. The party's programs and
platform, for the most part, retained the progressive outlook of the
resolutions that came out of the 1942 Port Hope Conference.

As time went on, there were rumours that John Diefenbaker,
who had come in third in the 1942 Winnipeg convention, would be a
candidate, and so would Donald Fleming, another of Michener's ac-
quaintances from the Albany Club. Quebec Conservatives were said
to have been impressed with Fleming because of an exchange in the
House of Commons when he defended the rights of French-speaking
Canadians. It was not until September 17, less than two weeks before
the opening of the convention, that Diefenbaker announced his can-
didacy; two days later George Drew followed suit.

The die had been cast, and Michener realized that the agreement he had with Drew, that they would seek re-election to the Ontario Legislature at the same time, no longer held. The fact that his
chief was in the running for the national leadership presented an
opportunity for him to participate in federal politics, and although he
had enjoyed work at Queen's Park, he had always seen Ottawa as his
ultimate destination. On September 24 Roland Michener resigned as
provincial secretary. He wrote to Drew that "the past two and a half

years, though strenuous, have been happy, first because of the har-
mony and mutual respect which has characterised your cabinet, and
secondly by reason of the fine spirit and quality of the civil service
with whom it has been my pleasure to work." He added that with the
assurance of a by-election gone, he had no intention of continuing as
minister without a seat in the legislature.

As might be expected, Michener was a strong proponent of
Drew for the leadership, but, as he had done at the 1942 convention,
he spent most of his time at the 1948 convention with the policy committee. The work of the committee went smoothly enough, especially
as its chairman, Fred Gardiner, saw to it that the delegates kept their
comments brief and to the point, but there was trouble over two questions in the proposed resolutions.

The first contentious issue, Michener recalled, was over the
sale of wheat. Two Manitoba delegates, John Macdowell and G.S.
Thorvaldson, objected to the recommendation that farmers have
a choice between selling their wheat through the wheat board or on
the open market. They argued that the wheat board should be
disbanded and an open grain market be re-instituted. However,
Gardiner put off the discussion until the Progressive Conservative
expert on agriculture, Lieutenant-Colonel A.J. Ross, MP for Souris,
could attend the meeting; he was able to persuade the delegates to
adopt the party's proposal that farmers should have a choice. The
other issue was the resolution outlawing the Communist Party of
Canada. This was meant to appeal to Quebec and the authoritarian
and right-wing Duplessis regime, but it outraged many delegates who
saw it as an unwarranted attack on basic civil liberties. It brought John
Diefenbaker to his feet arguing that the resolution would only make
martyrs out of Communists and thus help them rather than hurt them.
Enough votes were rounded up to pass the resolution outlawing the
Communists and make it a plank in the party's platform.

It looked as if the Ottawa convention would be a coronation
for George Drew. He had led the party to two great electoral victories
in the heartland of Ontario; he was the sort of winning politician
whom the Tories needed after so many years in the wilderness, although that image was somewhat tarnished by his personal defeat in
the last provincial election. Still, he was their best hope, their "white
knight," and there was an assumption at the Ottawa convention that
there was an informal alliance between Drew and Duplessis. Because
both men, as premiers, had opposed the welfare policy of the federal
government, the delegates assumed that Quebec's formidable Union

Nationale machine would be at the disposal of Drew if he were leader of the national Progressive Conservative Party. The press and particularly George McCullagh, the publisher of the *The Globe and Mail*, were ardent boosters of George Drew.

There was excitement and great expectations, and Roland Michener shared in the enthusiasm of the Ontario and Quebec delegates for his former chief; on top of everything, Drew had received the ringing endorsement of the party's Quebec organizer, Ivan Sabourin. Michener paid no attention to the support that John Diefenbaker seemed to be getting from the galleries although he did admit that the "Western Populist," as he was disparagingly called, put on a better performance than the last time. The election on Sunday afternoon was a foregone conclusion: George Drew won on the first ballot with 827 votes to 311 for Diefenbaker and 104 for Fleming. The convention exploded in an outburst of wild applause, and the delegates left Ottawa feeling that they had at last got a man who would lead the Progressive Conservative Party to victory in the next federal election.

They did not have to wait for long. Prime Minister Mackenzie King had announced his retirement in the spring of 1948, and the Liberals had actually had their leadership convention in the month before the Conservatives'. It so happened that there was no contest at either of these political meetings because Louis St. Laurent was the Liberals' "crown prince" and on August 8 he was formally chosen to head the party and become prime minister. The next year Prime Minister St. Laurent decided that he should have a mandate of his own and called an election for June 27, 1949.

Michener returned to his law practice, which he had had to surrender during the two and a half years that he had been provincial secretary; his old firm had missed his counsel and was very glad to have him back. However, he soon found that he was dividing his time between Toronto and Ottawa, between law and politics. As the new national leader of the Progressive Conservative Party, George Drew found himself with new advisors and a new staff; he wanted to have someone whom he knew and could trust and so he called on Roland Michener to help him. For a few months until the 1949 election Michener worked as a party official in Ottawa. "We set up a little research committee," he said. "we devised a few programs for the party and wrote a few pamphlets and documentary brochures for election purposes. I also helped to organize the shadow cabinet."

On his visits to Ottawa Michener looked up his old friend, Mike Pearson, and on occasion they would have a game of tennis, but when he went to work for Drew, he found Pearson out campaigning in the Algoma East by-election. It had come as a surprise to Michener that Pearson had become a member of the Liberal Party and had been appointed Secretary of State for External Affairs; he had been sworn in as minister on September 10, 1948, the month after St. Laurent had been elected party leader but was not yet prime minister. It was an eventful year, 1948, a year of transition, the year that Michener turned to federal politics and the year that Pearson joined the Liberal government.

> Pearson and I didn't differ enough on any of the issues to make one think that we had different political party inclinations [Michener said]. I noticed that he called himself a small "L" liberal, and I thought he [Pearson] might just as well have been a Conservative as a Liberal, but he was a civil servant all this time and he had no intention of becoming active in party politics. He was happy with his public administration responsibilities in External Affairs. It was his whole life. But he had got to the point where he felt he couldn't accomplish more. He'd been through the ambassadorships and he had been undersecretary, but he told me he wouldn't accede to Mackenzie King's request that he become a member of the party and be appointed Secretary of State [for External Affairs] and run for [a seat]. But he did when St. Laurent became prime minister [elect]. It was the time of hand-over, transition, and [Pearson] pursued then a political career with the consequences we all know."

It was Mackenzie King who picked the backwoods riding of Algoma East for Mike Pearson, the university don and distinguished diplomat; a cynical move by the prime minister, perhaps, his revenge for having been turned down by his undersecretary, but politically astute because it was the best available, safe Liberal seat at the time (the encumbent was happy to be summoned to the Senate). Pearson had to be shown on the map that Algoma East was in Northern Ontario. As planned, he won the by-election on October 25.

Russel Boucher vacated Carleton outside Ottawa, which was then the safest Tory seat, for his new chief, and George Drew campaigned with "ammunition" provided by Michener and won the by-election handily on December 20, 1948.

After being elected to Parliament and becoming Leader of the Opposition, he asked Roland Michener to look into the state of the party's organization in Quebec and report directly to him. Michener came to the conclusion that the easy assumption at the convention that the Tories under Drew could win Quebec was not likely to be realized. He found that many ridings in the province had no local Progressive Conservative associations, and that the party headquarters in Montreal was torn by internal rivalries and petty jealousies. In an effort to clear up the problems in Quebec, Michener arranged for a meeting of Montreal and Quebec City PC leaders at Montreal's Mount Stephen Club in March 1949. The meeting decided that, despite the glowing reports of the Quebec organizer, Ivan Sabourin, a thorough study should be made of the party's organization in the province. When the study was completed, it made depressing reading: there was disorder in the Montreal headquarters and disorganization throughout the province and an extravagant waste of party funds.

As for the much-touted alliance with the Union Nationale, George Drew did pay a courtesy call on Maurice Duplessis and the two politicians shook hands for the press cameras. However, when Michener visited the Quebec premier to discuss election plans, he found him to be noncommittal with regard to helping the Progressive Conservative Party. All that Duplessis was willing to do was to say that the Union Nationale organizers would be free to work for the Tories if they felt like it. Even this limited support brought a surprising by-election victory in February 1949 in the riding of Nicolet-Yamaska, which had not been won by the Conservatives since 1911.

While he did not mind working as a grey eminence behind the scenes, Roland Michener was anxious to be a candidate in the coming federal election, and George Drew, who had come to rely on Michener, wanted him to take a seat in the House of Commons. With such support, it was not difficult to find a suitable riding in Toronto, especially as Douglas Ross, the Progressive Conservative member for St. Paul's, had decided to retire. The local riding association proved amenable, and Drew came down from Ottawa to speak at Michener's nomination meeting on the evening of March 21, despite the fact that it was "budget night" in the capital. The Conservative leader warned of the extravagance of the Mackenzie King – St. Laurent governments, while Michener concentrated on the party's social policy, which he had helped to draw up.

"This policy is not based on hand-outs by the government," he explained, "but on the great productivity of our economic system, which enables us to provide for the weak and the unfortunate as well as those who provide for themselves." There was noisy applause and wild enthusiasm at the St. Paul's nomination meeting and an election committee was set up under the direction of Charles Rea, the provincial representative for the area, and all present were urged to campaign for "our Leader's lieutenant."

Little concern was shown for the fact that Douglas Ross had won the riding by less than two hundred votes in 1945. Drew appeared to be doing well in the country and plans were made to promote the Progressive Conservative Party as never before. When Prime Minister St. Laurent called for an election in late June, cutting short the budget debate, the Tories were confident of victory. "The tide is clearly against the present government, too long in office," Michener told supporters in a campaign letter. The main points in his election appeal were: the PC proposals to extend low interest loans to families with limited incomes to buy homes, cuts in personal and business taxes, and his own record of public service. Flyers were distributed throughout the riding telling residents: "Roly Michener...will be calling on you."

Despite the all-out effort of the Progressive Conservatives under their new leader, Prime Minister St. Laurent and the Liberals swept the country: they won an unprecedented 190 seats (out of 262), almost 150 seats more than the Tories, who were reduced to a rump of 41 members. Throughout Toronto, the Conservative vote fell, and the Liberals triumphed. Although Roland Michener actually increased the Tory vote in his riding—he was the only one to do so in the whole city—it was not enough to win St. Paul's, which went to the Liberal candidate, James Rooney, by a plurality of 1,078 votes.

It was the second personal defeat in a year. Roland Michener was bitterly disappointed and disillusioned. He had really thought that George Drew, with all his experience as premier of Ontario and the electoral victories he had won in Canada's heartland, would be the answer to the Conservative Party's leadership problems and that he would do much better than John Bracken, who was really an aberration. Instead, he had done much worse. As might be expected, Drew wrote that he deeply regretted Michener's loss in St. Paul's. "There was no one whose defeat I felt more keenly because I had counted on your close association and support in the work here at Ottawa."

In this letter Drew suggested that favourable economic conditions at the time (there was an oil and mining boom and hardly any unemployment) were the real reason for his defeat. "Mr. St. Laurent summed up the situation, as accurately as it has been summed up, in a recent speech in Quebec when he stated that they [the Liberals] had all the trump cards and, with all the favourable conditions then existing, people were certainly in the state of mind to support them." Michener, on his part, blamed the early election call. They had plans for the reorganization of the party but they hadn't been fully worked out before they had to be put into effect. "We were caught," he said, "we hadn't got far enough under George's leadership to make headway and, of course, there was a new Liberal leader, too."

There was no doubt that the good times of 1949 and the snap election were factors in the disastrous rout of the Progressive Conservatives, but Roland Michener had to admit that George Drew's personality was also a "substantial factor." He had had people come up to him and say, "Well, if you had another leader, I would vote for you," not so much in the 1949 election but in the 1948 provincial election when Michener had lost his seat and the Conservatives had lost Toronto and its environs to the CCF. The perception was that Drew was not interested in the ordinary people, and Michener felt that he did give that impression. He had a stiff military bearing, and he had been a military man with a distinguished war record, which made it easy for the Liberals to call him "Colonel" (he was a lieutenant colonel) and portray him as a stuffed shirt.

Yet at the same time, Michener had a "great admiration" for him. Drew had a thorough understanding, as a lawyer, of the principles of parliamentary procedure and also the federal system. He had had the experience of governing Ontario, and he had been, in Michener's words, "an excellent administrator in the sense that he gave the lead." Although he seemed shy and aloof when meeting people at a large gathering, he was great company with a small group or at a party. He was a "man's man always, a handsome man with a fine bearing, and a very good speaker, an exceptionally good speaker.

"He knew how important public speaking was," Michener said, "because he told me that I ought to learn to speak as well as he did. I hadn't at that stage and I don't think I ever did. I've heard him make magnificent addresses without apparently any notes or any planning, but I'm sure that he had planned them."

Some people regarded George Drew as being too pro-British and too considerate of the Imperialist past, but Michener denied this. He said that Drew never let sentiment influence him in any way, and if there was a conflict of interest between Britain and the Commonwealth, on the one side, and Canada on the other, there was no question where Drew stood: "he was a thorough-going and very devoted Canadian." He had the reputation of being a reactionary, which, Michener said, was unfair and was belied by his record as premier of Ontario. Drew had opposed family allowances and denounced them as a bribe by the Liberals to win votes in Quebec, and was called a reactionary for this; but Michener said that the family allowances were an infringement of provincial rights and that Premier Duplessis had been against them. When Diefenbaker came out in support of family allowances at the convention, he was not expressing the view of the great majority of Conservatives at that time.

The fact that they were very good friends made it difficult for Michener to assess Drew's failure as party leader. He was very sound, very responsible, and had good intentions, but he could not make people aware of his qualities and aspirations. His public personality was not warm enough to be really attractive; it did not match his oratorical abilities. There were undoubtedly many factors involved. George Drew was too much of an old- fashioned Tory, too much of an establishment figure, for the modern postwar generation; that was evident on the hustings, and Michener believed that "the public form pretty shrewd ideas of people's characters." Drew might not have been the right man for the right time, and yet, if he had not had to resign because of ill health in 1956, Michener thought that Drew would have been able to capitalize on the great fight he had put up in the pipeline debate and could have ousted the Liberals in 1957–58 although he would not have got as many seats as Diefenbaker did.

❧ 9 ❧

FRENCH AND THE
FEDERAL SCENE

As GEORGE DREW'S "LIEUTENANT ," Roland Michener was sent
to Montreal to report on the organization of the Progressive Conservative Party in Quebec which, by his account, was in a sorry state. It
was there that, for the first time, he came into direct contact with the
French language. Prior to that 1949 visit, he had been aware that
French was spoken in Parliament, as well as in Quebec and other parts
of the country, and was a political fact of life in Canada, but he had not
given it much thought. When he was a student, he had wanted to
learn French but it was not taught in Alberta schools then, and the
beginners' French class in his first year at university was as good as
useless and he did not continue. He was too busy with jurisprudence
at Oxford to bother about another language, although he wanted to go
to Paris after receiving his BCL to study at the Sorbonne, but his father
was not encouraging and said that he had been long enough abroad
and should return and learn the language at home if he wanted to.

It was not suprising that in Toronto, as a rising young lawyer, Michener should not have heard French spoken, but the same was true in the Northern Ontario mining towns where, in many instances, his clients were French-Canadian prospectors and mining promoters, but they always spoke English. It was also the case at Queen's Park where some of his colleagues, as members of the legislature, were Francophones but were so fluently bilingual that he could not tell that their mother tongue was French. As provincial secretary of Ontario, his officials spoke English and he did not know whether any of them were French Canadians. George Drew spoke no French and the Francophones on his staff, as premier and when he became national leader of the Progressive Conservative Party, were bilingual and spoke no French in the office, all of whose paperwork, as Michener well knew, was in English.

When Roland was in Ottawa, visiting his father or working for Drew and the Tories, he would often spend some time in the House of Commons, listening to the debates. There was no simultaneous interpretation at the time—it was to be introduced by the Diefenbaker government when Michener was Speaker—and whenever a member got up and spoke in French, the House emptied. Very few English-speaking members knew any French and, in any case, as Senator Edward Michener remarked, there was nothing of importance ever said in French and any ministerial statement or pronouncement on policy was always made in English.

However, during that mission to Montreal in 1949, Roland Michener did run into the French language, and found it to be an upsetting experience. At the Progressive Conservative Party headquarters the officials were bilingual, but they consulted each other in French and Michener would have liked to have known what they said since he was making an investigation of the party's organization in Quebec. But it was when he had the meeting of "Bleu" leaders at Montreal's prestigious Mount Stephen Club that he found his inadequacy in French most trying. The business of the meeting was conducted in English and most of the prominent Quebec Conservatives were Anglophiles and thoroughly bilingual, but during the informal reception much of the conversation was in French. Whenever Michener joined a group, they would switch to English and he found that embarrassing. It would be impolite for them to have done otherwise, as he would have been left out, an uncomprehending stranger in their midst. As a result, he would have liked to have been by himself and was quite glad when the meeting was over.

It was an object lesson for Michener, and he realized that he would have to have a working knowledge of French if he was to pursue his ambition of a federal political career. There was, of course, the example of George Drew who had got by without French because his wife Fiorenza,* who was multilingual and was fluent in Portuguese and Spanish as well as French, could act as his interpreter, especially at social functions. In the same way, Norah Michener spoke French so well that Pierre Trudeau delighted in talking to her in French. (She was also multilingual because she learned to speak Italian.)

Norah Evangeline (Willis) Michener had an extraordinary early education for a English-Canadian girl who was born on the prairies and grew up in Western Canada. When she was four years old and living in Boissevan, Manitoba, where her father, Robert Willis, was the bank manager, a French teacher, who had been hired by the local school, arrived in town; she could not find suitable accommodation until she met Norah's mother, Sarah Jane Willis, who said that she would give her board and lodging as long as she talked French to her daughter. Thus, Norah grew up bilingual, and while she lost some of her French through lack of use, "she picked it up again remarkably quickly," as her husband said, "and she spoke French better than most people."

It was not because of its importance in Canada, or the fact that it was the stepping-stone to political success in the country, that Norah kept up her fluency in French but because it was a great language with a great literature and she liked reading French books. She was a scholar. She got a degree in history and economics at the University of British Columbia and graduated from the Normal School in Vancouver. She was musical and studied and taught piano at the Toronto Conservatory of Music. After her daughters were old enough to go to school, she returned to the academic life and took philosophy at the University of Toronto and the Pontifical Institute of Mediaeval Studies.

She had a love of learning, Roland Michener said. "She learned Latin because it was one of the basic subjects she had to take for her doctorate degree in philosophy. It took her twelve years to get her degree. [She could only be a part time student because she had to look after the house.] She had four years of Italian with two good teachers,

---

*Fiorenza Drew was the daughter of the famous Canadian tenor, Edward Johnson, and his Portuguese wife, Viscountess Beatrice da Verga d'Arneiro. After his singing career was over, Johnson was manager of the Metropolitan Opera from 1935 to 1950. He died in his birthplace, Guelph, Ontario, in 1959.

and when she finished, she could speak Italian as well as they could. She was mistaken in Firenze [Florence] for an Italian." Diana, her second daughter, remembered reading a philosophy text to her mother while she was up a ladder painting the house. Norah received her doctorate at the University of Toronto in 1954 — the same year that Diana got her baccalaureate in biochemistry and physiology.

Norah's doctoral thesis was on the French philosopher Jacques Maritain, who was a visiting professor at the University of Toronto in the early fifties. She took lectures from him and from another well-known philosopher, Etienne Gilson, who was also teaching in Toronto at the same time. Her doctoral thesis was source material for her book *Maritain on the Nature of Man in a Christian Democracy*, which was published in 1955. However, Norah did not confine herself to philosophical treatises; she also wrote a cookbook under the nom de plume of Janet Peters. The cookbook, a collection of her recipes and articles that appeared in *Canadian Homes and Gardens*, was published by the magazine with the title *Janet Peters' Personal Cookbook*. In an introduction, Norah wrote of the civilized art of dining. The cocktail party had become the favoured entertainment in private homes because of the "disappearance of help," but she said the important thing about dinners was "the opportunity they give us for relaxed, unhurried conversation with our friends under the most ideal and intimate circumstances," and she set out a method of giving small sit-down dinner parties without too much labour for the host and hostess.

Both Roland and Norah, who was called "Nonie" by the children, were modern parents and treated their daughters as equals and always included them in the conversation at the family table, which was often on politics and current affairs. While there was no pressure on Joan, Diana, and Wendy to be outstanding students, it was obvious that Norah wanted them to follow her in scholarly achievements and, above all, she wanted them to know French and have the advantage of a second language. With that in mind, she sent her eldest, Joan, on exchange visits to live with a French-speaking family in Quebec City, and put Diana and Wendy in the Convent de Jesus Marie de Sillery, just outside Quebec City.

Non-Catholic girls, especially those without French, were not welcomed in this convent, and the Sisters of Jesus Mary, and particularly the acting Mother Superior Ste Tharcisius, were horrified at the mere idea, but Norah was determined that her daughters should be educated in French. So she contacted a friend, Abbé Arthur Maheux, who was the archivist at Laval University at the time—he had been the man who was mainly responsible for the pasteurization of milk in Quebec—and the abbé was able to get a special dispensation from the Papal Nuncio so that Diana and Wendy could go to the Sillery convent.

The Michener girls had gone to Bishop Strachan, the private school in Toronto, and there was a backlash from the authorities there. They said that it was a bad decision to send them to a Roman Catholic institution, that it would ruin their education. Norah was not persuaded, and Wendy, who was eleven years old and in Grade Eight, started at the convent the year after the war: she had "no French except for a few words," her father said, "and she did one year there and came back speaking and understanding French." In 1947–48, Diana, who was fifteen and in Grade Eleven, also spent a year at the convent. It was a traditional classical education that the Sisters of Jesus Mary provided, and the girls had to have special tutors in order to keep up with mathematics and physics and other science subjects taught in Ontario schools.

In 1950 Roland Michener took the family to study French at Laval University's summer school; it was the first of many expeditions to Quebec City in pursuit of the second language. That first year Wendy, who was a natural linguist, was in the top class with her mother, while her father was in the beginners' class. Joan, who was a good deal older than the other two, had got married and did not go to the summer school. Norah was anxious that her daughters should be able to speak French as well as write and read the language. "She made sure that our daughters were bilingual, and they were," Michener said and added ruefully, "with her husband, she was not so successful."

Not only were the Michener daughters bilingual but, with the exception of Joan, they had university degrees.

Joan Willis Michener Rohr, born October 3, 1927, wanted to be an artist; after graduating from Havergal Ladies' College, she took two years at the Ontario College of Art. She met a young American history professor who was a licentiate at the Pontifical Institute of Mediaeval Studies where her mother was taking courses; they were married in September 1948 in the Newman Club Chapel at the University of Toronto. Joan had become a Roman Catholic. A couple of years after their marriage they moved to the United States: Professor Donald Rohr got his Ph.D. at Harvard and taught history at Williams College in Massachussets and Brown University, Providence, Rhode Island. Joan gave lessons in painting and sculpture. She had two daughters.

Diana Mary Louise Michener Schatz, born April 13, 1932, followed in her mother's footsteps with a doctorate but in biochemistry rather than philosophy. She got her doctorate at the University of Toronto in 1958 and for a time worked as an assistant clinical chemist at the Toronto General Hospital. The government accepted her proposal to set up training courses in medical technology and, in 1966, she was made executive director of the Toronto Institute of Medical Technology, a diploma-granting body that specializes in teaching the technological side of medicine. In August 1960 Diana married Roy E. Schatz, a high school teacher in French and German who later became an educational officer with the Ontario Ministry of Education. She had two daughters and a son.

Wendy Roland Michener Lawrence, born March 8, 1935, graduated from school with six languages, but her baccalaureate from the University of Toronto was in English literature. She met a fellow student at the university, Leslie Lawrence, who worked as a set designer; they were married in 1957 and spent the next three to four years in Europe, visiting theatres. Wendy became an accomplished journalist and film and theatre critic; she wrote under her maiden name. After a family Christmas at Government House in Ottawa, when all the daughters and their children were present, Wendy returned home to Toronto, where she was taken suddenly ill and died on New Year's Day 1969. She was thirty-four years old and left, beside her husband and parents, two daughters. A Wendy Michener annual lecture at York University and a Wendy Michener film award have been set up in her memory.

Roland Michener had a hard struggle to become bilingual. He took courses, and as soon as he knew that he was going to Ottawa as a member of Parliament, he obtained French recordings and practised pronunciation and attempted to improve his vocabulary. Then there were the six weeks of French at the Laval University summer schools. When he was in the Speaker's Chair, he could read from a prepared statement and was always able to rely on the simultaneous interpretation, if he did not understand what was said in French, but there would be no such aid when he was Governor General; he had to be able to carry on a conversation in both languages. He had French lessons three times a week with a good teacher. "We would read *Le Devoir*," Michener said, "and discuss it in French and I didn't do too badly, but it was late in [the day to become really bilingual] ." Even in New Delhi, when he was Canadian High Commissioner to India but knew that he might become Governor General, he had regular French lessons from a French teacher who lived in the Indian capital.

"I tried very hard at times," Michener said, but admitted that it was very difficult for a person in his fifties to acquire another language. "If I'd only had the courage of my conviction [and studied French at an early age]," he went on, "I would have been bilingual by the time I got into the House of Commons."

After his defeat in the 1949 federal election, Roland Michener returned to his law practice again. He was always a hard worker, and able to get along very well with new associates, according to Robert Cranston who joined Lang Michener in 1940 and was the senior partner at the time of the firm's great expansion in the seventies and early eighties. There seemed to be more permanence about his return this time, although at the back of his mind Michener had the thought that he was not going to end his political career with a defeat. He would keep his hand in, but another election was a long way off. He became an active member of the Toronto Progressive Conservative Businessmen's Association and a couple of years later was its president.

The early fifties saw a mining boom in Northern Ontario and Michener's interest was aroused, particularly by the work of the brilliant scientist Dr. Norman B. Keevil, a Harvard Ph.D. and former University of Toronto professor of geophysics. Dr. Keevil was the first to introduce airborne magnetic surveys for geological mapping; he had been a "boffin," as scientists working for the war effort were called, and recognized the peacetime potential of the U.S. navy's secret airborne detector, which "had spotted every submarine passing through Gibraltar"; and he had acquired the Canadian rights to the equipment when it was declassified. The first time he tested it was in the summer of 1947: when the plane was flying over Northern Ontario, he "flipped the switch and in half an hour hit the biggest magnetic anomaly" over Temagami Lake. The aerial survey was followed by exploration work on the ground, where he identified a huge copper ore body on an island in the middle of the lake. Dr. Keevil obtained the necessary claims and, in 1952, Michener incorporated the Temagami Mining Company Limited.

It was going to cost a great deal of money to bring the property into production and so Dr. Keevil, with Michener's legal assistance, gave an option to Anaconda, and during the next year or so the huge American mining company spent three hundred thousand dollars in exploration work on the Temagami island. "They never drilled where I said they should drill," Dr. Keevil said, "They knew better." All that they uncovered was a long mineralized area of low-grade nickel and copper, and the Anaconda officials were disenchanted and decided to give the whole thing up. There was no big mine here, and they said to Dr. Keevil, "Take it back. We don't want it any more. Here's the results of our exploration work. You can have it for free. We give up the option."

Thus the Temagami resources were returned to him. But Dr. Keevil felt sure that he was right and that there was a rich copper deposit on the island; so he decided to test the special anomaly that he had mapped. The first hole that he drilled in this formation went through almost solid chalca pyrite that graded 30 percent copper for fifty-eight feet; it was the largest body of pure chalca pyrite anywhere in the world! All that had to be done was to dig it up and ship it to a smelter. The discovery drill hole was made in October 1954, and by April 1955 an open pit mine was in operation and continued producing millions of dollars' worth of copper for seventeen years.

One of the problems that Dr. Keevil faced was that Temagami Lake, a long, narrow body of water some sixty miles north of North Bay, was a resort area. There were hundreds of cottages around the many "fingers" of the lake, and the cottagers were up in arms when they heard that there was to be a mine in their midst to exploit the world's biggest copper deposit. However, Dr. Keevil saw to it that there was little mess or pollution and the protests died down when the cottagers realized that they would benefit from the mining operation to the extent of having better roads and getting electricity as well as telephones.

The success of Temagami made it possible for Dr. Keevil to embark on his career of assembling a great mining empire. He began taking over established companies, including famous old Teck Hughes, which made more than a hundred million dollars in the years when gold was twenty dollars an ounce. Temagami was the foundation of the Teck Corporation, which was to become one of the biggest natural resources conglomerates in the country. The name "Teck" came from Teck Hughes, and Dr. Norman Keevil's royalist sympathies were evident in the way that he dropped the plebian name of the mining engineer, Hughes, but retained the name of the royal German duchy of Teck for his paramount corporation. (The small Northern

Ontario mining community of Teck, site of the Teck Hughes mine, was named in honour of Queen Mary, the consort of King George V, who was Princess Mary of Teck.)

After his defeat in the 1962 election, Roland Michener, who was as much a royalist as anyone, was named chairman of Teck. "We gave him sabbatical leave to become High Commissioner to India and Governor General," Dr. Keevil said with a chuckle. As an old professor, he preferred "sabbatical" to "leave of absence." He saw to it that his son followed in his scholarly footsteps, and Dr. Norman B. Keevil Jr., who became president of Teck recently, received a Ph.D. for mineral exploration from the University of California in 1964. When he left Rideau Hall in Ottawa, Roland Michener returned to the chairmanship of Teck.

In May 1952 the Progressive Conservative Association of St. Paul's riding in Toronto held a nomination meeting and once again chose Roland Michener as its candidate. It was more than a year before Prime Minister St. Laurent was to call an election, but Michener was glad of the time and made the best use of it. He did a systematic canvass of the whole constituency and held public meetings in various quarters so that he could meet the people. He knew that he would have to work very hard to defeat the encumbent, Jim Rooney, and while there was a certain amount of disenchantment, rather than disillusionment, with the Liberal government, Michener did not sense any marked swing to the Conservatives: "Uncle Louis," as St. Laurent had become known to friend and foe, was still very popular.

The 1953 election, when it was called in June for August 10, caught Canadians by surprise because there had seldom been a federal election in midsummer. In fact, it was the conventional wisdom that this was quite the wrong time to have a vote because the farmers would be out harvesting and the townsfolk away holidaying. In any case, it was too hot for politicking. Roland Michener was about to leave for England; as general secretary of the Rhodes Trust in Canada, he was going to Oxford to participate in the fiftieth-anniversary celebrations of the Rhodes scholarships. There was a hurried change of plans. Norah went in his place while he stayed at home to campaign in his Toronto riding of St. Paul's. (It was not the first time that Norah had taken her husband's place at Rhodes scholarship functions, which were still all-male affairs at that time. Ted Jolliffe remembered Norah attending a Rhodes Scholars dinner at the Toronto Club which Roland could not be at because his father had just died; she was the only woman present at this black tie affair, and Jolliffe said that she carried off her surrogate role with easy assurance.)

Although Michener's team in St. Paul's was ready for an election, after months of preparatory work, many of his workers had to join their families on vacation for at least part of the summer campaign. Nevertheless they rose to the occasion and made up for the absentees with longer hours. It was the sort of hot and humid weather for which Toronto was infamous, and Roland Michener recalled that he lost fifteen pounds in that election. His issue was tax reform, but whether that made much impact on the local level was difficult to discern. When Norah returned from Oxford, she took her turn on the stump and spoke in Italian to the sizeable Italian community in the riding. Diana, who had campaigned for her father since she was ten years old, was among the troops in the trench warfare of door-to-door canvassing where most constituencies were won or lost.

On the night of August 10 there was excitement and suspense at Progressive Conservative headquarters in St. Paul's, with their candidate maintaining a slim lead of a few hundred votes. Finally, at 9.45 P.M., the issue was decided: with all the polls reporting, Roland Michener had won with a margin of 515 votes over Jim Rooney. It was a personal triumph for Michener because it was the only change from Liberal to Conservative in the city of Toronto. Nationally, the 1953 election had been another disappointment for the Tories: there had been no swing to them and while the St. Laurent government was down from its record number of 190 seats, it still had an unassailable majority of 170 seats; the PCs had picked up ten seats to count 51 in the House of Commons, still an abysmally small number, while the CCF and the Social Credit parties had made gains.

Michener was elated. He was on his way to Ottawa where he had always wanted to go. He told his supporters, "Our victory in St. Paul's was only achieved by the devoted assistance of hundreds of people, many of whom gave up their holidays to help." In retrospect, he realized that his career might have been very different if a few hundred had voted the wrong way, for his Liberal opponent. He would probably have not run again—three defeats in a row would have been too much—and he would have gone back to his prosperous law practice and made a lot of money and finished up as a judge.

Although he revelled in the euphoria of the election night result of having turned a riding around which was the supreme political achievement, he was unhappy about the way Canadian voters "let one party have too much power for too long." It was not healthy, and he saw signs of the Liberal Party's being dominated by machine politicians and corrupt elements. He was to say that, as a result of his election in Toronto St. Paul's, "I also established, perhaps, a new concept of political morality at the time because I caught the opposing forces [the Liberals] in a scheme to take thirteen hundred or twelve hundred votes away [from me] by putting false names on the revision list."

The Michener team in the 1953 election campaign consisted mostly of alert and bright young businessmen who kept a close watch on the other candidates; they could not understand why so many people went to the Liberal Party headquarters to put their names on the revision list compared with those who came to the Progressive Conservative headquarters. Once the revision of the voters' list was completed, the Tories began to check up and, Michener said, they found that there were two or three false names at each polling station; they were assigned addresses where nobody lived. For instance, there was an apartment house under construction on Avenue Road, and there were three couples on the revision list who were supposed to live there. But nobody lived there—it was just a concrete skeleton at the time. The false registrations were so distributed that twenty people could have voted the whole twelve hundred or thirteen hundred by moving from polling station to polling station.

"We sent letters to all these people [on the revision list]," Michener said, "registered letters, and most of them came back as 'nobody at that address.' So we immediately complained to the Chief Electoral Officer." *The Globe and Mail* heard of the falsifications and carried the story on its front page, along with photographs of the places where the voters were supposed to live but nobody lived. After such exposure, there was no chance of the false names being voted, and the Liberals lay low, asserting that they had had nothing to do with this attempt to rig the election.

If the scheme had worked, and they had been able to get away with voting the false names on the revision list, Michener would have been defeated. Soon after the 1953 election was over, there was a nine-day trial of the three or four people involved, two of whom were found guilty and sentenced to six months in jail. Michener was somewhat surprised at the lightness of the penalty but was philosophical about it, saying that they had done him no harm. The

Liberal candidate, Jim Rooney, was not charged and was evidently not implicated; it came out in the evidence at the trial that his followers had devised the scheme and carried it out without his knowledge.

In November 1953 Roland Michener took his seat in the House of Commons; as might be expected, he was warmly greeted by his old chief, George Drew, who said that he was looking forward to his assistance and advice. Michener was not among strangers because there were friends and associates from the Albany Club days on the opposition benches: Donald Fleming, who had been first elected in the postwar election of 1945; and Jim Macdonnell, who had been one of Roland's mentors at the Port Hope Conference (he had also been elected in 1945, but had lost his Toronto Greenwood seat in the 1949 election, only to regain it at a by-election later that same year); and George Hees, the dashing army officer who had helped to defeat General A.G.L. McNaughton in the wartime by-election, who was the member for Toronto-Broadview. Then there was his friend, Mike Pearson, the Secretary of State for External Affairs, who crossed the floor to shake his hand; Mike was esconced in the government front benches while Mitch languished so far away in the back benches that he had difficulty catching the Speaker's eye.

Shortly after Parliament met, Michener made his maiden speech. He spoke of his major concerns during the past election campaign: an increased supply of low-interest mortgage loans (the average interest rate on first mortgages at that time was around 5 percent) to assist families buying their first homes; improved availability of inexpensive natural gas (the TransCanada Pipelines was in the planning stage and would eventually lead to the great upheaval of the pipeline debate), and more legislation to help veterans and the disabled. It was no great oration but the sort of bread-and-butter speech that private members make during the debate on the Speech from the Throne, which was when Michener spoke.

∾ 10 ∾

T - TO - T,
BACKBENCH MP

ROLAND MICHENER HAD at last achieved his boyhood ambition of becoming a member of Parliament. It was no vaulting ambition, and he was quite frank in saying that he had never had any hope or desire of being prime minister like so many other politicians of his acquaintance. He was sure that, from the time he was first a candidate, George Drew had this high office in mind as his ultimate objective; and John Diefenbaker, whom he got to know after being elected, often told the story of how, as a newspaper boy, he had met Sir Wilfrid Laurier on a station platform in the prairies and had sold him a newspaper and told him that he, Diefenbaker, was going to be prime minister someday. All that Michener wanted to do was to follow in his father's footsteps to Ottawa.

However, he had left it a bit late: he was fifty-three years of age when he was introduced to the Speaker as the new member for Toronto St. Paul's. At that age he had assumed some costly commitments and obligations, and there was no way that he could meet them or maintain his standard of living on a member's pay—the sessional indemnity at the time was six thousand dollars and there was seldom more than one session in a year. As a lawyer he had been earning twenty-five to thirty thousand dollars a year. So Michener decided that he would have to continue with his law practice while being an MP and taking part in the debates in the House of Commons.

Many others were also working at home at their old jobs while serving as MPs in Ottawa; they were mostly from Montreal and Toronto or from places within an overnight train ride of the capital. Known as the "T-to-T" members, they arrived in Ottawa on Tuesday morning and attended sittings of the House from then until late Thursday evening, when they took the night train to Montreal or the overnight sleeper to Toronto. This allowed them three days, with Saturday included, in their profession or business and three days in Parliament, and the process of government was adjusted to meet this schedule, so that there were no major decisions or divisions on Monday or Friday and the budget was brought down in the middle of the week. Michener was a T-to-T member, although he maintained that he took the train on Sunday night from Toronto to Ottawa and was in the House from Monday to Thursday; but he did miss some Mondays, as an examination of the votes during the pipe-line debate showed.

Of course, those who represented constituencies beyond the two-hundred to two-hundred-and-fifty-mile radius of Ottawa, such as the members from Northern Ontario, Eastern Quebec, the Atlantic Provinces, and the West, could not very well have another job. This did not matter so much in the case of many Liberal and Conservative members from the hinterland since they were well-to-do and had large supplementary incomes, although it did mean that the older parties had difficulty recruiting bright young candidates in places that were far afield of Ottawa. But most of the CCF and Social Credit members had to get by on six thousand dollars a year; they had to maintain two homes, and some of them were reduced to penury and living in rooming houses in Ottawa.

It was typical of the attitude at the time that such discrimination against members from beyond the Toronto–Ottawa–Montreal triangle should be tolerated. As the apologists said, most of the MPs came from that triangle, and they represented most of the population. The Liberal Party, which had been the government for some twenty years, recognized this as a fact of power politics: it did not have to be beholden to the members from the outer reaches of the country. They were "beyond the Pale." Still, the whole T-to-T system was wrong; it was an anachronism, a reflection of a more leisurely period at the turn of the century when Parliament met for only a few weeks a year and a gentleman (there were no lady members) could continue to be a lawyer or doctor or businessman and at the same time an MP even if he lived in Vancouver.

By the 1950s the sessions were stretched over the full year, with a month off for Christmas and a couple of months' vacation between July and September, although the House had been known to sit in the clammy heat of an Ottawa summer. Michener found the T-to-T system exhausting: he worked seven days a week, practising law in Toronto on Friday, Saturday, Sunday — he found that he could get more done on Sunday — and sometimes Monday and the rest of the week being backbencher in Ottawa. If he did not keep fit, and he played as much tennis as he could, he was afraid that he would have a nervous breakdown.

Shortly after taking his seat as an MP, Michener rented an apartment on Metcalfe Street; Norah joined him occasionally in Ottawa but she also spent a lot of time looking after the family in Toronto. It was a comfortable and convenient apartment and he kept it all the time he was in Parliament.

Since he had an abiding interest in foreign affairs and had been an active member of the Canadian Institute of International Affairs (CIIA) for almost a quarter of a century, Roland Michener was appointed to the Conservative caucus's committee on external affairs. The committee chairman was John Diefenbaker, and at the first meeting he asked Michener to be vice-chairman. It was the first time that they really got to know each other, and Diefenbaker was affable and went out of his way to be friendly, although he knew that Michener had worked for George Drew and supported him at the last leadership convention. In a way, each man complemented the other's ability on this committee: Diefenbaker had a strong emotional attachment to Britain and the Commonwealth, and, in that, reflected the sentiment of most English-speaking Canadians; Michener was a strong Commonwealth supporter as well but his participation in the CIIA had made him aware of new trends in the world, of the North Atlantic Alliance, of the growth of the Commonwealth and of the developing nations through decolonization.

In fact, in the spring of 1954, Michener went on a tour of India and Pakistan that was sponsored by the Institute and, on his return, was able to acquaint caucus colleagues with the attitudes of the leaders of these newly independent countries toward Canada, and the concerns of Asians generally. (This was a time when Indo-Canadian relations were very close as a result of the mutual understanding between Nehru and St. Laurent.) It was on this tour that Michener met a young Quebec professor, Pierre Elliott Trudeau, whom he found to be rather quiet and unassuming. Trudeau had wanted to go on this tour and, since there was room for one more, the CIIA agreed to his joining the party as long as he paid his own way, which he did.

Roland Michener was a member of the Canadian delegation to the Tenth General Assembly of the United Nations, and he and Norah spent some six weeks in New York during the early fall of 1955. This was an occasion when he could get together with Mike Pearson—although the delegation was headed by Paul Martin, who was Minister of National Health and Welfare at the time, the External Affairs Minister was expected to take part in the UN debates—and Michener recalled going with Mike and Maryon to various parties, including one at Sir William (wartime agent known as "Intrepid") Stevenson's home. Actually, the only times that Mitch and Mike met socially in Ottawa were at diplomatic parties, and Roland was invited to more of them than the average backbench MP because he was a Rhodes Scholar. In fact, he recalled, at one such party the British High Commissioner, Lord Amory, noticing that he was wearing a Vincent's Club tie—the Vincent's Club was an athletic club to which Oxford "Blues" belonged.

The House of Commons showed very little interest in what was going on abroad, and Michener said, "It's just amazing how seldom there was a debate on foreign affairs." He could not remember an occasion when he and External Affairs Minister Pearson took opposite sides on an international issue or were involved in the discussion of such an issue. He was not on the House's External Affairs Committee, which never met in any case, and the only time that matters effecting the department came up was during consideration of the estimates (expenditures). "Then the question was whether the ambassador had spent too much for a mirror in his drawing room, or something like that," Michener said, "rather than anything to do with foreign policy."

Most of Michener's four years as a backbench MP were spent in the field of tax reform. As a member of the House's Banking Committee he pressed the government to provide tax shelters for those saving for retirement. At the 1942 convention, the Progressive Conser-

vative Party had promised that "consideration" would be given to a
pension plan for the self-employed, and although this was left out of
the Tories' 1948 platform, Michener campaigned personally in his
riding on the old proposal he had helped to draft. As a lawyer he faced
this problem whenever he filed his income tax returns, but he realized
that it went beyond lawyers and doctors and the professions to all
who were self-employed: to farmers, fishermen, shopkeepers, sales-
men, small businessmen, actors and artists, and such.

He spoke of the "injustice" of a tax regime that allowed those
who were employed and on payrolls to deduct the contributions they
made to their pensions and did not grant the same privileges to those
who worked for themselves. Michener first suggested during debate
on amendments to the Income Tax Act in 1954 that there should be tax
shelters for the pension funds of the self-employed, only to have the
then Minister of Finance, Douglas Abbott, scornfully dismiss his proposal as "simplistic" and say that he had been struggling with this
question for seven or eight years without being able to find a suitable response. Such criticism did not faze Michener, who raised
the matter again the following year in the Committee on Ways
and Means. There was a new finance minister, Walter Harris, who
congratulated Michener on his "excellent" speech and said that his
ministry was studying the problem.

Once again, despite such blandishments, no progress was
made, and the injustice with regard to the taxation of the self-
employed and the employed continued. In 1956 Michener returned
to the argument that he had made in previous years. This time he
could refer to the way that the British Chancellor of the Exchequer
Harold Macmillan had handled the problem: tax exemptions would
be allowed on pension contributions to a limit of five hundred pounds
(later raised to seven hundred and fifty pounds) or 10 percent of
the earned income in any one year. He quoted Macmillan as suggest-
ing that the beneficiaries of these deductions would range from "city
accountant to village grocer." Michener called this "a serious attempt
to deal with what so far has been an insoluble problem to the Minister of Finance and his predecessor," and added, "I suggest, Mr.
Chairman, it is high time that the issue be met squarely and fairly and
that this measure of injustice and discrimination ... in our income tax
law ... should be eliminated without further delay."

Finally Roland Michener's persistence paid off in Walter
Harris's 1957 budget. Along with a meagre six dollar increase in the

universal noncontributory old age pension, which did the Liberals a lot of harm in the ensuing election campaign (the finance minister was dubbed "Six Buck Harris"), it was announced that legislation would be introduced which would allow the postponement of taxes on limited amounts of income set aside as retirement savings. This was the beginning of the Registered Retirement Savings Plan (RRSP) that was to prove so popular and so beneficial. Donald Fleming, the Tories' finance critic, hailed the announcement as a "Conservative victory," which led Minister of Trade and Commerce C.D. Howe to remark, in an aside that was loud enough for *Hansard* to record, that that would be the only one this year. Little did Howe realize what a year of triumphs 1957 would be for the Progressive Conservative Party; not only would the Liberal government be defeated but he himself would lose his seat.

It was natural for Michener, with his mining experience, to lead the Opposition's attack on the proposed reduction in the subsidies paid to the gold mining industry. Although he pointed out that there had been a substantial increase in the wages paid miners and that a number of mines had had to close, he could not get the government to change its "fixed intention." He did elicit a reply from the finance minister when he urged the government to make a further, concerted attempt to get an increase in the price of gold (thirty-five dollars an ounce). The United States was still on the gold standard, and Walter Harris pointed out that Washington fixed the price of the gold content of the U.S. dollar and thus would be loath to agree to any increase.

Since the abortive federal-provincial conferences of 1945–46, the provinces had had to sign limited agreements on tax sharing with Ottawa, and when this matter came up in the House, George Drew had attacked these agreements as being no solution to the basic problem of a fair and adequate financial division between the provinces and the federal government. Michener dusted off speeches he had made while provincial secretary for Ontario; he criticized Ottawa for its disregard of provincial autonomy and for taking over too many tax areas. His arguments, however, fell on deaf ears, because the federal government had no intention of changing its relations with the provinces.

Then there was the long and bitter struggle over the Defence Production Act, which would have continued the temporary powers granted the government during the Korean War, and was a prelude to the tumultuous pipeline debate. It would have given Howe, who was minister of defence production as well as minister of trade and commerce, the right to fix prices and to force any manufacturing company to accept a defence contract under terms set by the minister; it was a sign of the authoritarian attitude of the economic czar of the St. Laurent government, which was further demonstrated by the arrogant way that Howe invoked closure during the pipeline debate. The Progressive Conservatives were appalled. Michener and the rest of the Tory caucus saw the legislation as dictatorial and a threat to political and economic independence.

All progress on the measure was brought to a halt by what amounted to a Tory filibuster, which was organized by Jim Macdonnell. George Drew gave a speech lasting four hours and twenty-three minutes; Roland Michener spoke at every stage of the Bill's passage through the House of Commons. When Howe, who was a self-made businessman and disliked academics, and Rhodes Scholars in particular, questioned Michener's qualifications to criticize the measure, Michener replied that he knew enough about the issue, and added, referring to Howe's American background, "I have lived my whole lifetime in this country, and I do not think the minister can make the same assertion." Tempers were frayed, and in the end Prime Minister St. Laurent had to meet with Opposition Leader Drew, and a compromise was worked out allowing the government to retain the wartime powers for another three years. They did not last as long as that for, when John Diefenbaker became prime minister in 1957, he saw to it that these extraordinary powers were abrogated.

The angry defence production debate, the uproar in the House over the authoritarian behaviour of the minister and the way that he spurned the Opposition, had not taught the St. Laurent government a lesson, as was shown in the repeat performance, only more raucous, of the pipeline debate. By now the Liberals were beyond learning; they had come to believe that they were the "natural governing party" and that they could not be overthrown in any election. St. Laurent appeared listless and tired, Michener said, and seemed to have given the reins over to his super-minister, C. D. Howe, who was on an ego trip of historic proportions. Since 1950 Howe had been working on the construction of the TransCanada PipeLine, the longest ever pipeline, which was to bring natural gas from Alberta to the factories and homes of Eastern Canada. It was to be an undertaking comparable to the Canadian Pacific Railway, and Howe, the American-born engi-

neer, saw himself in the company of Sir John A. Macdonald, the Scot-
tish-born lawyer, as a builder of Canada. The pipeline would be a
further transportation link binding the country from west to east, and,
like its predecessor, the CPR, it would have to follow an all-Canadian
route through the wilderness of Northern Ontario, where for hundreds of miles there was so little habitation.

When his friends, the Texas oilmen who were to build the
pipeline, advised him that the best way to get around the Great Lakes
was through the Midwestern states, Howe would not bend. It was
Northern Ontario or nothing. When the New York bankers refused to
come up with the money "without the definite prospect of an American market for gas," Howe was "shaken," according to William
Kilbourn's account,* but nevertheless determined to get his way. The
government, if he, Howe, had anything to do with it, would take the
place of the bankers and make a short-term loan so that TransCanada
could go ahead, and, while there was some argument in cabinet, the
minister saw to it that this was done. Furthermore, Howe was insistent that construction should begin in 1956.

At first the government refused to admit that it was going to
provide a loan to TransCanada, and St. Laurent derided "such speculation in the newspapers," but that did not stop the questions in the
Commons. There was a sense that the Liberal cabinet was divided on
this issue, which was just what the parliamentary inquisitors needed
to get them on their feet. They were in full cry during the first week of
May 1956, and Diefenbaker was pointing an accusatory finger at
Howe and fulminating about the cavalier and contemptuous manner
with which he was treating Parliament. Insults were traded as Opposition members became more and more frustrated with the way their
questions went unanswered.

There had to be a decision soon if construction was to begin in
1956, and the cabinet met at the beginning of the second week in May
and agreed to take the plunge, after Howe had pleaded with the other
ministers "to let him have his way once more, to crown his career with
this final splendid accomplishment for Canada." The cabinet agreed
not only to put up the money but to work out a way of getting the plan
through Parliament by June 7, the deadline for construction to begin
that year. When Howe told the House that the government would
make a loan to cover 90 percent of the construction costs, his an-

---

*Much of the background to the historic pipeline debate is taken from *PipeLine* by
William Kilbourn. Although this book was published in 1970, it is regarded as an
authoritative work.

nouncement was greeted with groans and jeers. Davie Fulton called it "a treaty of surrender" and George Drew asserted that this was a general invitation to America to come to Canada "to be financed to the extent of ninety cents on every dollar." The rest of the week was occupied by procedural wrangles, the purpose of which was to prevent the government from introducing the bill.

Michener took part in the debate with what he described as "a great deal of enthusiasm." He spoke on the bill only once; usually his interventions were on side issues that would permit a vote and take up time. Howard Green acted as a quarterback for the Conservatives and Michener recalled him saying, "Come on, guys, don't let it stop!" and he would put his hand on a member's shoulder and say, "Your turn, you'd better get ready to go on the floor." It was not until May 14, the beginning of the third week in May, that the government was able to bring in the Northern Ontario Pipe Line Corporation bill, the legislation designed to loan two hundred and eighty million dollars of federal funds to TransCanada to build the pipeline. The delaying tactics of the Opposition meant that there were only nineteen days of debate left before the June 7 deadline.

In introducing the bill, Howe made a powerful speech that seemed to impress members, judging from the attentive silence with which it was received, but when the minister ended by announcing that closure would be invoked at each stage of the debate to limit discussion, there was an immediate uproar, and cries of "dictatorship" and "guillotine." The Tories had expected the axe to fall at some time during the debate but here it had been dropped before discussion had begun. They could not believe their good luck: they had been handed the best possible issue. They did not have to come to grips with the pipeline proposal; they had something much more fundamental before them and that was democracy itself, the contemptuous manner with which Howe and the Liberals were treating Parliament. As Michener said, "We were being muzzled before we had said anything, we considered that as an insult." Furthermore, the Tories could charge, as they did, that the government in suppressing debate had something to hide, perhaps a pay-off to Clint Murchison and the Texas oil men who controlled TransCanada.

Although Michener did not play a leading part in the watershed pipeline debate, he did take part in the discussion of the bill. The Northern Ontario Pipe Line Corporation, he said, was being set up as "a crown corporation for the purpose of lending money, not to Canadians, but to non-Canadians." He wondered whether the American corporations that "owned 83 percent" of TransCanada were not more interested in bringing Alberta gas to the United States than to Eastern Canada for the benefit of Canadians. "If they had any serious intention of doing [the latter]," Michener said, "it is fairly evident that corporations with those resources could do it if they wished. So when they fail and come to the government for help, one is justi-fied in questioning the wisdom of getting mixed up in a complicated arrangement that is neither private enterprise nor crown corporation but a confusing mixture of the two." It was a "patchwork solution" to a common and important objective, but not only was it that, he as-serted, but the minister in his enthusiasm to get the job done quickly "has forced on this House a method of procedure which is patchwork and wholly undesirable."

On one occasion Michener caught Howe out on the price of gas: the minister had assured the House that it would be less on the Canadian side than for export. However, Michener pointed out that a statement made earlier indicated that, for the first three years, the gas would be sold at a price that would be cheaper in the United States than in Canada. "It was a minor thing," Michener said, "but I took some satisfaction in calling Mr. Howe's attention to it." The minister said that it would have to be corrected because the law did not allow Canadian gas to be sold outside Canada for less than the price charged Canadians.

In the end the government's huge majority and closure made sure that the June 7 deadline would be met and the bill passed in time for TransCanada to begin construction that year (although a strike of American steel workers producing the pipe upset the schedule). The tumultuous debate, which at times approached bedlam, destroyed more than it built. There was the popular and amiable Walter Harris, the finance minister and government House leader: he was consid-ered to be the Liberal most likely to succeed St. Laurent, but his con-duct in pushing the bill through the Commons, and the fact that he had to move the motion suspending Donald Fleming for refusing to obey the Chair, brought his political career to an end. And there were many others, including St. Laurent and C.D. Howe, and, of course, the Liberal government.

However, the immolation of the Speaker, René Beaudoin, largely self-inflicted, was the real tragedy of the pipeline debate. A handsome man who had a reputation for courtesy and fairness, Beaudoin was spoken of as a possible Permanent Speaker, if that office was created. Michener admired him greatly and said that he was very fluent in both languages and that he was so knowledgeable about parliamentary procedure that he was busy writing a book on the subject. There were two contradictory demands on the Speaker during the pipeline debate: the first was to maintain the impartiality of the Chair, and the second was to see that the government's timetable for its legislation was met. As points of order succeeded points of order and rulings were constantly challenged, Beaudoin began to show signs of strain.

Finally, one night when the debate seemed to be coming to an end, the Speaker fell into a trap set by Colin Cameron, the grey fox of the CCF; Cameron knew how proud Beaudoin was of his high office, and when he drew attention to two letters-to-the-editor in an Ottawa newspaper criticizing the Speaker's conduct and proposed a motion of privilege, Beaudoin not only accepted the motion but instructed Cameron on how to present it. "We all went home rejoicing that night [Thursday, May 31, 1956]," Michener recalled. "We had a motion that could not be superceded, and until this was disposed of, the government's business of the day could not be called." Walter Harris was horrified; he could see a whole new debate stretching out beyond the June 7 deadline. Beaudoin realized that he had blundered — but how was he going to redeem himself and get out of this impasse?

The next day, "Black Friday," the Speaker returned to the Chair and, in a *mea culpa* statement, said that he had made serious errors, that there was no breach of privilege, and he proposed that the business of the House revert to where it had been on Thursday at 5:15 p.m., before Cameron's intervention. In other words, René Beaudoin, who looked "really shaken," according to Michener, was turning the clock back. Amid mounting tumult and chaos, the Speaker grimly proceeded with the business as if it were Thursday, May 31, at 5:15 p.m., as William Kilbourn said, and all that had happened thereafter had not occurred. There was nothing now that the Opposition could do to obstruct the passage of the bill except to protest, which they did loudly and at length while the Liberals added to the pandemonium by banging their desks and singing such disparate songs as "Onward Christian Soldiers" and "Alouette." Beaudoin made no attempt to restore order. "I was very sorry for him," Michener said, "but what he did was unforgivable."

If there was a victor in the pipeline debate, it was surely the Conservative leader, George Drew, who was relentless in resisting the government's attempt to ride roughshod over Parliament, and yet he became one of its victims. He had worked so hard during the month or more when the House was in an uproar over the issue that he had a relapse of the meningitis that had put him in hospital in the fall of 1954. It was a tragic irony, as Michener said, that George Drew should have exposed the Liberal government for the corrupt and authoritarian regime that it had become after twenty-two years in power, only to have to retire and let the benefit of what he had done, the public support that he had created, go to his arch rival, John Diefenbaker.

Roland Michener had been such a close confidant and advisor to George Drew that he was acclaimed as the "leader's lieutenant" in the 1949 election campaign. However, as a T-to-T member, he did not have time to do much for Drew, although he did look into the question of a Progressive Conservative Research Department to provide the PC caucus with information on current issues. Michener had suggested the establishment of such an organization in 1949, and he was able to draw on the experience of the research department that served the British Conservative Party in making the recommendation again. As a result, a research department was set up at PC headquarters in Ottawa and an economist from Queen's University, Donald Eldon, was engaged as the party's first full-time researcher.

Although Roland and Norah were entertained on several occasions by George and Fiorenza Drew at Stornoway, the official residence of the Opposition Leader in Ottawa, they did not see as much of each other as when Roland was a minister of the Ontario government and George was premier. At that time the Drews lived on Rosedale Road in Toronto and were immediate neighbours of the Micheners (their house was 5 Rosedale Road). Still, Roland was a good friend and loyal supporter of the Conservative leader and might have been expected to have had some advance notice of his retirement, but he read about it in the newspapers. "I didn't know how serious his illness was," Michener said, "and I didn't believe that he would have to retire, so I carried on as though he would recover and all would be well."

At no time, amid all the sound and fury of the pipeline debate, did George Drew give any hint that he was on the point of collapse. "No, he didn't," Michener said, "He would fall down dead rather than admit that he was exhausted." So Drew soldiered on. He kept going till the debate and the session ended, and only then would he bow to the fact that he was seriously ill. It was when he was in a Toronto hospital and his doctor, who was a famous physician and knew his patient's condition well, warned that he could not carry on, that it was a matter of life or death, that Fiorenza and his friends, among such top federal Tories as Jim Macdonnell and Earl Rowe and Grattan O'Leary, persuaded him, reluctantly and with some difficulty, to sign the letter of resignation.

This was the beginning of the great change in the Progressive Conservative Party and in Canadian politics.

∾ 11 ∾

SPEAKER AS
SECOND CHOICE

GEORGE DREW'S RESIGNATION caught everyone by surprise and came as a shock to Roland Michener and most other Progressive Conservatives; they could not believe that their leader, who had a military bearing and looked ruddy and robust, could be so sick that he was unable to carry on. Since Parliament was not in session, members were scattered across the country and only a few of those in the hierarchy were at Drew's hospital bedside. Word of his resignation came from radio reports and the front pages of newspapers (Canadian television was in its infancy in 1956), and the MPs' reaction varied from excitement and elation to sorrow and depression. The politicking began immediately on the telephone, with Mike Starr, who was not part of the so-called Ontario clique in the Conservative caucus, lining up his friend, Allister Grosart, who had managed Drew's successful leadership campaign in 1948, to work this time for John Diefenbaker.

Michener himself was busy with his law practice; he had known Drew for so long and had been such a close colleague and friend that he felt his retirement personally. It was the end of a chapter in his own political career, and the party had lost a great advocate. He did not know whom to support now, or indeed whether he wanted to support anyone. He knew that Diefenbaker would be the person most likely to succeed Drew, but there were soon other candidates in the running, Davie Fulton and Donald Fleming, and they were friends. Michener felt that Davie was "rather shocked" when he told him that he was not saying openly whom he would support, and he was not encouraging his constituents to support any one of the three candidates; they would be free to vote for whom they thought would be best for the party. "From a selfish viewpoint," Michener said, "I could see no good reason for opposing Diefenbaker, which I would have to do if I supported either Fulton or Fleming."

At the end of November 1956 there was an emergency session of Parliament to deal with the Suez Crisis and the United Nations Emergency Force; UNEF, as it was called, was established as a result of the initiative of Mike Pearson — a proposal that was to win him the Nobel Peace Prize. British and French forces had invaded Egypt in an ill-fated attempt to reassert themselves as Imperial powers by retaking the Suez Canal, which the Arab leader, Colonel Gamal Abdel Nasser, had nationalized a few months earlier. It was a disastrous move, and there were fears that the conflict might spread, especially since the Soviets threatened to come to the aid of Egypt. At the United Nations, Pearson, acting quickly to cool down the situation, proposed a peacekeeping force made up of troops from some of the smaller member nations, to separate the antagonists and provide them with a way out. Since UNEF was a result of Canadian initiative and was to be commanded by a Canadian, General E.L.M. Burns, it was taken for granted that much of the force would be made up of Canadian troops, and it was to authorize the dispatch of these troops that Parliament was recalled.

Pearson's initiative had been well received throughout the country, and the Liberals expected the emergency session to be a mere formality, but they did not realize the amount of resentment there was at the way the government had failed to support Britain. When the House met, Earl Rowe, who, with the resignation of George Drew, was acting Leader of the Opposition, launched a bitter attack: he said that Suez was Britain's lifeline and here was the Canadian govern-

ment siding with Nasser and the Soviet Union. His speech so aroused
Prime Minister St. Laurent that he replied angrily, and with more
candour than political sense, that he had been "scandalized" by the
way the large powers used the veto at the United Nations "when their
own so-called vital interests were at stake," and then he declared that
"the era when the supermen of Europe could govern the whole world
has and is coming pretty close to an end."

This brought Howard Green to his feet. "I suppose," he said of
St. Laurent, "he considers that all the supermen are in the Canadian
government. If they are not all in the Canadian government, then I
presume the opinion of this same Prime Minister is that they are in the
United States government." John Diefenbaker expressed his regret
that "Canada should have permitted the use of words which cannot
hurt those at whom they are directed but will raise the hopes of
Communists everywhere in the world and will bring solace to the
Khruschevs and Bulganins."

Michener was torn between his feeling for Britain—"I am and
have been a Britisher from birth," he was to say — and his support for
the Charter of the United Nations. He did not like the way that the
United States had forced Britain and France to back down, but what
they were doing was contrary to the UN Charter. "Inwardly," he had
to admit, "I really didn't go along" with the Conservative attack on
the St. Laurent government over their lack of support for Britain. He
expressed "satisfaction that Pearson had the courage and ability to
suggest an easy way out of the war."

However, when Michener spoke in the House, he was critical
of the United Nations Emergency Force. He had just returned from a
meeting of NATO parliamentarians in Paris; there had been a week of
discussions with some two hundred legislators from fifteen countries,
and Michener was impressed with the leader of the United States
delegation, Senator Lyndon B. Johnson. He admired the way that
Johnson was able to get delegates to come around to the American
viewpoint. It was quite a diplomatic feat. He referred to the NATO
conference during his address in the Commons and said that he
agreed with Pearson when he said that "the great need at this time
was to close the ranks of the Western alliance and to restore and to
present a solid front."

NATO, he asserted, was "a regional arrangement under the
Charter of the United Nations." He was impressed, Michener said, by
the fact that "NATO possesses the only international police force in the
world today," and wondered why the United Nations was not using

NATO to deal with the situation in the Middle East "instead of the improvised force [UNEF]" that was the subject of the present debate in Parliament. He sought to excuse the action that Britain and France had taken by saying that they were attempting to restore law and order. "In fact," Michener asserted, "the law itself, if you are an Austinian*, as I am, depends for its validity on there being sanctions." In other words, he believed that Britain and France were enforcing peace and security, and he warned "that we must bear the responsibility of having substituted this sort of undefined, novel international policeman [UNEF] for a [British and French] force which was certainly competent, at least at the stage that it had reached, to deal with the Egyptian dictator and his forces and to separate the Israelis and the Egyptians and occupy the Canal Zone."

It was apparent that Michener expected the United Nations Emergency Force to take on the role of the British and French troops in the Suez and keep "the Egyptian dictator," as he called Nasser, in order; and only later did he acknowledge that UNEF depended on the consent of the parties involved, and that meant the consent of Egypt. He damned the force with faint praise, calling it "idealistic in the sense that it is adding some material force to moral opinion as expressed in the United Nations." With the hangover of Imperialism and the British connection at the time, it was difficult for most Canadians to understand or sympathize with Egyptian or Arab aspirations or concerns, and that was evident in the uproar over the Queen's Own Rifles. When Mike Pearson heard that this was the infantry battalion that the Canadian government offered to contribute to UNEF, he knew there would be trouble. "Here we were," Pearson wrote in his memoirs (*Mike*, vol. 2), "sending in the Queen's Own, wearing essentially a British uniform with UN badges. The Egyptians had just been fighting the Queen's Own. When I voiced my misgivings to our Minister of National Defence [Ralph Campney], his reaction was so immediate and violent that I did not pursue the subject."

As a result, the military brass had their way, and the battalion was moved to Halifax and billetted on the aircraft carrier, HMCS *Bonaventure* (formerly HMS *Magnificent*), which was to carry the contingent, together with equipment, to the Middle East. However, the Egyptians were adamant: they would not have the Queen's Own

---

*John Austin (1790–1859), English jurist and lecturer on the principles of jurisprudence and international law. A collection of his lectures published posthumously was entitled *The Philosophy of Positive Law*. He expressed the view that force was the only effective guarantor of the rule of law.

Rifles. In fact at one point, Nasser did not want any Canadians in the United Nations Emergency Force because, he said, they were too closely associated with the British; but he was talked out of this. After two weeks, and many pointed and acerbic questions by the Tories and much chagrin and embarrassment on the part of the government, the Queen's Own were deboarded from the aircraft carrier and sent home to Calgary, and service and supply troops were dispatched to Egypt. It was not a glorious beginning for the peacekeeping force, and seemed to confirm Michener's view of it as idealistic but ineffective.

While the Conservatives had shown the Liberal government to be bunglers on the issue of UNEF and, if not anti-British, certainly not very friendly to the British, which, in the climate of the times, would count for votes, they were deeply involved in the extraordinary democratic exercise of choosing a new leader. As Michener expected, the majority of the Conservative caucus was for Diefenbaker but he did not real-ize that it was as much as forty of the fifty members. Yet, despite this overwhelming support, there was an attempt made, by Dick Bell and those in the party hierarchy who had been at Drew's bedside when he resigned, to stop Diefenbaker. They decided to approach the would-be candidate of the 1942 Winnipeg convention, Sidney Smith, who was by now president of the University of Toronto, but Smith turned them down, saying that his doctor forbade it and he was too old.

Roland Michener was not part of this vain effort to overturn the Diefenbaker bandwagon. Ever since Drew's resignation, Michener had kept as low a profile as possible. He had to meet with those members of his constituency association who were going to Ottawa to be delegates at the convention, and he told them that he felt that Diefenbaker would be chosen but that he did not think that he had the best qualities for leadership: he was too self-centred, too much of a prima donna, too intent on his own authority, and not the sort of man to trust other people. However, Michener would not disclose his po-sition or even whether he would vote for or against Diefenbaker. He would leave them free to vote as they saw fit.

As everyone expected, John Diefenbaker won easily on the first ballot (he got 773 votes to Donald Fleming's 393 and Davie Fulton's 117). Michener, as he said, limited his activities at the Conser-vative leadership convention to the policy committee, and he did not take much part in that. He avoided like the plague the different groups supporting the various candidates, and it seemed as if he would have just as soon disappeared into the rickety woodwork of the

Coliseum, Ottawa's dingy cowpalace in which the convention was held. He never let on whom he voted for, and even thirty years later he was reluctant to disclose that the secret ballot he cast was for Donald Fleming.

Obviously, Michener's covert behaviour at the PC Convention was because he knew that Diefenbaker was going to win the leadership and he wanted to keep in his good graces, but there was another reason, which was that he had such a fine sense of manners that he did not want to offend his friend Davie Fulton by letting on that he had voted for Fleming. As for Diefenbaker, Michener's strategem, if it was that, failed, because the Chief had the simple credo that those who were not for him were against him. The Conservatives met in Ottawa during the second week in December 1956, and there was a period of four months, until the 1957 election was called, when Diefenbaker was Leader of the Opposition and occupied the Leader's ornate office in the Centre Block of the Parliament Buildings, which the acting Leader, Earl Rowe, had hastily vacated. Yet, in all that time, Michener could not remember ever being invited to the Opposition Leader's office. He was sure that Diefenbaker met the Conservative caucus after being elected leader, but that meeting did not make much of an impression on him, and he knew that many Tory members — mostly those who had supported Diefenbaker at the convention — were in and out of his office all the time.

Still, there could be the explanation that Michener was a backbench MP, and a T-to-T one at that, who had not, according to his own account, been spectacular. But he had a presence and experience as a provincial minister and there were only fifty PC members, and Diefenbaker had worked with him on the caucus's external affairs committee, although that committee was not highly rated. "I didn't make any splash in the House of Commons," Roland Michener confessed. "Nothing spectacular — I was there and I took part when it was necessary." It is true that he left so little a mark that, except for *Hansard*, he is not mentioned in any accounts of the pipeline debate or of UNEF and the Suez Crisis or of Parliament generally during that period.

As a half-time member of Parliament — which was what, as a T-to-T member, he really was, the other half-time being a lawyer — Michener could not have been expected to do much better. Yet he had set his heart on coming to Ottawa, on following in his father's footsteps; that had been his ambition since boyhood. But, as pointed out earlier, he had left it too late. By the time he had become a member of Parliament, his domestic commitments made it impossible for him to devote his full time to the House of Commons. In many ways, Roland was much more responsible than his father, who moved capriciously from one house to another and left his wife to pick up the pieces, but less adventurous. Still, if he had done more as an MP, and backed Diefenbaker when he knew he was going to win the leadership, he would not, in all likelihood, have scaled the heights of public service and become Governor General. And if Drew had not fallen ill and had become prime minister, Michener would have certainly been appointed a cabinet minister, and possibly minister of External Affairs, which is what he wanted. But that, too, might have been the end of his career.

The fact that John Diefenbaker became leader of the Progressive Conservative Party was one reason why Prime Minister Louis St. Laurent called an early election; he could have gone to the people in the fall of 1957, which would have been the traditional time to do so since it would have been four years into his mandate, but he wanted to go as early as it would be decently possible, in the spring of 1957, in order to take advantage of the fact that the Tories had a new leader. St. Laurent shared, if not inspired, the Liberal view of invincibility, and was confident of winning against Drew but, as he told Lionel Chevrier, he was ten times more confident of winning against Diefenbaker.

With the dissolution of Parliament on April 12 and the election called for June 10, 1957, St. Laurent felt that enough time had elapsed since the pipeline debate for its nastiness to have been erased from the all-too-short public memory. That was also the view of many Conservatives, including those close to their new leader; they said that it was a year old and people would have forgotten about it, but Diefenbaker insisted that the trampling underfoot of the rights of Parliament in the pipeline debate was the issue, and he would make it the issue. Michener agreed that "the dominant factor" in the 1957 election campaign was "our stand on the pipeline" against the ukase of an arrogant and autocratic government. He believed that this moral issue counted for much more in Toronto than the Suez Crisis and the charges that the Liberals were anti-British, although he said that the latter might have had a greater impact on the more traditional loyalties in the countryside.

Once again an attempt to rig the election in the Toronto riding of St. Paul's came to light when a group of nuns complained to Michener's campaign headquarters that the revised voters' list— some two thousand names had been added to the 1957 enumeration—showed a married couple living at their convent. There was no such couple at their address. Michener immediately assigned some young Conservatives to the case, and they found that one hundred and fifty names had been wrongfully added to the voters' list. By this time it was the end of May and Michener decided to go public with the evidence. He took a reporter and photographer from *The Globe and Mail* on a tour of the riding, pointing out the parking lot where a Mr. and Mrs. Norm Poole were listed as living, the municipal waterworks where a Mr. and Mrs. Roy Hardy were supposed to occupy Apartment 311, and an apartment building, still under construction, allegedly occupied by four voters.

Quite obviously, there was widespread voter fraud, and the other candidates reacted to these charges by coming up with charges of their own. James Rooney, who was running again for the Liberals, told the press that his agents had discovered twenty-six false names on the voters' list, while the CCF hinted darkly at revelations they would make. The chief electoral officer, Nelson Castonguay, appointed Ontario Chief Justice James McRuer to investigate, and after the election the RCMP laid charges against members of the Rooney campaign for fraudulently adding names to the voters' list.

In his riding, Michener could feel a surge of support, especially toward the end of the campaign. George Hees, whose Toronto riding of Broadview was close to St. Paul's, said that the turning point came three weeks before election day when Diefenbaker was wildly cheered in a big and well-staged meeting in Vancouver: it was then that the Conservative campaign really took off. "I felt sure," Michener said, "that we would make substantial gains but whether it would be enough, I didn't know. But I was hopeful." In St. Paul's, Michener got the biggest majority ever in the history of the riding. Usually there was a narrow margin of a few hundred to a thousand votes, whether a Liberal or Conservative was elected, but on the night of June 10, 1957, there were great celebrations at the constituency association's headquarters when it was shown that Michener had 6,657 more votes than his Liberal and CCF opponents; in 1958 he had a plurality of 11,001.

They were heady days for Tories, the days of mid-June 1957; for the first time in twenty-two long years they had won a federal election and would form the government. There was a moment of uncertainty when there were rumours that the Liberals might carry on in the hope that the CCF would keep them in power; after all, the Conservatives had only seven more seats, with 112 to their 105, only five more if the Liberal Labour and Independent Liberal were counted. But St. Laurent soon quashed these inspired reports and turned the government over to Diefenbaker.

Roland Michener had difficulty concentrating on his law practice in Toronto as his thoughts kept straying toward Ottawa. He had plans to go fishing with a friend, Arthur Walwyn, but before he went he decided that he had to see Diefenbaker and offer his services as an elected Conservative and a loyal member of the party. So he rang Ottawa and got an appointment.

There was a lineup of people on the second floor of the Parliament Building's East Block where the prime minister's office was located, but Michener had no trouble getting to see Diefenbaker. He was glad to hear that the Chief, who was in a cordial mood, had been considering a suitable job for him, or, as he put it, what he could most usefully do. "I was thinking," he reported Diefenbaker as saying, "that you might be parliamentary secretary for External Affairs because I'm keeping that portfolio for myself." Michener said that he would be very pleased to accept this position. However, the prime minister elect had not made up his mind yet, but he said that he would get in touch with Michener before Parliament met, when he should have "a better idea of who should be where."

As might be expected, people in the Department of External Affairs were "extremely interested" as to who would be their new minister, and John Holmes, who was assistant undersecretary at the time, said that they were delighted to hear that Roly Michener might become parliamentary secretary. They were aware that Diefenbaker was keeping the portfolio but they were sure that he would find it too great a burden and then the parliamentary secretary would become Minister. Or so they hoped. Holmes and others in the department had been with the Canadian Institute of International Affairs and knew Michener from his association with that body; they considered that his background and understanding of foreign issues made him ideally suited for diplomacy. Actually, Michener did talk to Holmes about his possible involvement with the department; at the time Holmes was acting as Diefenbaker's external affairs secretary, but there was no *sub rosa* campaign to get Michener appointed. "No," Holmes said, "nobody in External would have dared to do that."

The people in the department were disappointed that, in the end, Michener did not get the job, and, as they expected, the prime minister found External Affairs more than he could handle. He turned the portfolio over to Sidney Smith, the president of the University of Toronto.

> We were pleased with the appointment [Holmes said]. For one thing, we had a minister. Trying to deal with the prime minister, with all the things that he had to do, was hopeless. Everybody liked Sidney and he couldn't have been nicer. He had the kind of academic background which should have made him a good minister, but we were dismayed to find how little he knew of international affairs. He had no time to read his papers because he was plunged almost immediately into a by-election. The poor man got terribly rattled [in the House of Commons]. That was very sad. Roly would have been so different.

So Michener went fishing. Time passed and he heard nothing, except that George Drew was to be the Canadian High Commissioner in London: it was one of the first things that Diefenbaker did on becoming prime minister. Michener wrote to his old leader and friend, congratulating him on his appointment; he said that he had no idea what to expect from Diefenbaker: "I do not know what is in store for me. I hope further responsibilities, but I am delighted that you have accepted the London post. It keeps you in public service and in a position for which you are peculiarly fitted." Diefenbaker had said that he was only appointing a proportion of his cabinet when the Progressive Conservative government was sworn in on June 21, 1957, with some ministers doubling up, and he did not name any parliamentary secretaries.

The Commonwealth Prime Ministers' Conference was due to be held in London shortly after the swearing-in ceremony, and Diefenbaker was determined to go despite the fact that he had so much to do at home. The new Canadian prime minister became an instant hit with the British public by announcing that he would call a Commonwealth trade conference; he went on a triumphal tour of Britain, which was climaxed by an address to a large and enthusiastic audience in the Albert Hall.

Months went by. Diefenbaker completed the selection of his cabinet and appointed a number of parliamentary secretaries (they were called parliamentary assistants at first), but Michener's name was not among them. He continued to practise law and wait. Then, at last, the call came: Michener was summoned to Ottawa at the beginning of October, less than two weeks before Parliament was due to open. Diefenbaker told him that he had offered to nominate Stanley Knowles, the prominent ccFer and authority on parliamentary procedure, to be Speaker of the new House of Commons, but if Knowles refused, he wanted to propose Roland Michener. There was no doubt in Michener's mind that Knowles would refuse and Michener said as much to Diefenbaker and that he would get ready for the position. He would have preferred to have been minister of External Affairs and even parliamentary secretary, but he recognized that the Speakership was a prestigious if onerous appointment.

He consulted the Clerk of the House and visited the Speaker's Chambers where he found René Beaudoin still writing his book on parliamentary procedure. They exchanged pleasantries. Beaudoin had been re-elected and continued as Speaker until the new Speaker was elected; he worked until the last day in his old office where all the necessary reference books were, and Michener believed that he had more or less completed his manuscript. But Beaudoin made only one appearance in the new Parliament and then disappeared.

Madame Beaudoin called on Michener when he became Speaker and told him that René had left her for another woman (whom he later married) and that she had no means of support. "I sympathized with her, "Michener said, "and advised her as best as I could, but there was not much that I could do." Beaudoin had gone to the United States, to Nevada, where he found that he could not practise as a lawyer, and had to take a menial job. His manuscript came to light when he tried to get it published, but Michener said, "I never heard from him myself and I don't know what happened to it."

When the Twenty-third Parliament met on October 14, 1957, Roland Michener was nominated by Prime Minister Diefenbaker and seconded by the Opposition Leader, Louis St. Laurent and unanimously elected Speaker of the Commons. Later Michener was to complain that not until that very day did he know for certain that he was going to be Speaker, but this was not done deliberately to keep him on tenterhooks: it was just John Diefenbaker's way of making appointments. Mike Starr, who was one of the Chief's earliest supporters, did not know until the day he was sworn in that he was to be minister of Labour, and Bill Hamilton only learned that he had been picked as postmaster general on the way to Government House for the swearing-in ceremony.

It was a hectic day for Michener, October 14, 1957, but a triumphant and historic day as well, for it was the day that Queen Elizabeth opened Parliament. Not only was it the first time that the monarch had presided at this function but the first time that television had covered the proceedings. The dull red Senate Chamber shone brightly in the glare of the klieg lights, which gave out so much heat that the temperature was said to have risen almost fifteen degrees Fahrenheit during the hour long ceremony. Her Majesty found the going hot, or so it was reported, but bore it with fortitude and read every word of the Speech from the Throne, first in English and then in French, which took some forty minutes. It was, by all accounts, a brilliant affair. At the summons of the sovereign, conveyed by Black Rod, Mr. Speaker Michener, resplendent in his newly acquired black silk gown and tricorne hat, led the MPs from the Commons Chamber across the Hall of Honour to the door of the Senate Chamber and as far as "the bar." The new Speaker made the traditional claim of the rights and privileges of the legislators, and every time he spoke and every time the House of Commons was mentioned by the Queen, he doffed his tricorne hat. There could not have been a more splendid beginning to his Speakership.

❧ 12 ❧

Speaker and
Prime Minister

When Roland Michener became Speaker, he found that a simultaneous interpretation system was in place in the House of Commons. All the equipment had been installed during the six months when there were no sittings, from the time of the dissolution of the Twenty-second Parliament to the opening of the Twenty-third Parliament; each desk had been fitted with its own microphone, and booths for the interpreters had been built into the corners of the chamber so that they matched the oak panelling and were hardly noticeable, and in the front of the Ladies' Gallery, directly opposite the Speaker's Chair, was a control panel operated by a technician. "It [simultaneous interpretation] began as by magic," Michener said, "on the first day of the Twenty-third Parliament, and went on successfully ever after."

There was no doubt that simultaneous interpretation was a boon to most members, and it added considerably to the efficiency of Parliament. Michener remembered that, as a backbench MP, he had always intended to read the translation of a speech in French in the next day's *Hansard*, but never had. Simultaneous interpretation also added to the accuracy of the reporting of the Commons because the whole proceedings were taped and there was an oral record. It made for better-informed debates since the interpreters who were turning the French into English or the English into French came close enough to the substance and meaning of a speech without providing an absolutely correct version, which would have to wait for the translation in *Hansard*.

It meant that the Speaker had greater control. He would have liked to have had a switch on the side of the Chair so he could silence a member by switching off his mike, but he did not have one. However, when he rose, the technician in the gallery directly opposite him would turn off all the mikes except his. That gave the technician unusual power, which was an anomaly of the system, but Michener could not think of any other disadvantage.

Although the Diefenbaker government took the credit for the introduction of simultaneous interpretation, it was unlikely that it initiated the system. The St. Laurent government must have decided on it and ordered the electronic equipment, but the Diefenbaker government put it into operation, and, as Michener said, "I'm sure that Diefenbaker was keen to have it for more reasons than one." Aside from the advantage of simultaneous interpretation, the earphone with which each desk was provided made it easier for anyone hard of hearing, as Diefenbaker was, to understand what was being said in the House. On many an occasion, when he did not have his earphone on, Diefenbaker would be heard asking his seatmate, Donald Fleming, "What's he saying?" In summing up, Michener said that simultaneous interpretation "made life much more livable in the House of Commons."

Just as the electronic revolution started in Parliament when he became Speaker, so Michener was faced with the issue of the first electronic journalists. The Parliamentary Press Gallery, which came under the jurisdiction of the Speaker, refused to grant membership to radio reporters, and without that membership the radio reporters could not cover Parliament. The older newspapermen who ran the Press Gallery felt that their profession as parliamentary correspondents was being threatened by this rag-tag bunch of young, inexperienced newsmen. The radio reporters appealed to the Speaker, and Michener solved the problem by giving them part of the diplomatic gallery. "Fortunately, there weren't many of them," Michener said, "and I was able to set aside four seats with everything [including simultaneous interpretation] piped into them." The first few electronic journalists were the beginning of an invasion, and soon the older newspapermen could no longer, like Canute, hold back the tide and, in 1961, accepted radio and television correspondents as full members of the Parliamentary Press Gallery.

The Speaker's Chambers included a suite of offices and a dressing room, as well as Room 16, which Michener used as a dining room, but there were two bedrooms upstairs "which John Hamilton had captured before I had taken the Chair." There was great competition for the inadequate amount of office space in the Centre Block, and John Hamilton, a prominent Toronto lawyer who was the Tory member for York West, simply expropriated the bedrooms when the St. Laurent government was defeated, and turned them into offices for himself. "I didn't like to disturb him after he got settled there," Michener said, "but those two bedrooms would have made a great difference to my wife and me." All that the Micheners had — and now Norah spent most of the time in Ottawa when Roly was Speaker — was the small apartment on Metcalfe Street.

However, soon after taking the Chair, Michener was assigned Mackenzie King's house at Kingsmere; he was the first Speaker to have the "Farm House," which had been refurbished by its owners, the National Capital Commission, as a summer residence. "That was a great boon to me," Michener said, "because it gave one an escape for the weekend. I found it made being Speaker a lot more tolerable, as it was a complete break [with Parliament]. I seldom entertained there. Just my wife and I went there and I rested over the weekend and I did my homework, which included memorizing the faces and names of the Members and their constituencies. You had to have two things right on your tongue, the Member's name and the name of his constituency, because one time you use his name, Mr. So-and-So moves ... and another time, it is the Honourable Member for So-and-So ... That was one of the difficulties of sitting in the Chair."

Another difficulty was administration. Since there was not enough office space, some members of Parliament had to double up, and secretaries had to be shared. Only the Centre Block of the Parliament Buildings was at the disposal of the legislators; it came under the jurisdiction of the Speaker of the House of Commons, and only a little more than half of that because the Senate Wing was a separate administration under the Speaker of the Senate. The East Block had the Prime Minister's Office and the Department of External Affairs, while the West Block had the Ministry of Fisheries and offices of other assorted bureaucrats. The accommodation of the Commons was squalid, a throwback to the old days when there were fewer members and shorter sessions. Michener did his best to help: he cleared some officials from offices in the Centre Block, and by the time he left the Speaker's Chair each member had a room of his own and a secretary; but the improvement in legislative quarters really came when the West Block and later the Confederation Building were taken over by Parliament. Then the members had not just one office but a suite of offices and not one secretary but a support staff.

Parts of the Centre Block, such as the Parliamentary Library and the restaurant, were jointly administered by the House and the Senate, but Michener got along well with the Speaker of the Senate, Mark Drouin. They were good friends and they worked as a team. "We had quite a smooth time," Michener asserted, but recalled, "There were complaints about the way the lobsters were cooked. It didn't suit the Maritimers that they weren't boiled in salt water."

On October 14, 1957, the day that Michener was elected Speaker of the Commons and the day that the Queen opened Parliament, it was announced that Mike Pearson had been awarded the Nobel Peace Prize for his initiative in establishing the United Nations Emergency Force and resolving the 1956 Suez Crisis. As Pearson said in his memoirs (*Mike*, vol. 2), the news came as a complete surprise to him, and helped to brighten up the gloom of his single room in the basement of the Centre Block where he had had to move as a result of the change in government. Michener, in the Speaker's fine chambers, was delighted that his friend had received this award which "he so well merited," but all the excitement of that day made him think that the announcement of Pearson winning the Nobel Prize was made just before the Liberal Leadership Convention. Pearson actually received the award in December when the Liberal Convention had been called and the race for the leadership was on. "I thought," Michener said, "what a great advantage to receive the Nobel Peace Prize just before a leadership convention. Too bad we haven't one for Paul Martin." Pearson's election as Liberal leader on January 16, 1958, was a foregone conclusion.

Michener's first experience as Speaker was with the Diefenbaker minority government, which could have been a very tense and awkward situation but actually turned out to be easier in some ways than the huge majority government of the Twenty-fourth Parliament, where he came into conflict with the prime minister. While

Diefenbaker had such a narrow margin of a handful of seats in the Twenty-third Parliament, he was not concerned about being voted out of office; in fact, he was anxious to be defeated so that he could ride the current of public opinion to a majority government, which he did in 1958. Thus the Twenty-third Parliament was regarded as an interim affair, and, as Michener said, "of no consequence except to prepare for the next election, and each party tried to do the best it could to improve its own position for the inevitable election."

As a result, tempers became short toward the end; everyone was watching and waiting for the prime minister to act; on February 1, 1958, Diefenbaker disappeared from the House of Commons, and returned, by his own account (*One Canada* vol. 2), at "a minute or so after six." He had gone to Quebec City where Governor General Vincent Massey was in residence to secure the dissolution of Parliament. Jimmy Gardiner was speaking and Michener took the Chair to say that it was six o'clock when the prime minister rose to make a statement. Mike Pearson, who was by now Opposition Leader, objected and demanded the right of reply. Others wanted to know why he should be given the floor when it was six o'clock. The Speaker said that if the prime minister was to give notice of what he suspected, there would be no more proceedings. It took fifteen minutes for Diefenbaker, who wanted to get in his political licks, to say that he had a writ of dissolution and that Parliament was no more.

Pearson was furious, and the Opposition reaction was stormy. In his memoirs (*Mike* vol. 2) Pearson said that at six o'clock the Speaker should have left the Chair and recessed the House: "This was the only quarrel I ever had with my good and old friend, Roland Michener." It should have been by unanimous consent of the House of Commons that Diefenbaker made his statement, and Michener assumed that it had been granted, since it was for a government spokesman to outline the following day's business. He admitted that he was wrong. It was a bitter ending to his first Parliament and only Pearson came to the traditional farewell party that the Speaker gave on dissolution. "Mike said he was sorry and then left," Michener recalled. No other member showed up. There was no explanation for this, unless the MPs were rushing off to start their campaign.

The Opposition members might just as well have come to the party: there was nothing that they could do to halt the juggernaut of the Diefenbaker Tories. The Social Creditors were wiped out, the CCF reduced to eight seats with their leaders M.J. Coldwell and Stanley Knowles defeated, and the Liberals cut down to a rump of fewer than fifty members; but Mike Pearson survived to lead the party and fight other elections. When the Twenty-fourth Parliament met on May 12, 1958, Michener found the atmosphere to be very different. The Progressive Conservative government, which had barely filled the seats on the Speaker's right, now overflowed and filled half of the seats on the other side. It was not that the Tories were in a triumphant mood but that the remnants of the Opposition were so subdued compared with their cantankerous behaviour in the last Parliament — and, after their massacre at the polls, they did lie low at first. While every election resulted in about a hundred new members, there were many more than this as a result of the Diefenbaker landslide, and most of them knew nothing about Parliament.

"They all wanted to talk," Michener said. "The first thing I had to get into their heads was that it was a debate and that in a debate there have to be alternate speakers, and that you can't have two on the same side without hearing from the other side. It was not a great issue and the Conservative Whips helped by explaining that they could have as many speeches as the Opposition but no more. If the opposition quit, then they could all talk one after another as long as the time allotted for the debate."

If the new members knew even little about Parliament or Ottawa, their spouses knew less, and it was no wonder that Norah Michener was asked to provide instruction on etiquette in the nation's capital. The *Memorandum for the Wives of Members of the Senate and the House of Commons* was written "in response to a discussion which took place at a meeting of the Parliamentary Wives' Association in May 1958," shortly after the Twenty-fourth Parliament opened. It was a small mimeographed booklet, twenty-one pages long, in which Norah said that the best definition of protocol was "international good manners" and laid out the rules for good manners at Government House, at diplomatic receptions, and in the House of Commons and the Parliamentary Restaurant.

The *Memorandum* begins by saying that MPs and their wives should call on the Governor General "immediately after arrival in Ottawa." This would be done by signing the Visitors' Book at Rideau Hall. The wife of a member should write: "Mr. John Smith, MP., and Mrs. Smith." It would be incorrect to put down "John Smith MP and Mary Smith" because "this signature gives no indication if Mary is a wife or daughter and the man's title is omitted." Replies to invitations from Government House should be in the third person and handwritten. If invited to a ball or formal dinner at Rideau Hall, ladies should wear evening dresses and long white gloves; they would remove the gloves "completely" at the table. After any hospitality at Government House, the Visitors' Book should be signed "if possible, within three days." On the other hand, "always write a small note of thanks" for a party at an embassy.

Much of the booklet is taken up with information about the Parliamentary Restaurant and the galleries of the House of Commons, which would be of value to any newcomer. Members and their wives were entitled to use the Parliamentary Restaurant; they could take guests there but one or other of them would have to accompany them. There were three private dining rooms, and the *Memorandum* tells how to use them for parties and says: "It is usual to leave with Mr. Villeneuve [the maitre 'd] tips for the waitresses." As for the galleries, cards would be needed for admission to the Members' and Ladies' Gallery and could be obtained from the Sergeant-at-Arms, while the Public Gallery was usually open to anyone. Then, there is a short account of titles and precedence. The Governor General should be addressed the first time as "Your Excellency" and the second time as "Sir," the prime minister as "Mr. Prime Minister," a cabinet minister as "Mr. Minister," and so on.

Norah Michener's brief on manners and customs in Ottawa was well received by the vast majority of the new MPS' wives; such a guide had long been needed and it could have been prepared by no better a person than the wife of the Speaker: Mrs. Michener was an authority on etiquette and had written about it (and the culinary arts) under the name of Janet Peters. The criticism was that its approach was too patrician for Canada. There was great emphasis on the curtsy. "Women curtsy when presented" to the Governor General. "At the end of the function, the Governor General will leave .... Curtsy as he goes by." "Make a full curtsy to His Excellency." While that might have been the height of good behaviour at the time, the curtsy was on its way out and was to be done away with officially when Roland Michener became Governor General. Then there were the cards when calling on a diplomat: "take with you one card of your own and two of your husband's"— the reason for the husband's two cards was that he called on the ambassador and on the ambassador's wife. Most of the new MPS' wives did not have cards of their own and, in any case, the three-card call had gone out with the wing collar and the top hat.

The fact that the *Memorandum* was addressed to wives and took for granted a man's world might have had a negative impact because the women's movement was beginning, but it would have had no effect on the wives of the new Conservative members. They were more likely to resent the upper class tone of the booklet since the party under Diefenbaker had become much more populist. Then there were those who felt they did not need any instructions in etiquette, and were indignant at what they called "Madame Speaker's pretensions to teach them manners." But they were a small minority.

The name "Madame Speaker," while said derisively, suited Norah since she spent almost as much time in the House as Roland. From her seat in the Speaker's Gallery she would send notes down to any member who was not comporting himself properly. When Alvin Hamilton, the former agriculture minister in the Diefenbaker government, crossed the floor of the House, just before the sitting began, to speak to an Opposition member, he received a note saying that this was not good behaviour. Alvin said that he laughed it off but others did not take it so kindly. Yet there was a need for someone like Norah to keep a watch on manners, and Hamilton was the first to admit this: he said that there was so little decorum in subsequent Parliaments. Diefenbaker was insistent that members be well dressed and did not like them to have pens and pencils in their breast pockets, and certainly not in a case in their shirt pockets. In this the prime minister had Norah's full support.

At the beginning of the Twenty-fourth Parliament, Michener's relations with Diefenbaker were such that he wondered whether the prime minister would nominate him for Speaker again. He had heard reports that Diefenbaker was dissatisfied with the length of Question Period during the previous Parliament, that he thought that Michener favoured the Opposition, and that he had too many friends, like Pearson, on the other side. Michener emphasized that this was just gossip, that Diefenbaker never said so to him. It was only when the prime minister had decided to renominate him as Speaker that he let it be known that he was concerned about Question Period. Michener reported that Diefenbaker said to him:

"What do you think you could do about cutting short the Question Period? I said that is not within my power. I said the House could put some limit on it, but I don't try to prolong it; I try to cut it off and get on with the business of the day. Well, he said, I would like to be assured that you will do your best to keep the questioning under control."

There was no time limit on Question Period, and, as Michener said, as long as a member got up, he was entitled to be heard. On the average, the Question Period lasted for three-quarters of an hour,

which was not too long, but there were many occasions when it went
on for two hours or more. Mr. Speaker Michener tried to keep it short:
"I wouldn't let people go on with unlimited supplementaries [follow-
up questions]. I would knock them down if they asked the wrong
person. I would say that is not the responsibility of this minister,
or that is not a question, it is an argument. What is your question?"
Despite his best efforts he was not always able to keep control of
Question Period or Motions that preceded Question Period, and the
Opposition by means of procedural arguments about privilege or
principle could turn it into a heated debate. Without a time limit
Question Period could get out of hand and undoubtedly did exacer-
bate the Speaker's relations with the prime minister. However, a time
limit was not adopted until some years after Roland Michener had
left the Chair.

While Diefenbaker did not protest publicly about the
Speaker's rulings during Question Period and the amount of latitude
that he allowed the Opposition, he did let it be known that he was
not very happy with the situation. On his part, Michener denied that
he "consciously favoured the Opposition" although he admitted that
he "did his best to keep them on foot and not have them submerged
by weight of numbers" on the government benches. Sometimes the
prime minister would argue with the Speaker about a point of order.
"If he thought I was unjust, he would say so," Michener said, "And if
I thought he was right, I would drop it." However, on May 25, 1959,
Prime Minister Diefenbaker allowed his indignation over a Speaker's
ruling in favour of the Liberals' assertion of "trickery" get the better
of him and he refused to sit down when called to order. There was a
lively exchange back and forth between the Chair and the government front bench and further points of order. "It got so complicated,"
Michener said, "nobody knew what we were talking about."

On another occasion the Speaker was faced with a dilemma.
He wanted the prime minister to withdraw a remark he had made, but
what would he do if Diefenbaker refused? "I was greatly troubled,"
Michener recalled. "I said to myself, nobody would ever name the
prime minister, particularly one who has two hundred and eight
members behind him. What shall I do?" He decided the only way out
was to use diplomacy. He spoke of the right honourable gentleman
being a great authority on parliamentary procedure and asked him
what he would do in the circumstances, and suggested that the House
might be adjourned for fifteen minutes to give him time to consider

his options. In the end there was no adjournment, and while not backing down fully, Diefenbaker did withdraw enough to save the honour of the Chair.

By his own reckoning, Mr. Speaker Michener did not initate any very radical procedural changes in the House of Commons. He did preside over a committee that sought to, and did, improve the rules. Aside from the brawling cockpit of the Question Period, Michener's conduct of the business of the House was gracious and courtly and much admired by most of the Conservative and Liberal members, as well as by the handful of ccFers who became New Democrats during his time in the Chair. (The founding NDP convention was in Ottawa in 1961.) Officials of Parliament, who had seen Speakers come and go, regarded Michener as one of the finest; he had maturity, authority, and a "regal bearing." Erik Spicer, the Parliamentary Librarian, said that Michener came closest to being the "ideal" Speaker: "he had the presence, he had the appearance, he had the experience."

Paul Martin thought that Michener was "one of the best Speakers that we ever had." Mike Pearson had a great respect for his friend, and Martin said that Pearson told the Liberal caucus that "he hoped that under Michener there would embark a very constructive period of cooperation," which did not work out "because we were a vigorous opposition and the Speaker controls the House." In fact, Martin "felt that Roly was an unnecessary constraint" and, on one occasion, asked to speak to him in his Chambers. Martin complained that the Speaker "had been too severe in his handling of myself." They had a very frank discussion. "I often remember that," Martin said, "I came out of that meeting with great respect for him because I think if I had been in his position and he had been in mine and had attacked me as I had attacked him, I wouldn't have been as complacent as he proved to be."

There was a right of appeal against a Speaker's ruling during Michener's time in the Chair—it has since been abrogated—and it had been used very freely at times, especially against Mr. Speaker Beaudoin's rulings during the pipeline debate. However, there was only one appeal against Mr. Speaker Michener's own rulings and that did not come from the Official Opposition but from one of the small band of socialist members, Frank Howard. It was a trivial matter and was overwhelmingly rejected. Still, Michener was proud of the fact that there was only one appeal in the five years that he was in the Chair.

As for Mr. Speaker Michener's important rulings on parliamentary procedure, the most memorable was over the Pallett Affair. John Cameron Pallett, an Ontario lawyer and member of Parliament for Peel, was alleged to have instructed an independent appraiser to put as generous a valuation as possible on the land of a former client that was being expropriated for Malton Airport, later named the Toronto Lester B. Pearson International Airport. He was also said to have negotiated with the minister of Transport on the matter. However, the valuation of $17,330 was not accepted by the government, and when the case was taken to court, the compensation for the property was fixed at $11,200 and interest. The Opposition Leader, Mike Pearson, moved that the member's actions be examined by the House's disciplinary committee, the Committee on Privileges and Elections, and Pallett was a choice target for the Liberals since he happened to be the Tories' Chief Whip at the time.

In making his ruling, Mr. Speaker Michener said that while the judge was critical of Pallett for influencing the appraiser, he was more critical of the appraiser for allowing himself to be influenced. Furthermore, the member did not stand to gain or profit for himself by anything he did, nor were any public funds improperly paid out. In fact, the amount paid out (the compensation of $11,200 and interest) was determined by due process of law, in other words, by the judge himself.

"In my view," Michener said, according to *Hansard*, "simple justice requires that no honourable Member should have to submit to investigation of his conduct by the House or a committee until he has been charged with an offence." It was open to a member to bring charges, but no one had done so. "Did he [Judge J. T. Thorson] intend or imply that the honourable member's conduct was an offence against the independence or dignity of the House of Commons, about which as a former member of that House he would be cognizant and alert? He does not say so," Michener went on. "There is no direct charge of this kind in the judge's observations about the honourable Member for Peel, nor has any member of this House taken the responsibility himself of saying that such a charge must be implied from such observations or of saying what the charge is. Instead, the supporters of the motion say in effect, 'Let the committee see if there is anything of this kind with which the member could be charged.'" Michener ruled that the motion did not involve a *prima facie* case of privilege and was therefore disallowed.

While the Speaker's relations with Prime Minister Diefenbaker were sometimes strained, Michener was one who always looked on the bright side and tended to laugh off irritations and difficulties. The two men got along well enough together, but they were never close, although Michener said, "I'm happy to acknowledge him as a friend and call him John." He did not know what Diefenbaker's attitude to him was, but they had a mutual respect for each other. There was once, and only once, that the prime minister asked the Speaker to come and see him. He had a report, Diefenbaker said, that Michener had purchased from a diplomat a Lincoln automobile that had been brought into the country without duty. Michener denied that he had dealings with a diplomat; he had bought a secondhand Lincoln, it was true, but from a dealer and he had paid him his price, and that was all there was to it.

Diefenbaker expressed his relief that there had been no attempt to evade duty, and, as if to make amends for this inquisition, he said: "You know, I am not a very trusting person. There are only three people in my life time whom I really trusted, absolutely trusted." That was how Michener recalled the conversation, and, as he said, there were Diefenbaker's two wives (the first wife, Edna, died in 1951) which took up two of the three, but who was the third? Could it have been David Walker or Senator William R. Brunt, who was killed in an automobile accident? Michener did not pursue the matter but felt that it was an insight into Diefenbaker's real feelings, and his character.

There was no doubt that Roland Michener had the right temperament to deal with a prickly personage such as John Diefenbaker; he was calm, judicial, and never took umbrage, no matter how much he was provoked. But Norah was different: she was much more emotional and she did not have a high regard for the prime minister or, as Roland put it, "she sized him up pretty well and knew his weaknesses." But, he added, "she was on the side of his wife whenever she heard about their differences," and that she and Olive Diefenbaker were good friends. Diefenbaker, whose antennaes were sensitive as far as personal relations were concerned, knew of Norah's attitude, and there were rows.

One of them was over the chandeliers in the Speaker's Chambers. Norah, who had very good taste and could have been a professional interior decorator, said that the main chandelier was not big enough for the room and that the two smaller chandeliers on either side of the fireplace should match. At Roland's suggestion, she rang

Howard Green, the minister of Public Works, and told him that she knew a man in Montreal who had beautiful chandeliers at a very cheap price. They were put up, and the way that Diefenbaker heard about this, according to Michener, was when Olive said to him, "You should see the lovely chandelier the Speaker has in his chambers." The prime minister was furious at such "extravagance" and refused to allow payment for the main chandelier, which was reputed to cost seven thousand dollars. Michener said that although it was worth five thousand dollars, it only cost five hundred dollars and he paid the bill. Norah was very annoyed, but Roland treated the matter lightly and used to say that the chandelier was his and he would take it with him when he left the Speaker's chair. In the end, Public Works paid for it, and "I said to Norah, if you can get my money back, it's yours; so she kept after the chandelier maker [who had been paid twice] until he paid her back."

Then there was the occasion when Norah was travelling on her own in Europe (Roland was leading the Canadian delegation to the Commonwealth Parliamentary Conference in Australia at the time). She visited the Canadian Ambassador in Paris and signed her name in the book: *Norah Michener, La Presidente, Ottawa*. A little later on, Diefenbaker was in Paris and saw this inscription, and when he got back to Ottawa he got hold of Norah and said, "What right have you to put *La Presidente* as your address in Ottawa?" Michener reported that Norah told the prime minister that *Le President* was French for "Speaker," and it was on the brass plate of the door to the Speaker's Chamber; hadn't he seen it? Diefenbaker wouldn't believe it until he took a look for himself; it was a door through which he passed regularly because it led to a small room that he used as a retreat from the Commons, but he had never noticed the brass plate. (The present brass plate reads *Le President* and, beneath it, *Speaker*.)

Although Michener considered it an amusing incident, he seemed to feel that Norah was being a bit elitist by writing the French for Speaker in the embassy book, but he said that in her travels through Europe he "gave her carte blanche, which was a silly thing to do." However, Norah was a woman of strong convictions and felt that her husband's role had never been fully appreciated by Prime Minister Diefenbaker, whom she abhorred, or by Parliament and that "Le President" was a much better job description than "Speaker." She was his greatest supporter and she campaigned tirelessly to raise the importance of the position of Speaker— too often it had been a consolation prize for not getting into the cabinet. The Speaker had to be

ROYAL VISIT. The Governor General escorts Queen Elizabeth to her aircraft after her seven-day Centennial visit, July 1967. (Associated Press Photo.)

BENELUX TOUR. Queen Juliana welcomes the Governor General at dockside in Amsterdam, April 1971. (Foto National Persbureau N.V., courtesy Roland Michener.)

CARIBBEAN VISIT. Michener tries out a native bow and arrow in a village in Guyana, February 1969. (Courtesy Roland Michener.)

ARCTIC TOUR. Norah and Roland Michener watch an igloo being built in Frobisher Bay, April 1969. (Courtesy Roland Michener.)

KEEPING FIT. Jogging was an everyday exercise for the Governor General. (*Toronto Star.*)

Practising for the Grey Cup kick-off. (Courtesy Roland Michener.)

Joining the cheerleaders' chorus line in N.W.T. (UPI/Bettmann Newsphotos.)

TAKING THE SALUTE. The Governor General, in the summer uniform he designed himself, with Norah and Colonel Strome Galloway, on Canada Day, 1972. (Courtesy Roland Michener.)

RUNNING ANTELOPE. The Governor General becomes a Blood Indian Chief in ceremony at Standoff, Alberta. (Courtesy Roland Michener.)

SCALING THE PEAK. At eighty, Roland Michener climbed the mountain in the Rockies that was named in his honour. (Courtesy Roland Michener.)

HIGH KICKING. In his retirement Michener keeps fit. (*The Globe and Mail,* Toronto.)

HONORARY CHAIRMAN. Michener continues his mining interests with longtime friend Dr. Norman B. Keevil. (Courtesy Roland Michener.)

STILL JOGGING. Roland Michener with Rosedale Elementary School students in Toronto. (*Toronto Star.*)

DOCTOR NORAH. As Chancellor of Queen's University in Kingston, Roland Michener confers an honorary degree on his wife. (Photo by William O'Neill.)

"I invited them to come to Ottawa," Michener said, "and they all came, the Speakers and Clerks, and we decided on having a regional meeting every year." The first regional meeting was held in Quebec in 1960. As the founder of this group Michener was regularly invited to the meetings and attended a couple of them after leaving the House of Commons.

Another innovation was the Canada – United States Inter-Parliamentary Exchange, which was formed as a result of the initiative of Prime Minister Diefenbaker and President Eisenhower during the latter's visit to Ottawa in the summer of 1958; the two leaders felt that a better understanding of each other's legislatures would be achieved by having joint meetings of selected groups from Congress and the Parliament of Canada. Roland Michener and Mark Drouin, the Speaker of the Senate, met with their opposite numbers in Washington and designed a format of two meetings a year, alternating between the two countries. There were to be twenty-four from each side, with the congressional delegation divided equally between the House of Representatives and the Senate, while the parliamentary delegation had a preponderance of members from the House of Commons. At Michener's suggestion, wives were made parties to the visits. There were usually a couple of days of conference and couple of days of sightseeing, and Michener remembered the first meeting in Washington when they were shown NORAD (North American Air Defence Agreement) headquarters in Colorado and flown there and back in the president's plane.

The idea of a permanent Speaker or a continuing Speaker had been considered in the past; it made sense, provided the encumbent was unanimously acceptable to the House. Then his experience would not be wasted. There was strong support for Michener to keep the Chair among members of Parliament and especially academic observers of the parliamentary scene who greatly admired his style. The Liberals were in favour of his continuing, and Paul Martin said that Mike Pearson would have been happy to have seen Michener as a permanent Speaker, and so would Stanley Knowles, the acknowledged authority on parliamentary procedure. At the end of the Twenty-fourth Parliament, H.W. Herridge, the acting Leader of the New Democratic Party (formerly CCF), paid a glowing tribute to Michener's conduct in the Chair and, "for those reasons," said that "during recent months there has been a growing interest in the House, and in the party for which I have the honour to speak this afternoon, in the proposal that we should have a permanent Speaker."

A private member's bill had been introduced from the Conservative benches that would have given the Speaker a special constituency, Parliament Hill or the House of Commons. However, Michener, who, as he said, "was quite ready to participate in the establishment of that kind of tradition," did not think this was a very good approach. Nor did he believe that the Speaker should be a functionary. He preferred the British system whereby the Speaker would run in the normal way as his party's candidate, but, if it was the consensus that he should continue in the Chair, there would be no real contest since he would not be opposed by candidates of the other parties. The only trouble with this would be that the constituents in the Speaker's riding would be more or less disenfranchised, but Michener said that he came home every second or third weekend and gave better service to his constituents than the average member "for the simple reason that the Speaker has more prestige and a better entrée to the bureaucracy; he gets more attention."

While Michener's support was strong among members of Parliament, it was weak among cabinet ministers. Their view was that he let the Opposition get away with mayhem. Alvin Hamilton complained that Paul Martin would turn his back on the Speaker while attacking the government and would not be called to order. "The trouble with Michener was that he wanted to be liked," Hamilton said. "A Speaker should not be liked but respected."

On the other hand, Howard Green, another Diefenbaker minister, thought that Michener was "a very good Speaker" and had words of praise for his wife. However, Michener could be faulted for his conduct of the daily Question Period. Patrick Nicholson said that he allowed it to be "wantonly protracted" until it became a "damaging consumption of Parliamentary time." The oral questions were supposed to be about "matters of urgent national importance," and Nicholson said, in his book, *Vision and Indecision*, Michener should have ruled out of order the argumentative questions and insisted that the trivial questions be put on the Order Paper.

It was Michener's view that the Opposition parties would not have opposed his re-election if there were some indication by the prime minister that he would be asked to continue in the Chair. However, Paul Martin said, that might have been Pearson's position but it was not the Liberal Party's, and, in any case, they already had a candidate (Ian Wahn) in the field. And John Diefenbaker kept silent. But Michener was not really worried; he was sure that, on the basis of his record as Speaker, he would have no trouble being re-elected.

The accolades that he received on the last day of the Twenty-fourth Parliament made him all the more confident that he would be returned as a member and Speaker again.

On April 18, 1962, when Michener adjourned the House after Prime Minister Diefenbaker announced that he would be seeking dissolution of Parliament the next day, it was generally assumed that the government would be returned with at worst a reduced majority. Certainly, the Progressive Conservative members were in a confident mood as they tossed their order papers in the air and boasted about winning the election, which was to be held on June 18. They did not count on the effect of continuing high unemployment and the run on the dollar that resulted in devaluation in the middle of the election campaign.

When the Tories came to power in 1957, the Canadian dollar was quoted at slightly more than $1.06 U.S. which almost every one considered to be too high. The finance minister, Donald Fleming, tried to get the dollar down and did succeed in lowering it to $1.03 U.S. It remained at this level for some time but then it began to fall; there were signs of a downward pressure even before the election was called, and, afterwards, the situation grew worse with what amounted to an organized campaign of selling it short. At the beginning of May the government decided it had to act and pegged the Canadian dollar at 92.5 cents U.S.; this devaluation would prove to be beneficial because it would help the export trade and stimulate the economy. However, there was no time to explain this to the people, so this sudden lowering in the value of the currency had a psychological impact on Canadians and did not inspire confidence in the way that the Conservatives were running the country. It gave the Liberals an issue they were quick to exploit with the "Diefenbuck," which had seven and a half cents cut out of it. Nationalist pride was hurt: the Conservatives lost all but one of the seats bordering the United States. There was no doubt that this devaluation in the middle of an election campaign was the biggest single factor in the Tories' loss of ninety-two seats: the Diefenbaker government, which had had the greatest majority in history, was reduced to a minority government.

Roland Michener knew that this was going to be a very different election from the landslide of 1958; the great expectations of the Diefenbaker government then had not been realized. Yet he was not too concerned because he felt that his re-election was assured because of his record as Speaker. He had been nominated as Progressive Conservative candidate for St. Paul's, but he had inquired of the chief electoral officer whether there would be any objection to his being put on the ballot as the Speaker, and found there was none. "I was tempted to do it," Michener said, "but it wouldn't have been fair to leave my [PC] riding association without a candidate as the election came on, so I decided to run as the party's candidate." However, he based his campaign on his own activities, especially after the devaluation of the dollar; in other words, he attempted to run as an independent although an official Conservative candidate. His strategy failed. He lost by twenty-seven votes to Ian G. Wahn, the Liberal candidate, who had been campaigning in St. Paul's riding for some two years.

It was a bad blow for Michener, made worse by the fact that it was unexpected. He had upheld the neutrality of the Chair on every occasion and, as a result, had been a prime candidate for the yet-to-be-established office of "permanent" Speaker in the Canadian House. "I'd been in the Speaker's Chair for five years and two Parliaments," Michener said. "And, if I continued as an active partisan, it would reflect on my independence, and I didn't want that to happen." Thus, his defeat in the 1962 election marked the end of his political career. On previous occasions he had been able to absorb disappointments such as this and maintain his cheerful disposition, but this time he was bitter; he felt betrayed. Nothing, not the best possible public service, could influence the fickle electorate in the big cities. He had been an outstanding Ontario minister, only to be defeated in the provincial election of 1945. He had been praised as an "ideal" Speaker but rejected by the voters in 1962. Michener said that if he had his life to live over again, he would never run in a city riding; he would pick a constituency in the country where there was much more political stability.

This was the dilemma of a Speaker: he was expected to be impartial in the Chair but had to be re-elected in a partisan contest. Furthermore, there was no real security, unlike the British House where a Speaker, when he left the Chair, was assured of a good pension and even a peerage. The only preferment for a Speaker in Canada would be appointment to the Senate, and Michener would have liked that. He wanted to end his public career as his father had done in the plush sanctuary of the Upper House, but Prime Minister Diefenbaker would have none of that. He said, "You go back and win that riding, you can win it and we need it." So Michener returned to private life. When the Twenty-fifth Parliament met at the end of September 1962, the Leader of the Opposition, Mike Pearson, while supporting the nomination of the new Speaker, Marcel Lambert, paid a tribute to the previous Speaker, Roland Michener: "He has deserved well of his party, of this House, and indeed of his country."

If Michener had been elected as the member for Toronto-St. Paul's, he knew that he probably would be elected Speaker again, despite the Conservative chief's opposition to him. Prime Minister Diefenbaker would have nominated Marcel Lambert, as he did at the opening of the Twenty-fifth Parliament, and then the Opposition Leader, instead of supporting the prime minister's nomination, would have proposed Roland Michener. It was more than likely that Mike Pearson would have had enough votes to return his friend to the Chair. The Liberals had ninety-nine members and could count on the leaderless NDP, who had eighteen members (Tommy Douglas had been defeated in the 1962 election and was scrambling around trying to win a by-election, which he did some weeks after Parliament met). That would have given Pearson one hundred and seventeen votes to one hundred and sixteen for the Tories, but there were thirty Social Crediters, twenty-six of them from Quebec, led by a Westerner, Robert Thompson, who was a complete novice to Canadian politics and was overcome by the fact that he held the balance of power. Judging from the way he behaved, Thompson would have supported the election of Michener as Speaker.

That would have brought about a parliamentary crisis. Diefenbaker was not the kind to accept defeat, and the Chief and his followers would never have recognized the Chair. It was not the kind of situation that Michener, with his view about the impartiality of the Speakership, would have wanted, and it was a good thing that he did not have to face it and was defeated.

Norah accompanied Roland when he went to 24 Sussex Drive, the prime minister's official residence, to discuss the question of his being appointed to the Senate. They had tea in the dining room; and Olive poured and John sat slumped in a chair with a walking stick at his elbow. He had tripped and broken his ankle, and this crippling accident on top of the disastrous election results had a psychological impact on Diefenbaker; he was depressed and no longer his wisecracking, story-telling self. No, no, he said to a Senate appointment, there would be an election soon, and he wanted Michener back in the House. Then he turned to Norah: "You can persuade him to run. Why don't you help me and get after him?" Norah said that she couldn't and wouldn't try to make Roland go back to party politics. Diefenbaker stood up and, whether deliberately or not, put his walking stick in front of Norah's chair so that she could not get up. "I moved off," Roland said. "I didn't want to get mixed up in this tussle." Eventually Diefenbaker moved away from Norah and the Micheners left 24 Sussex Drive.

Although Michener found it "quiet and comfortable" to be back in his law practice and once more chairman of the Teck Corporation, which had grown considerably during his years as Speaker, it was not long before he was returned to public service. There were many people in business and politics who felt that he had been shabbily treated by Diefenbaker, but it is doubtful that this was why Manitoba Premier Duff Roblin appointed him to head the Royal Commission on Local Government Organization and Finance. In October 1962 Michener put paid to his political career when he announced that he would not be running again in Toronto–St. Paul's, and it was probably then that Roblin decided to seize the opportunity to engage someone with such superb qualifications for the job. At any rate, Roland Michener became chairman of the provincial commission (he was the only outsider, the other four commissioners were Manitobans) on February 13, 1963, just a few days after the third Diefenbaker government collapsed and the country was faced with a second election campaign in less than a year.*

There were other provincial commissions similar to the Michener Commission in Manitoba and they were all parallel to the Royal Commission on Taxation, which had been appointed by Prime Minister Diefenbaker in 1962. In fact, one of the first meetings that the Michener Commission had was in Ottawa with the Carter Commission. (The Carter Commission was named after its chairman, Kenneth Carter, who asserted that "a buck is a buck" and should be taxed no matter how it was acquired. This commission laid the foundation for the 1971 tax reform when a capital gains tax was introduced.) In the early sixties, all levels of government in Canada were concerned about their finances and the great changes in society that had occurred since the war. There was a resurgence of provincial power and the tide had turned from the time when the central government did everything.

*With his cabinet in shambles and ministers deserting him left and right, it was fully expected that Diefenbaker would be slaughtered at the polls; there were predictions that the Tories would be lucky to retain forty seats. However, when the government was defeated and the election called, Diefenbaker seemed to revive and fought what was probably his greatest campaign; he returned with ninety-five seats and denied Pearson a majority government.

Michener enjoyed his work with the Manitoba Commission and travelled extensively throughout the province, holding meetings in Winnipeg and other centres. One dominant feature in his report, which was published at the end of April 1964, was the statement that too much of the general welfare state expense was being borne by real estate property owners and householders. The commission recommended that the province take over this ever-increasing expense and that it be paid for by the retail sales tax; the province should also assume responsibility for the construction and maintenance of the main roads and bridges. The Michener Report proposed that school boards be amalgamated and municipalities be concentrated in regional groups.

It was back in 1962 that Mike Pearson had first raised the prospect of another public service role for Roland Michener; Mike, knowing that his friend was disappointed at not being appointed to the Senate, sought to comfort him. "He even suggested," Michener said, "the possibility of being Governor General, which was rather a surprise to me but appealed very readily to my wife. She said, 'That's a good idea,' right from the beginning." This suggestion was taken as just a kindly gesture since Pearson was not yet prime minister, although it was not long before he came to power in 1963. Michener did agree that a posting as diplomat would be "an additional purification of my partisanship" for the vice-regality, but he indicated that he would not go anywhere. At one point Pearson wanted him on the Bilingual and Bicultural Commission, but Michener refused, saying, "I've already got a commission and I'm fully occupied as its chairman."

Then Prime Minister Pearson rang Michener to say that Nehru had died and that "we would like to have a high commissioner with political experience because there's a feeling that Nehru's departure might lead to breakup or upheaval in India." The prospect of going to New Delhi appealed to the Micheners. Roland had turned down Australia and would not have accepted Washington (which was not offered to him) "because it would have been too much like being at home"; he would have preferred London but India was a good second choice. Both Norah and he had visited the country some ten years earlier and "were very much intrigued by the differences between East and West," and Roland agreed to go and, as he said, went very quickly.

He spent part of July and much of August in Ottawa, being briefed by the Department of External Affairs and learning how to be an ambassador. By September 1, 1964, he had taken up his duties as Canadian High Commissioner in India. The Micheners sailed on the *Queen Mary* to Britain and flew from London to New Delhi, a long thirty-two-hour flight in those days. While in London, Roland met his predecessor, Chester Ronning, who had been seven years in India, the longest tenure of any Canadian envoy. They talked about the assignment, and Ronning said how much he had enjoyed his time there. He had been on friendly terms with Nehru and Canadian-Indian relations were good, but the importance of Ronning's mission was that he was Canada's China expert (he spoke Chinese fluently) and kept in touch with the Chinese through their embassy in New Delhi at a time when Canada did not recognize the People's Republic and had no contact with Peking. While High Commissioner to India, Ronning was co-opted for the Canadian delegation at the 1961–1962 Geneva Conference on Laos; he proved to be a valuable go-between because he had got to know the Chinese Communist leader, Chou En-lai, at previous meetings. The only outcome of the Laos conference was the creation of the Indo-China Commissions, of which Canada was a member.

While Ronning was considered to be a bit of a radical by some, possibly because of his association with the Chinese Communists, he nevertheless enjoyed the imperial sport of tiger shooting, according to Michener. Ronning had been the guest of the Maharao of Kota, who had a jungle full of tigers and used to hold tiger hunts; he staged one, at Ronning's request, for Prime Minister Diefenbaker during his visit to India. Michener never went tiger shooting and said that he was not at all interested, but he got to know the Maharao of Kota "because he had the habit of coming to see us in Delhi and he liked our ammunition." The Indian prince was an international-class trapshooter, and Michener saw him shoot a hundred rounds without missing a clay pigeon.

Lal Bahadur Shastri had succeeded Nehru as prime minister; although virtually unknown outside India, he was a leading member of the ruling Congress Party from the key province of Uttar Pradesh and had served with distinction in previous governments. He was described as a "dimininutive and gentle" man by Michael Brecher in his book, *Succession in India*, and he was the perfect compromise candidate in that, ideologically, he was in the centre between the left and right wings of his party. He was an able politician and a hard-working and honest administrator, in fact, so hard-working that Michener said that he worked himself to death. There was no doubt that Shastri's quiet humility helped him to succeed the charismatic Nehru, who was the father of his country; Lal Bahadur had no enemies and his choice could be rationalized by Congress moguls as a temporary, stop-gap measure — which, as it happened, proved to be true. When he was named leader, Shastri emphasized continuity by saying that he looked forward to the "continued association with us" of Nehru's daughter, Indira Gandhi; she became his minister of Information and Broadcasting. Michener got to know the new Indian leader well and accompanied him on his official visit to Canada in the summer of 1965.

It was at Tashkent, in Soviet Central Asia, that Lal Bahadur Shastri succumbed to a heart attack, his second after becoming prime minister. He had gone there to attend a summit conference with General Ayub Khan of Pakistan and Soviet Premier Alexei Kosygin, who acted as mediator, to settle the war over Kashmir in August and September 1965. The Micheners happened to be in Kashmir when the fighting began and had to hurry back to New Delhi. The dispute over Kashmir, which was largely Moslem but had a Hindu maharajah who had opted for India at the time of partition, was a running sore in Indo-Pakistan relations for years. It had reached the point in 1965 that the Pakistanis decided to take Kashmir by force; they were well armed and they had been provided with tanks and planes by the United States, and, as Michener said, "they thought that they could romp through the Indian troops the way the Moguls used to do." However, they were brought to a crashing halt on the plains about two hundred miles from Delhi and the Indian commander, General Muchu Chaudhuri, told Michener that they lost seventy-five tanks in the battle. Chaudhuri was to become Indian high commissioner to Canada in the following year.

Michener was in constant contact with Ottawa during the conflict. New Delhi was not close enough to hear the sound of battle but there was a blackout in the capital because of the odd air attack; Michener counted two Pakistani bombing raids, which "weren't very wholehearted." The question was "whether we should send our wives and children and unnecessary staff home." Arrangements were made to fly the Canadians out, "but we decided to hold off" for a while, and then the war was over: it lasted three weeks. There was not really a truce but a cessation of hostilities, and it was to reach a permanent settlement that Shastri had gone to Tashkent in January 1966. The agreement had been signed and Shastri had given in to Ayub and accepted some conditions that he knew were going to be difficult to explain in India, and Michener wondered whether worry over this brought on the fatal heart attack: he died in the early morning of January 11, 1966.

The cremation of Lal Bahadur Shastri was an experience that Michener would not easily forget. He and Norah had been on holiday in Hong Kong when they got word of the Indian leader's death; they took the first flight to Delhi and got back just in time to welcome J.R. "Jack" Nicholson, the post master general, who had been sent to India to represent Prime Minister Pearson at the rites. They went first to Shastri's house to express their condolences to the widow, and then, at nine o'clock, set out in the high commission's car for the two-and-a-half-mile drive to the burning ghat on the sacred Jumna River. They crept along through the solid mass of a million people and by noon were in sight of the cremation. "We arrived just in time to see the son of Mr. Shastri put a light to the sweet-smelling camphor wood pyre," Michener recalled. Gandhi and Nehru had been cremated on the banks of the Jumna, and memorial parks had been created for each of them; there would be a third dedicated to Shastri.

Once again India was faced with a succession, and Michener, a keen observer, reported every move and backroom manoeuvre to Ottawa. It took a week before the Congress MPs in a secret ballot voted almost two to one for Indira Gandhi; thus Nehru's daughter succeeded Nehru and a democratic dynasty was in the making; there were to be few breaks with the ruling family and Shastri's had been the first. In the beginning some thought of Mrs. Gandhi as a weak leader, but Michener felt that, although her upbringing made her seem quiet and ladylike, "she was a very strong-minded woman." Norah got to know Indira so well that she was included in the annual family tribute to Nehru; Nehru's elder sister, Madame Vijayalakshmi Pandit,* who had been a distinguished diplomat and was the first woman and Asian president of the UN General Assembly (1953), was at these small gatherings in the garden behind Nehru's residence, and a certain rivalry existed between the aunt and the niece that developed into real hostility when the niece became prime minister.

Michener told a "simple little story" about Norah having lunch with Indira one day: "Mrs. Gandhi said to her, `Now that you're settled, is there something you're lacking or that I can do for you?'

*Some idea of the Englishness of the Nehrus is evident in the fact that Madame Pandit was known as "Nan" in the family, while Jawaharlal's younger sister Krishna Huttesingh (she was married to a wealthy mill owner) was called "Betty" by her friends.

And my wife said that she would like a Siamese cat. 'That's very fortunate,' Mrs. Gandhi said. 'My Siamese cat has just had kittens.' So they brought around two little Siamese cats and my wife chose one — and that was the beginning of a pair that we brought home with us." (The first cat, a female, was named Sita, after the Indian goddess, while the second cat, a male, was called Ram, after the Indian god who was husband to Sita.)

While Canadian-Indian relations were generally very good, there was one bone of contention: the Indo-China Commissions, which were a by-product of the Vietnam War. India was the neutral chairman of these commissions, while Poland represented the Communist bloc and Canada the West, although Paul Martin, the External Affairs minister at the time, vigorously maintained Canada's "independence," which would have been a denial of the "troika" structure of these Cold War vehicles. There were three such commissions, one each for Vietnam, Laos, and Cambodia. The Indian foreign minister, Swaran Singh, who kept a tight rein on the Indian appointees, was a very agreeable man but Michener found him to be "very susceptible to the views of the Communist bloc." The commission had clear evidence that North Vietnamese troops had entered Laos, but the commission turned a blind eye and would not report it to the Geneva Conference. "Nothing could be done about it," Michener said, "unless India would concur with us that there was a clear breach of arrangements — but India would not." There was one time when he thought he was getting somewhere in having the matter referred to the Geneva Conference, but "the whole thing blew up, much to my disappointment." As Michener said, the Indo-China Commissions were one of his major preoccupations in India.

Another was the Canadian aid program. Its biggest undertaking was a hydroelectric power project in Madras: Michener said that a seven-mile tunnel was being built to divert the water that flowed down the Nilgri Hills, where the rainfall was the heaviest in India, from the Arabian Sea to the Bay of Bengal; there would be five power stations on the way down and irrigation for a vast area of farmland. He also visited other Canadian projects, such as the nuclear power plant in Rajastan and the experimental atomic reactor at Trombay, across the water from Bombay.

There were two potential famines in India while Michener was high commissioner. In 1965 the monsoon failed and this reduced the country's grain yield to the point where there would have been severe starvation if it had not been for Canadian and American aid. "We put in a million tons of wheat," Michener said. "This was added to the ten million tons that the United States supplied, and I figure that, between us, we had sustained the lives of sixty-six million people during that crop failure." The same was done in 1966 when a serious crop failure occurred in Uttar Pradesh. At the height of the food shortage Maurice Strong, who was head of CIDA (Canadian International Development Agency) came to India, and Michener got the Indian Air Force to fly them over the worst of the drought areas. "It was so dry," Michener said, "that the land was parched and cracked. And where there was an artesian well, you could see about an acre or so of green where things were growing."

As he had been given a watching brief on politics in India, Roland Michener spent a good deal of time in the Lok Sabha, the Lower House of the Indian Parliament. There was also the personal interest he had, as a former Speaker, in a country's legislative process. He had met the Speaker of the Lok Sabha, Hookam Singh, at Commonwealth Parliamentary Association meetings, and considered him an old friend. Michener said that Mr. Speaker Singh was not as firm or as decisive as he might have been, with the result that he did not succeed in getting everybody to sit down when he stood up. "You'd sometimes find six people standing, talking, and gesticulating, and the Speaker standing, too," Michener said. "It took a little while to sort that out."

The Lok Sabha, like the Canadian House of Commons, had simultaneous interpretation, but instead of two languages, there were six official languages, although, as Michener pointed out, there were really fourteen major languages in the country, some of them as different as Russian and English, and hundreds of dialects and minor tongues. Language was a serious problem for India and Michener was high commissioner when the language riots occurred in 1965.

These bloody disturbances were a direct outcome of the country's constitution, which had been drafted in the late forties during the first fine rapture of independence. Nehru was one of its main authors, and there are parts of the constitution that bear the imprint of his elegant hand, for Jawarhalal Nehru, who was educated at Harrow and Cambridge, was one of the greatest writers of English; his style was much admired and he wrote an autobiography that was a best-seller. It was always his regret that he was not as conversant in his native language of Hindi as in English, and therefore was insistent that the constitution should recognize Hindi as the national language. It was to be expected that an Indian language would replace English, which was, after all, the language of the imperialist British Raj. The mistake that Nehru made was to set a time limit: Hindi was to replace English as the language of the central government fifteen years after the constitution came into effect, which it did in 1950.

So 1965 was to be the year of linguistic change. The trouble was that, while Hindi was spoken by more people than any other Indian language, it was confined to two-fifths of the population in the north, and the people in the south regarded its imposition as a threat to their economic livelihood. If Hindi replaced English as the *lingua franca* of the subcontinent, then the non-Hindi-speaking people, the majority of Indians, would be at a distinct disadvantage to the Hindi-speaking minority in the competition for the highly prized central government jobs. The Tamils rose in revolt and Madras was in flames; railway stations were blown up and government buildings burned; hundreds of protestors were killed. There was no trouble in Delhi, Michener said, but the situation was serious in the south, and it was resolved by the simple but unconstitutional expedient of putting English back as the language of the central government, of big business, and the elite.

It was ironic that blood should be shed to retain the old colonial language of English, but English put all the diverse races of India on an equal footing as far as a *lingua franca* was concerned. When Michener visited the Lok Sabha, he sat in one of the boxes for distinguished visitors which was fitted for simultaneous interpretation, but he never used the earphone. All the debates, when he was there, were in English.

However, the authorities would not give up the dream of having Hindi as the national language. They had had to back down in restoring English but they took a step forward by instituting a system of trilingual education: the children of India would learn English, as an international language, Hindi as the national language, and a local language — if Hindi happened to be their local language, then they would have to learn Tamil, Malayalam, or another Indian language. Some educationists were appalled; they said that this concentration on language would mean that the Indian children would have no time to learn anything else. Roland Michener was bemused by this system of trilingual education; he knew how hard it was to become bilingual because he himself was taking regular French lessons in New Delhi in anticipation of becoming Governor General of Canada.

ᔥ 14 ᔥ

TWENTIETH
GOVERNOR GENERAL

WHILE THE EXTERNAL AFFAIRS DEPARTMENT, which was never pleased with the appointment of an outsider to one of its diplomatic posts, would have rated Roland Michener's mission to India below that of Escott Reid, a fellow Rhodes Scholar, and that of the multi-purpose Chester Ronning, who were both career diplomats, Paul Martin, the External Affairs minister at the time, considered him to have been "certainly one of our best High Commissioners." Michener, Martin said, was always pressing for more assistance, more aid for India, much more than the Canadian government allowed. He got to know the ministers in the Indian government, and the prime ministers, and, Martin went on, "We could see that they respected him very greatly."

As Prime Minister Pearson expected, Michener was in New Delhi at a time of great political upheaval and social change, and would be able to use his experience as a former politician to good effect. Whether or not Pearson, who had himself been a career diplomat, really believed this to be an advantage, it was certainly the best way of getting his old friend "purified" for the subsequent role of Governor General. Michener had been sent out ostensibly because of fear that India might break up following the death of Nehru, and there was no doubt that the Pakistani attack in the year after he became High Commissioner was due to misapprehension of India's weakness and disunity under Nehru's successor, Lal Bahadur Shastri. The war lasted but three weeks, and the plans to evacuate Canadian women and children from New Delhi were cancelled. Michener got to know Shastri well and, on his death, was an interested observer at the second succession, that of Nehru's daughter, Indira Gandhi.

Then there was the revolt in South India against the attempt to make Hindi the national language. The rioting in India occurred at the same time as the rather more subdued struggle for bilingualism in Canada, but Michener did not attempt to draw any inferences or conclusions. He merely reported the facts to Ottawa with little comment, as he did with New Delhi's reaction to its humiliating reversal and the government's bizarre attempt to salvage its language policy by making India a trilingual country.

Roland Michener regarded India as a most satisfying assignment. He toured the country and visited all but two of the provinces, but what impressed him more than its prospects and problems (of which there were many, including famine and a rigid caste system but most of all language) was India's close ties with the Commonwealth. Not only was it by far the largest member but it was the greatest initiator and innovator: it was the first republic to be accepted in the family of nations headed by the British monarchy, and was always trying to strengthen this essentially loose and amorphous organization. In 1965 a Commonwealth Secretariat was formed, and, perhaps because of Indian prompting, Prime Minister Pearson asked Michener if he would like to be the first secretary general of the Commonwealth. "I don't think that this was generally known," Michener said, "but Mike offered me the job, but I turned it down, as I'd rather take the chance on becoming Governor General." A Canadian was to become the first secretary general of the Commonwealth: he was Arnold Smith, a career diplomat who was also a former Rhodes Scholar.

Norah did the usual things that a diplomatic wife was supposed to do: she joined an international group of women to raise money for famine relief, and she acted as a hostess which, as Roland said, was not an easy task in India, "where you have to boil all the water for twenty minutes before you drink it and where every vegetable has to go through a purifying solution for twenty minutes. It doen't improve the vegetables but it improves your health." However, Norah had other interests. As a religious philosopher, she was intrigued by Hinduism, with its pantheon of gods and belief in reincarnation, and, whenever she could, would discuss the subject with a fellow philosopher, Dr. S. Radhakrishnan, who was also the president of India. She had an appreciation of Indian art, and the Micheners returned home with a collection of Indian paintings, including several by the modern Indian artist, Arup Das, as well as sculptures that, a friend said, was "as good as any private collection in Canada."

It was on Michener's initiative, while he was in India, that the Shastri Indo-Canadian Institute was established as a memorial to the late Indian prime minister; this was a major diplomatic achievement because the organization has, over the years, contributed greatly to better understanding between India and Canada. The Shastri Institute came about largely because of Michener's friendship for Shastri, and here was a case where Michener's political experience counted, according to Geoffrey Pearson, Mike Pearson's son and a career diplomat. "Politicians are interested in each other," Geoffrey said; "they are less interested in professional diplomats." The Shastri Institute, which is now based in the University of Calgary and has been going since the late sixties, fosters cultural and academic exchanges. It was started off, Michener said, by a generous grant from the Indian government of three million rupees (the equivalent of two hundred and fifty thousand dollars at the time).

Another memento of Michener's time in India is the fine equestrian statue of King Edward VII in Queen's Park, Toronto. This came about largely as a result of the enthusiasm and persistence of Henry R. Jackman, a prominent lawyer and businessman and former Conservative member of Parliament for Toronto Rosedale, who had "a passion for statuary," as Michener put it. Jackman believed that the mark of a great city was in the statues that graced its boulevards and parks, and while Toronto had its share of these, it had none of a man on horseback, which, in Jackman's view, was a serious oversight. He looked everywhere for a suitable equestrian statue, but could find none until he heard that there were several available in India.

Even before the Raj left, the Indians began tearing down the old imperial statues; this was a spontaneous mob action and left some of these monuments rather badly damaged. However, after independence, it became government policy to rid the country of these all-too-solid reminders of British rule, and there was a systematic and properly conducted removal of these statues, most of which were cast in bronze. They were carted off and dumped in government storage yards, a strange and sombre assembly of larger-than-life images, some lying flat on the ground, others leaning drunkenly against each other, of Queen Victoria at every age, of viceroys resplendent in their uniforms and plumed hats, of generals on prancing steeds, and others, like King Edward VII, riding on horseback as if to review a parade.

There was no market for these hefty relics of Empire: the Indians could have had them melted down, but that was somehow seen as an affront to the British, who were now their associates in the Commonwealth, and so they were glad to hear of Jackman's interest in the equestrian statue of King Edward VII in a park between New and Old Delhi. (The bases and plinths were not removed with the statues, but were left intact, like so many empty tombs dotting the cityscapes, probably because they were expected to support future Indian statuary.)

Michener moved quickly to get what Henry Jackman so greatly desired and found that the Indians, at the government department that dealt with such matters as the storage of obsolete memorials, to be most cooperative. They said that the only charge would be for crating and shipment, but Edward on his horse was of such a size that it could not be shipped in one container but had to be cut up into three pieces. When the three carved-up bronzes reached Toronto and were fitted together, it was done with such skill that not a seam shows. The total cost came to some twenty-five thousand dollars, which Jackman considered a bargain for an equestrian statue of such quality and workmanship.

It was one of Michener's last official acts in India, but when he was Governor General he received word that there was a bureaucratic foul-up. So he wrote a letter to External Affairs Minister Paul Martin on July 19, 1967, which said in part:

> The Ministry of External Affairs [in India], through Mr. Kannim Pilly, confirmed the Indian government's willingness to give the statue, and tenders were received for its removal and shipment, but I have just heard from Mr. Douglas Hicks, the acting High Commissioner, that the Indian government would like an official request from the Canadian High Commission. They may anticipate that there are still some Indians who value these relics of British rule.

Michener must have written the last sentence with his tongue in his cheek, but it was a diplomatic way of excusing the amount of red tape in India. At any rate, Martin gave his approval, and the equestrian statue of heroic and imperial proportions arrived in due course and was assembled and erected on a mound in Queen's Park just behind the Ontario Legislative Assembly.

On March 5, 1967, Governor General Georges Vanier died. Some six months before, Roland Michener, on one of his visits home, saw the fine old soldier and diplomat who had served with such distinction as the Queen's representative for seven years. Vanier told Michener that he was "very intent" on being Governor General during Canada's Centennial year. He said that he knew that he was infirm and had been warned that he was not really strong enough for the arduous task of being host to so many official visitors, but he was determined to carry on. A deeply religious man, Vanier said that he believed that "God will give me strength." Michener wondered whether Vanier knew that he was speaking to a probable successor, and came to the conclusion that he must have done so because of all the speculation in the media.

During much of the last year of General Vanier's life, Madame Vanier substituted for him at many of the functions requiring his presence.* She opened conferences, she received delegates, she hosted receptions and dinners. For the last few months the Governor General was bedridden; occasionally he would struggle downstairs for dinner, but he could not stay for more than an hour. A grande dame of the old school, Pauline Vanier looked and behaved like a vice-reine and enjoyed her work. However, Prime Minister Pearson and the government were becoming more and more concerned about General Vanier's condition. All the plans for the sixty official visits of heads of state or heads of government during the Centennial year had been made. The menus for the banquets had been arranged and coordinated between the Prime Minister's table and the Governor General's so that visitors would not eat the same meal twice; the invitation lists had been drawn up. It was only months away from the opening of Expo 67 and the flood of visitors, and the government had to know whether Vanier could carry on and act as the country's host, so Pearson insisted that he should have a thorough examination by the best specialist.

---

*There was a similar situation a decade later when Governor General Jules Léger was incapacitated by a stroke, and his wife, Madame Gabrielle Carmel Léger, had to substitute for him even to the extent of reading the Speech from the Throne at the opening of Parliament.

So they sent for the famous Boston heart specialist, Dr. Paul Dudley White, whose diagnosis was that General Vanier could not survive if he continued as Governor General. Privately, Dr. White gave the opinion that Vanier's heart was giving out and he could not live much longer. Prime Minister Pearson was disappointed: he had wanted Vanier, who was an old friend and colleague, to realize his ambition of being Governor General during the Centennial year, but now he had to go. To soften the blow, Pearson proposed an important but lesser role. He called in Esmond Butler, the secretary to the Governor General, and instructed him to ask Vanier whether he would accept a position as the federal government's host in Quebec City; he would be able to live in the Citadel, the official residence of the Governor General in Quebec City, and would receive foreign visitors, but he would not be Governor General. There was a negative response to Pearson's offer. No, the old man said, no, he was not interested. It was the last time that Esmond Butler saw Georges Vanier because the next morning the Governor General was dead.

"'If I'm not going to be Governor General, that's it,' and he willed his own death," Butler said, and his view was borne out by others, including Michener who felt that after Vanier knew he could no longer continue in office, his interest in life faded: "He was holding himself together by his will and he just let go and died."

General Georges-Phileas Vanier was in his seventy-ninth year when he passed away. His body lay in state, first in the ballroom at Rideau Hall, then in the Senate Chamber of the Parliament Buildings, before being taken, on March 9, 1967, to the Basilica, the Roman Catholic Cathedral in Ottawa, for the first of three funeral services. It was an impressive ceremony, and, despite the cold, large crowds lined the streets of the capital to bid farewell to a governor general who was so well loved and respected, and stayed to watch the cortège move by slow march and with muffled drums to the railway station. The second funeral was held in the Roman Catholic Cathedral in Quebec City on the following day, and the third in May 1967 when Vanier's remains were interred in a crypt at the Citadel.

Michener learned of General Vanier's death from news reports in New Delhi and, because of the imminence of the head-of-state visits, expected to be summoned right away, but nothing happened. No telephone call. No telegram. Weeks passed and Michener began to worry: perhaps Mike was having difficulty with his cabinet ministers who did not like appointing a one-time Conservative. However, Paul

Martin said there was not a bit of recrimination in the Liberal caucus. "I don't think there was anybody inside or outside the public service who could qualify better than Michener," Martin said. "People just felt that this was a good appointment."

Finally, at the end of March, the call came, but it was indecipherable. Communication between Ottawa and New Delhi was by wireless telephone, which had a tendency to fade, and while Michener knew that it was the prime minister's secretary on the line and that Pearson wanted to speak to him, he could not get three words together that were understandable. It was the height of frustration for him to hear Ottawa's voice rising into the clear with a couple of words distinguishable and then disappearing into the garbled beyond. There was no comprehension, no meeting of minds, until the prime minister's secretary shouted over the static, "Telegram, telegram," and Michener understood and replied, "Telegram, telegram," and hung up.

At three o'clock the following morning a telegram was received from Prime Minister Pearson asking if Roland Michener would be good enough to allow his name to be presented to Her Majesty as the government's nomination for the next Governor General of Canada. "By Jove," Michener exclaimed, "I didn't know what to say, but it was there. It had come about against the greatest odds you could imagine, because Pearson wasn't even in command of a majority government. For five years he carried on, and if he hadn't carried on that long, I would never have gone to India, I guess, and certainly never become Governor General."

The Micheners got up, and Norah ordered a bottle of champagne and Roland scribbled a reply, saying that he was very glad to accept this great honour and, since the mission's telegraph operator was still on duty, immediately sent it off to Ottawa. A couple of senior officers at the High Commission, who had probably been alerted by the telegrapher, joined them, and "we were soon sitting around," Michener said, "talking about the future, drinking a little champagne, and wondering how all this could have happened."

While there were reports in the Indian press that the Canadian high commissioner was to be Governor General of Canada, Michener could not say anything about it until he received word that the Queen had accepted his nomination. There were requests for interviews, but all he could talk about, much to the chagrin of the Indian journalists, was his assessment of Indo-Canadian relations, how much his wife and he had appreciated Indian art and culture, and how much they had enjoyed their tour of the country. He gave a glowing account of his trip to Nepal to see King Mahendra, but the Indians seemed singularly uninterested—Michener was the first Canadian High Commissioner to India to be credited to the Himalayan mountain kingdom famous for its Gurkha soldiers. On April 5, 1967, the telegram arrived announcing the Queen's acceptance of his appointment but advising him that, because of the circumstances of Centennial year, the installation ceremony would have to be held in Ottawa on April 17. Michener had just twelve days to say goodbye to India, to have dinner with the Queen and spend a night in Windsor Castle, and to get home in time, as he said, to put together a little speech and be sworn in.

Meanwhile the secretary of state department in Ottawa went to work: it saw to it that the RCAF had its VIP Yukon ready to be dispatched to New Delhi, that suitable accommodation was booked at Claridge's Hotel in London, and that proper arrangements were made for Michener's arrival in Ottawa. Protocol demanded that, from the time of appointment, a governor general should be escorted everywhere, and an air force officer was assigned as an aide-de-camp. Esmond Butler also sent Colonel A.G. Cherrier of the Rideau Hall staff to meet Michener and accompany him back to Ottawa, although it was fully understood that the Secretary of State looked after the Governor General until he was installed, at which point he became the bureaucratic responsibility of Government House. In the midst of all this activity the Under-Secretary of State, G.G.E. "Ernie" Steele, a large bluff man, received a two-foot-long telex from Norah Michener in which she outlined a series of things that she wanted done: most of the items on the list were formalities that would have been taken care of as a matter of course, but there was a request for two thousand small parcels of Canadian flour that she wanted the air force to fly out to India so that they could be distributed as gifts and souvenirs.

"We almost broke up," Ernie Steele said, "but we got them. I think I said that the difficult we do immediately, the impossible may take a day or so longer. A few phone calls, and we arranged for the aircraft which was going to go out there to pick them up, and it was done."

It was a mad scramble to get out of India in time. Michener had only eight days to pack and say his official farewells, and there was party after party, all of which was a sign of his personal popularity and the high regard for Canada, and all of which had to be attended. The Canadian High Commissioner's residence in New Delhi was full of green tin trunks, which were the baggage the British favoured in the days of the Raj, and an inheritance that the Indians kept. Norah supervised the packing and answered demands to know where to put what. Some forty of these tin trunks, by Roland's count, were loaded on a big four-engined aircraft, and another lot of furniture was to come, but Michener said, "everything was looked after beautifully." There was only one stop on the flight to London, and that was at Beirut, where one of Norah's Siamese cats got lost. They searched high and low in the airport because they thought that the animal had got off the plane. In the end they had to take off without finding it, and once they were airborne, the cat appeared. It had been hiding in the springs of a mattress. There was a fully furnished bedroom on the VIP plane.

The first thing the Micheners did on arriving in London was to drive to Windsor Castle for the appointment with the Queen. It was a memorable occasion, the dinner party that night in one of the state dining rooms with its glittering chandeliers and the panelled walls hung with Gobelin tapestries and paintings of previous monarchs. Among the eighteen guests was another Rhodes Scholar, Arthur E. Porritt, who was to become Governor General of New Zealand. Although about the same age as Michener, Porritt had gone to Oxford in the fall of 1923, the year that Michener went down; he was a notable athlete and was captain of the New Zealand team in the 1924 and 1928 Olympic Games; after his time as Governor General, he returned to England and was elevated to the peerage as Baron Porritt. The Queen sat in the middle of the long dining table, with Roland Michener on her right, while the New Zealander was on the other side of the table on Prince Philip's right.

During the course of the dinner party, Michener said that the Queen encouraged him to go abroad on visits as the Canadian head-of-state. He reported her as saying to him: "I go abroad representing the Commonwealth, but I'm always accepted as the Queen of the United Kingdom. Nobody ever thinks of me as the Queen of Canada, and so I can't represent Canada on these state visits. I think that you should, in your role [as Governor General], encourage your government to send you on these visits." Prince Philip reiterated what the Queen said, and Michener replied that he was ready to do whatever Her Majesty wished.

Ernie Steele and an assistant from the Secretary of State Department, Carl Lochnan, went to London to meet Roland Michener and brief him on the procedures leading up to his installation. The undersecretary had brought with him the official warrant appointing the Governor General which had to be signed by the Queen. While the Micheners were at Windsor Castle, Steele took the warrant to Buckingham Palace and delivered it to the Queen's secretary, Sir Michael Adeane. The stopover in London was only for a couple of days; then the Micheners and the whole reception committee, Steele, Lochnan, Colonel Cherrier, the RCAF officer, and a representative of the Prime Minister's Office who had come over with the undersecretary of state, all boarded the VIP Yukon for the journey home.

There was some embarrassment in Ottawa at the delay in Madame Vanier's departure from Rideau Hall, and this became more acute with the impending arrival of the Micheners. The trouble was that Pauline had no home to go to, as the Vaniers had sold their house in Montreal and only had an apartment that was rented; then there was her hope and belief that the government would allow her to continue in the role of vicereine during Centennial year. The press had encouraged her in this view by saying, on the death of her husband, "Why not Madame Vanier for Governor General?" She asserted that the prime minister had suggested that she should carry on, and although this was denied, there was an impression among the Rideau Hall staff that Pearson had made an approach to her on the matter.

It is possible that the prime minister had done so; after all, they were old friends — Georges Vanier had been counsellor in London before the Second World War when Vincent Massey was the Canadian high commissioner and Mike Pearson was first secretary — and he was sorry for Pauline; as prime minister, Pearson had made promises that he could not keep. However, the probable explanation was that he had told Madame Vanier, at the beginning of 1967, that, while her husband was sick and virtually bedridden, she could substitute for him, as she had been doing so splendidly, throughout the Centennial year, and she took this to mean that she would be expected to carry on the viceregal role, even after the death of her husband.

In any case, when it was officially announced that Roland Michener would be the next governor general, Pauline Vanier made no move to leave. Finally Esmond Butler told Colonel Don McKinnon, the comptroller of Government House, that her furniture, ornaments, and other possessions, which were distributed throughout the building, should be tagged and moved into the "Tent Room." It was this more than anything else that made Madame Vanier realize that she had to leave Rideau Hall. She discussed her departure with Butler, and they agreed that, since she was so well known and so well liked, it would be better for the Micheners if she did not stay in Ottawa. An old friend helped her make up her mind: Mrs. Grace Pitfield, mother of Michael Pitfield, the senior mandarin who was later made a Senator, found a house for her in Westmount, and that was where she moved. (Eventually she decided to go to France to be with her son, Jean, at L'Arche, his home for handicapped men in Trosly-Breuil.) There were emotional scenes when Prime Minister Pearson and others bade farewell to Pauline Vanier as she left in the Governor General's private railway car for Montreal. It was the day before the Micheners moved into Rideau Hall.

When they arrived in Ottawa, the Micheners were put up in the newly acquired government guest house at 7 Rideau Gate — they could not move into Rideau Hall until Roland was installed as Governor General. It was at the guest house that Mike Pearson proposed that the custom of curtseying should be stopped, and those in the know felt sure that Maryon Pearson was the instigator of this: she could not see herself curtseying to her long-time friend, Norah Michener. Roland was happy enough to drop this old-fashioned and somewhat demeaning form of etiquette, but Norah, who had emphasized curtseying in her *Memorandum* to parliamentary wives and was a stickler for protocol, was not so pleased.

A small ceremony also took place when Secretary of State Judy La Marsh and her undersecretary, Ernie Steele, went to 7 Rideau Gate to welcome Roland and Norah Michener on behalf of the government of Canada.

At his installation, which was held in the Senate Chamber of the Parliament Buildings, Roland Michener was presented with the Great Seal of Canada, which was a rather weighty badge of office. He was handed this heavy object by the Clerk of the Privy Council, Gordon Robertson, and, as Michener said, handed it back before he dropped it. The Great Seal, which is much like a corporate seal, only larger, bears the official imprimatur of the Crown and is used on all laws, orders-in-council, and other federal government documents. In his short speech, after he was sworn in, Michener said that so quick had been his transition from New Delhi to Ottawa that he had the sensation of having run all the way. He alluded to the newly formed tradition that the Governor General should be a Canadian in the following words:

> However, we are greatly heartened, in entering upon our term of office, by the thought that the Governor General has come to represent the Canadian people as a whole and that, in addition to his necessary and

important constitutional functions, he now symbolises for Canadians the stability and continuity of their national life and and institutions. In consequence, all Canadians have a personal interest in the office and in helping the incumbent to reflect their hopes and aspirations for the future.

Fully a third of the speech was in French, and this was undoubtedly the work of Norah or, at least, she had given it polish and style, so the speech in its entirety was a joint enterprise. In the French portion Michener paid tribute to his predecessors, Vincent Massey, the first Canadian Governor General, and "Their Excellencies" General Vanier and Madame Vanier, and went on to say how saddened all Canadians were by the general's death and expressed condolences to his widow. As an authority on protocol, Norah knew that both the Governor General and his wife were entitled to be addressed as "Excellency." (Massey was a widower and his daughter-in-law acted as his hostess.) As if in applause, the cannons crashed out a twenty-one-gun salute on Parliament Hill.

Roland Michener was installed as the twentieth Governor General of Canada on April 17, 1967, just two days before his sixty-seventh birthday. As might be expected, there was a great birthday party on April 19 — a family affair with the three Michener daughters and their husbands, as well as Mike and Maryon Pearson and senior members of the Government House staff. It was like the good old times, like a rag at Oxford, with Mitch and Mike together again for fun and jollity, and Mitch proposed a toast to Mike, who would be celebrating his seventieth birthday in four days' time, on April 23. Mike got up and recalled all the birthdays they had celebrated together, and, as an eyewitness recounted, fumbled around, saying that there was someone else who had a birthday at the same time and who was always mentioned at their birthday parties but he couldn't remember who it was. At this, Don McKinnon rose and said, "It's Her Majesty the Queen, sir, her real birthday is on the twenty-first." Pearson appeared amused. "Ah," he said, "I knew it was somebody important, somebody as important as us."

❧ 15 ❧

HOST TO
THE WORLD

ONE OF ROLAND MICHENER'S first functions as Governor General was to review a guard of honour drawn up in front of the entrance to Rideau Hall. For this ceremony he wore the viceregal uniform, a magnificent livery all embroidered in silver with tassled epaulettes and a plumed fore-and-aft hat; actually he had on the uniform of one of his predecessors, Lord Bessborough. Michener had ordered his own when he was in London but had been warned that silver embroidery was a dying art and that the ladies who did the work were getting old and that it would be some months before he would receive the garment. He knew General Vanier had left Bessborough's uniform in a trunk at Rideau Hall, so he asked the dowager countess for permission to borrow it; she was the oldest of the widows of the governors generals, of whom five were living at the time. There was a precedent for this: Vincent Massey had borrowed Lord Tweedsmuir's, which was more his size. Lady Bessborough had forgotten about the uniform that General Vanier had apparently worn on formal occasions and never had one of his own. "Of course," she said, "go ahead and wear it, but I want it back eventually."

The new Governor General came out, resplendent in his new uniform, to take the salute, and after the ceremony he wanted to express his appreciation and held out his hand to the officer commanding the honour guard. The officer seemed taken aback; he had his sword drawn, but he quickly sheathed it and shook hands. It was a faux pas: Michener would have shaken hands as Speaker but in the viceregal uniform with its cavalry sword, he should have saluted. He did not make the mistake again.

Roland Michener liked the trappings of his high office, but he decided to follow the precedent set by his predecessors and wear only the Governor General's uniform on great state occasions such as the opening of Parliament. However, he was commander-in-chief of the Canadian armed forces and felt that he should have a different uniform when he visited military bases or presented colours, so he designed one for himself. He found that there was a viceregal tropical uniform that was white, like a naval officer's dress, with little decoration and no rank badge — "I've always made that clear with the armed forces that, although I'm commander-in-chief, I don't have a rank." The only trouble with this summer kit was that it included a pith helmet, which Michener did not think appropriate in these anti-colonial times, and he suggested to Buckingham Palace — he had to get royal approval for his new uniform — that an officer's peaked cap would be more suitable. Once there was assent, he designed a similar uniform in blue for winter wear.

Since women were being invited to the New Year's Day levy, Michener decided to move the reception from the dull and chilly formality of the Senate Chamber to the warmer and more attractive ambiance of Government House. There was a special levy dress for governor generals and he had inherited Vincent Massey's: the trousers with their gold braid fitted but the decorated morning coat was too small. So Michener had the decorations taken off Massey's coat and put on one that he had made in Ottawa. Thus he had a levy dress at little cost.

The enthusiasm that the new Governor General had for uniforms did not go unnoticed, and Michener recalled that the novelist, Mordechai Richler, said "I had all the good manners and appearance of a maître d'hôtel, and on another occasion he referred to me as being

'uniform mad.'" This was shortly after Richler had won the Governor
General's literary award; the writer knew that Michener did not really
approve of him and considered him "vulgar," and he refused to sign
the presentation copy of his book. Actually, the first literary awards
were a shock to the new Governor General: the poetry prize went to a
poem that was a string of obscenities. A Quebec nationalist was given
the prize for French literature, and when he went to accept the award
he made an impassioned plea for the independence of Quebec, and
said that he would give his prize money to the separatists. It was a
time of student revolt and the Canada Council, which was responsible
for picking the winners, seemed to feel that it had to reflect the underground morality in the awards. Michener was so disgusted that he
thought seriously of refusing to take part, but judging standards
improved, perhaps due to the fact that the Canada Council learned
of his concern.

As for his predilection for uniforms, Michener was quite un-
repentant. "I thought that panoply and ceremony were part of
monarchy," he said, "and if I were playing the part of the Crown
in Canada, I would not deprive those interested in such displays of
the privilege. So I didn't have any hesitation in proceeding with
[wearing] the customary uniform." Michener said that he was not
greatly interested in having a coat-of-arms, but Norah persuaded him
to apply to the College of Heralds, and he enjoyed designing it with
the assistance of Commander Alan Beddoe, who had a part in designing the Canadian flag. As Michener said, his arms were "a combina-
tion of significant things in my life."

The crest, which he used as his privy seal, was a lion holding
a Speaker's mace from the Canadian House of Commons. Since he
was the twentieth Governor General, his plain blue shield had the
Roman numeral twenty on it with a crown and a fleur-de-lys be-
tween the x's. The College of Heralds decided that as a distinguished
Canadian he was entitled to "supporters," which are the animals on
both sides of the shield. He chose two deer standing on their
haunches, one to signify Red Deer, Alberta, where he grew up, and
Hertford, his college at Oxford, whose crest was a deer; he had a
Quaker buckle put on one of the deer to show his Quaker ancestry.
He chose a French motto, *Libre et ordonné*, which he interpreted as
"Freedom in an Orderly Society."

It had been a hectic, almost frenetic, time since the Micheners
arrived in Ottawa and took up residence at Rideau Hall. There was all
the pomp and circumstance, the twenty-one-gun salute on Parliament

Hill, the reviewing of the honour guards, the uniforms and the silver braid, but Michener still had to face his most difficult test. He was expected to speak at the annual Parliamentary Press Gallery Dinner. As a member of Parliament he had attended a number of these functions, where politicians from the prime minister down were mercilessly lampooned, and knew that to address this ribald gathering would be an ordeal from which he could not escape. The speeches were supposed to be off the record and were expected to be witty rather than funny. His predecessor, Vincent Massey, had spent weeks working on his speech for the Press Gallery Dinner, and here he had only a few days, for the annual bash was to be held on Saturday, April 22, following Monday, April 17, when he was sworn in.

He began by expressing his gratitude that he had been picked and processed in time for the annual Press Gallery Dinner, which he described as

> ... a highly seasoned feast, very enjoyable to those parliamentary guests who can stand being peppered, but perhaps not such an unmixed delight to the thin-skinned (if there be any left). None dares to stay away for fear that what he might suffer *in absentia* would be more painful than what he might ward off by his presence. For me, during my five years as Speaker of the House of Commons, the relative immunity which I was accorded at these dinners left me free to raise my glass and lower my guard. The new role which qualifies me to re-enter this exclusive society appears to give me somewhat similar claims to enjoy myself at the expense of those who really drive the political machine. I say "appears" because one never knows what gifts you journalistic Greeks may put on one's plate.

Michener recalled that when he was Speaker his "old friends of the Press Gallery" had kept watch on his "postures, physical and metaphysical, in the Big Chair of the House of Commons" and how he, in return, concerned himself with "their working quarters and drinking habits." His description of the latter as being "somewhat clandestine because of the official morality on the Hill" drew guffaws from those who knew of the "blind pig" operated as an adjunct of the Press Gallery in the then drink-free Parliament Buildings. He was glad to see that the annual dinner had not lost "its excitement or sting." "On the one side," he said, "are the guests — those legislative reflectors of the public will — and on the other side the hosts — the self-appointed moulders of the public conscience, the two sides being engaged in friendly (at most times) but somewhat unequal combat. My observation as a relative non-combatant was that on one side the weapons were designed to draw blood but not to mutilate and that the defensive capacity of the phalanx of guests was greatly weakened by internecine sniping."

Michener started off well and drew laughter and applause from the black-tie audience that filled to overflowing the parliamentary restaurant. However, after a lighthearted consideration of his role as Governor General, whether it should be "held in suspense for some indefinite period while Canadians make up their minds what they really want," whether it should be that of a president or that of a national ombudsman, he grew serious by reiterating his view that a Canadian in the viceregal office was not only the representative of the Queen but "representative of the Canadian people." And he lost a great part of his audience when he ended with a paragraph in French, which most of them did not understand — there was, of course, no simultaneous interpretation at this party.

Still, Michener's speech was genial and urbane, like its author, and generally fitted the occasion. It was not up to the literary standard of Vincent Massey who, as has been said, worked long and hard on his addresses to the Press Gallery Dinner and even set the one that he delivered on April 28, 1956, in rhyming verse! (Massey included the latter in a collection of his speeches that was published, after he left Government House, in a book entitled *Speaking of Canada*.) But Michener's was among the better contributions of the governors general. However, there were duds such as that of a successor, Ed Schreyer, whose dull platitudes so bored the company that he suffered the indignity of being bombarded with dinner rolls.

After the Press Gallery dinner, Roland Michener had to get down to his real work of being host to the world for Canada's Centennial Party. On April 27 there was the official opening of Expo 67 in Montreal, which was the first Category One World Fair to be held in the Americas since the war, and a couple of days later the arrival of the first heads of states or heads of government and special envoys. There would be new guests every third or fourth day, May 3, May 8, two on May 10, May 14, May 16 when Queen Juliana and Prince Bernhard of the Netherlands arrived; and so it went until the end of Expo on October 27. If Michener felt that he had been running all the way from New Delhi, as he said when he was sworn in, there would be no let-up: he would be running during the next six months of official visits.

Because the new Governor General had been in India while Expo was being built, he did not know about the power struggles and the political infighting that went on which led many to believe that the whole monumental project would never be completed and should be abandoned. But it was built, due largely to the management skills and driving force of the Montreal engineer Robert F. Shaw, and built on time. Michener was, as he said, enormously impressed by what he saw on his first visit: sixty nations participated in "Man and His World," or "Terre des Hommes," that was the title and theme of the World's Fair. There were the usual speeches at the official opening of Expo 67, and the Governor General lit the flame which was to burn in the Court of Nations, or rather he and the prime minister lit the flame. "I think I passed the torch to Mr. Pearson," Michener said, "and he stuck it in the oil and lit the flame."

Since this was his first visit to Quebec as Governor General, protocol demanded that he should pay his respects to the provincial government and the city of Montreal. There was no difficulty with Mayor Jean Drapeau, who had never stopped lobbying to get the World's Fair for Montreal, and Michener called on him in the morning before the official opening of Expo 67, but he was not able to establish his *bona fides* with the premier, Daniel Johnson, until the state banquet given that night by the provincial government in the Quebec Pavilion. The Quebec premier was the host and the new Governor General was the guest of honour and sat on his right; Prime Minister Pearson was on Johnson's left, Mrs. Pearson on Michener's right, and Madame Johnson on Pearson's left.

It was a splendid repast but it was the first time that a dinner had been given in the Quebec Pavilion, and the service was slow. During one of the interminable waits between courses, Maryon Pearson wanted very badly to have a cigarette, and Michener recalled, "She nudged me and said, 'Could you get Prime Minister Johnson to propose the toast to the Queen? I'm dying for a smoke, and so's the cardinal on my right. In fact, I think he's going to go to sleep if he doesn't have a smoke.'" Michener noted that the former premier of Quebec, Jean Lesage, and Premier John Robarts of Ontario left as though going to the washroom "but they obviously went out to have a smoke." However, Johnson was adamant; he would not concede anything to smokers. "No," he told Michener, "it [the toast to the Queen] will come in its proper order" — which was not until half-past eleven that night.

The first head of state visitor was Emperor Haile Selassie of Ethiopia; he arrived on April 30, just a couple of days after the official opening of Expo. The routine that was followed with regard to such visitors — and, of course, it applied to the Emperor — was that they were met at the Ottawa airport by the Governor General and the prime minister and were taken into the air force hangar for the brief speeches of welcome. Then the whole party drove to the Parliament Buildings, where a Guard of Honour was inspected and more short speeches were made. After that the Governor General took head-of-state visitors to Government House; prime ministers and special envoys were escorted to the official hospitality house, 7 Rideau Gate, or to hotels.

Emperor Haile Selassie had as his honourary ADC Robert N. Thompson, the former leader of the Social Credit Party of Canada who was then sitting as an Independent member of Parliament. Thompson, an old friend and advisor of Haile Selassie, had had a remarkable career in Ethiopia: he had been sent there during the war to train the air force as a result of his experience in Canada with the Empire Air Training Scheme. He became commander of the Ethiopian Air Force in 1945 and stayed on in Addis Ababa after VJ-Day as an educator, and was for a time the country's deputy minister of education. Besides Thompson, the Emperor's retinue included a couple of ministers and his grandson, Iskander Desta, who was the head of the Ethiopian navy. Michener wondered whether the latter had been brought along as a precaution because Haile Selassie's son had revolted when he had been left at home during one of his father's trips abroad.*

Perhaps the most extraordinary member of the Emperor's colourful retinue was his pet dog, Lulu, a tiny Mexican Chihuahua that was no bigger than one of the black squirrels in the park at Rideau Hall. Lulu went everywhere that his master went, and the Lion of Judah, which was one of Haile Selassie's titles, insisted on this. The Chihuahua was well behaved when the Emperor was in a reception line, and stood quietly by his foot, but under the table at a banquet the guests were to find that the dog was not so disciplined, and some of the ladies almost fainted. "The little dog would put his cold

---

*The 1961 revolt occurred when Haile Selassie was on an official tour of South America, but it was not the work of the crown prince, Afau Wossen, according to Robert Thompson. The *coup d'état* was staged by General Mengistu, the commander of the Imperial Guard, who held the crown prince as hostage and made him sign a paper supporting the rebels. As a result, the press reported that Afau Wossen had led the uprising against his father and did not make any correction because of subsequent events. The army and navy remained loyal and had put down the revolt before the Emperor returned. Thompson asserted that Iskander Desta was Haile Selassie's favourite grandson, the son of his favourite daughter.

nose against a lady's silk stocking," Michener said, "and she would jump and look at her neighbour to see which one was getting fresh. We could see what was going on. It was so funny. You'd think that Lulu would be a female," he went on, "but it turned out to be a male — somebody saw it cock its leg against a piece of furniture."

Esmond Butler had a vivid recollection of Haile Selassie's arrival. As he made his way to the reception hall, he discovered that Norah's two Siamese cats, Sita and Ram, had caught a chipmunk and brought it indoors. The chipmunk was still alive, and, as cats do, they kept pouncing on the poor creature and playing with it. "I knew about Lulu, the Emperor's pet dog," Butler said, "and I was convinced that the cats would make short work of him, and I tried desperately to get them outdoors — and I succeeded just as Haile Selassie and Lulu entered Rideau Hall."

At the dinner party that night Robert Thompson sat on the opposite side of the table to the Emperor who was flanked by Governor General Michener and Prime Minister Pearson; Thompson was to act as interpreter, and while Haile Selassie's English was quite good, he preferred to have some of the questions translated into Amharic because it gave him more time to consider his reply. "Bob," he would say, "you tell them this." Toward the end of the banquet the Emperor seemed to get angry. "Why are you not wearing your Ethiopian decorations?" he demanded of Robert Thompson, who replied that he didn't have any. The Emperor did not seem to believe him and repeated the question again, and got the same reply, that Thompson had no medals.

When the party withdrew to one of the drawing rooms, Haile Selassie accepted the fact that he had neglected to give his Canadian friend and advisor any decorations when he was in Ethiopia, and was determined to make amends. Right here and now. All of which was in Amharic, and Thompson had to tell Paul Martin what the Emperor wanted to do. The External Affairs minister appeared worried; he consulted Prime Minister Pearson who, in turn, talked to Governor General Michener. Then Pearson came over to Thompson and said that he could receive the decoration but "please don't wear it or say anything about it until July the first, when we're going to institute the Order of Canada." So the guests were shown into a small public room in Government House, and in the presence of the Ethiopian ministers and no one else, Emperor Haile Selassie made Robert Thompson a Grand Officer of the Star of Ethiopia, the highest honour that a foreigner could receive.

The next day the Emperor visited the Parliament Buildings and had lunch with the prime minister at the Country Club, which was across the river on the Quebec side of the capital. That was the protocol that was established for the official visits: the Governor General gave a dinner for every head of state, and the following day the prime minister hosted a lunch. If the guest was not a head of state, the pattern was reversed with the prime minister giving the dinner and the Governor General the lunch. Usually the official visitor and entourage then left by train for Montreal, to go to Expo, and, often, at half-past four that afternoon, just a couple of hours after they had gone, the next party was coming up the steps of Rideau Hall. There was a mad rush, Esmond Butler recalled, to change the sheets that were still almost warm and get everything ready for the new arrival.

It was an exciting time at Rideau Hall, but this kind of entertainment was also hard work. The Governor General had to be able to carry on a conversation with each visitor, and a brief was prepared for every one of them. "I no sooner finished seeing somebody out of the door," Michener said, "than I would go back and get the next party's brief and begin to bone up on the country, the state of its economy, its population and politics, so that I could be an agreeable and knowledgeable host. It was quite an education." There was only one occasion when Michener ran out of conversation or, more accurately, was unable to converse, and that was when he was beside the wife of an African chief who spoke no known language. No interpreter was around who could interpret, "so we sat there, the two us, and we couldn't communicate a word—it was very odd."

For Prime Minister Pearson the Centennial Year was, in one way, an even greater burden than it was for Governor General Michener. "Mike complained about eating too much," Michener said. "He had to come to my dinners and lunches. He was duty-bound to do so. But I didn't have to go to his dinners or lunches. So that he had to eat two meals for every one of our official guests, while I had to eat only one." Pearson was not the sort to eschew entertainment; he was a convivial man. Yet he found this round of banquets a strain: "If he had a free choice," Michener said, "he would not be having seven-course dinners or engaging in small talk, because they're not arranged as conferences. You usually have a lady on each side of you, instead of the man you want to talk to, and if she's charming that's some compensation. But they're not the best use of time."

Another who overate for her country was Judy La Marsh who, as secretary of state, was in charge of Centennial celebrations and was therefore a regular guest at these official dinners and luncheons. She complained about the constant service of maple mousse, a delicious dessert that she could not resist. "I don't remember that it was that frequent," Michener said, "but we did have an extra-good mousse with a maple flavour that had been my wife's mother's receipe." It was no surprise that statesmen like Judy should have suffered from extra poundage that summer because, by all accounts, the meals at Government House were culinary delights. This was due to the work of M. Zonda, the famous French chef, whom Roland Michener had inherited from Vincent Massey.*

The official state visitors came to Rideau Hall bearing gifts for Roland and Norah Michener. There was everything from a gold brooch with rubies and one with diamonds, gold bracelets and silver compacts, cigar boxes and cigarette cases, a couple of old silver brandy cups from Queen Juliana, chinaware and glassware, a dinner gong from Tanzania, a Persian rug from the Shah of Iran, a stuffed leopard from Kenya, a carved ivory tusk from Cameroun, lacquer boxes and books, framed portraits of the donors, and a silver inkstand from the Queen and Prince Philip. Actually, there was an exchange of gifts; the Micheners presented their guests with Canadian paintings, Eskimo carvings and prints, Indian baskets and masks, handmade glassware and pottery, jewellery and enamelware. The gifts were kept in a storehouse at the secretary of state's Department and, according to Judy La Marsh in her book, *Memoirs of a Bird in a Gilded Cage*, the government set a limit of four hundred dollars' worth of gifts for a head of state. Norah usually looked after the selection of gifts for each of their visitors.

---

*Vincent Massey had been approached to be the first Canadian Governor General, but after his wife died, he was asked again whether he was willing to undertake the viceregal role, and Massey was supposed to have said, yes, he would as long as he could get Zonda as chef at Government House. Zonda had the reputation of being the best chef in London; he worked for the Spanish ambassador, the Duke of Alva and Massey did not so much steal him as negotiated his release since the ambassador was returning to Spain. Zonda brought out a book of his recipes during Centennial Year. He was some seventeen years at Rideau Hall, and retired for reasons of health while Roland Michener was Governor General. Zonda returned to France and was no longer a chef, although he would occasionally be flown to California to supervise a dinner party for the wealthy tycoon and former U.S. ambassador in London, Walter Annenberg.

Not only was the Governor General involved in this giving and receiving but so was the prime minister, and Esmond Butler remembered an occasion during the visit of the prime minister of Australia when Mrs. Pearson got things mixed up. "She thought what they were giving was what they were receiving," Butler said, "She exclaimed, 'Oh, how beautiful!' to blue liqueur glasses and decanter on a blue tray, 'Oh, how beautiful.' I can still hear Mike saying, 'Maryon, we're giving it, not getting it.'" There were also gifts or *pourboire* for the servants at Government House, and Butler said that a formula was worked out whereby the guests left a tip of ten dollars a day; since few if any stayed more than two days, the sum involved was not very much, although head-of-states usually gave more. (The president of Cameroun was reported to have left fourteen and a half thousand dollars for the staff at Rideau Hall.)

There was a brief respite from the official visitors when the Queen and Prince Philip came to Canada on June 29, in good time for the July first celebrations, and stayed a week, and the Micheners could remain in the background. Since President Lyndon B. Johnson had paid a flying visit to Expo on May 25 and not come to Government House, the most momentous visit was to be that of the president of France, and it was to occur toward the end of July. General De Gaulle had chosen to come to Canada in a French warship, the cruiser *Colbert*, which would make Quebec City his first port of call. This posed a problem for the federal government and after some sticky negotiations with the Province of Quebec, it was agreed that the Governor General would receive him first when he set foot on Canadian soil, and then the premier of Quebec would take over; the French president would drive to Montreal, open the French Pavilion at Expo, and come to Ottawa where he would be the guest of Michener and the federal government. That was the plan.

Early in the morning of July 23 the viceregal party arrived at the Anse au Foulon (Wolfe's Cove) where the *Colbert* was docked; there were about five thousand people, mostly American tourists, in temporary bleachers that had been constructed under the cliff. Roland Michener stood at the foot of the gangplank, Norah was next in line, then Premier and Madame Johnson. The Governor General noted that the *Colbert* was not flying the Canadian flag, as she should have been, but only the tricolour. That was a discourtesy, Michener said, "but I don't think anyone complained." The warship's band played "The Marseillaise" and General De Gaulle marched down the gangplank, was received, and moved on, but there was no sign of Madame De Gaulle. Finally she emerged and stepped ashore a minute or so after the president.

Meanwhile, General De Gaulle had been taken over by Premier Johnson while Michener continued to greet the rest of his entourage. Esmond Butler, who was aware of the rivalry between Ottawa and Quebec on this matter, rushed up to the Governor General and said, "It's your job, sir, to be with the president." Michener stopped shaking hands, and, with a little pushing and shoving, rejoined the general. Then came the speeches, and Michener had a carefully prepared address, which was somewhat longer than usual, in which he made it clear that it was he, representing the Queen and the federal government, who welcomed the French president to Canada on behalf of all Canadians. The only trouble was that a helicopter kept circling overhead and drowned him out; at one point the noise was so loud that he had to stop speaking. Nobody heard what he said. It was a press helicopter, and Michener wondered whether the "buzzing" was by design or not, because the aircraft disappeared when Premier Johnson spoke and General De Gaulle responded.

After the official greetings the plan was for the Micheners to drive to the Citadel while the Johnsons took President and Madame De Gaulle to City Hall for ceremonies there and then to the Citadel. There would be two cavalcades, one federal and the other provincial, and this would allow the Micheners twenty minutes to change and receive the French visitors. But Norah got into the wrong car, the provincial car, and found herself sitting in the back seat with Madame De Gaulle and the premier's wife, who looked surprised and wanted to know why she was not with the Governor General's party. Norah was embarrassed but it was not her fault because she had been directed to the car by the Chief of Protocol, Chris Eberts, who had got his cavalcades mixed up. There was no time to change cars, and she went with the De Gaulles and the Johnsons to the City Hall reception and with them to the Citadel.

Michener had looked around for his wife, and was relieved and amused to see her arriving with the guest of honour. There was, as he said, a very representative group from the federal government, including the external affairs minister, Paul Martin, in the Grand Salon of the Citadel, and they had twenty minutes' talk with the French president, who appeared affable and friendly and expressed his pleasure at visiting Canada on the occasion of its Centennial. Then De Gaulle left and began his triumphant drive along the north shore of the St. Lawrence to Montreal, ending up on the balcony of the Montreal City Hall where he uttered the separatist slogan, *"Vive le Québec Libre."*

The Micheners returned to Ottawa to prepare for the French president's visit. A special seven-foot-long bed had been installed in what was known as the Queen's suite at Rideau Hall, and the French ambassador even wanted to see that it was the proper size. One hundred and twenty guests had been invited to the great state dinner that was to be given for him, and Zonda had promised an unsurpassed feast. Although the great chef had been fifteen years or more in Canada and regarded himself as a "demi-Canadien," this was to be the supreme moment in his life, to put on a banquet for General De Gaulle.

While Government House had no responsibility for the French president's tour of Quebec or the way that he was treated by the populace as a conquering hero, Michener did follow events on television and in the news media. There was consternation over De Gaulle's *Vive le Québec Libre* but the question was: did he know that it was the separatist slogan? Michener was glad to hear Mayor Drapeau tell the president that the French of Canada had got along for two hundred years without the support of France and were quite capable of looking after themselves, but he noted that the mayor had taken a long while to say that. Prime Minister Pearson's reaction was sharp: De Gaulle's behaviour was an intervention in Canada's domestic affairs and it was "unacceptable"; but, Michener said, there was a renewal of the invitation to come to Ottawa, although "I had the pretty shrewd suspicion that he wouldn't be coming."

At nine o'clock in the morning of the day he was to have arrived, the day of the great state dinner, External Affairs let Government House know that President De Gaulle was flying home. Norah went down to the kitchen to give Zonda the bad news. The chef was working on the desserts, which were sumptuous concoctions of cherries and cream; he had made spun-sugar baskets in which the desserts were to be served, and was in the process of decorating the handle of each basket with a bow of thick tricolour ribbon, also made of sugar. He had finished about ten of them, all spun and hardening. Zonda could be irascible, and one of the aides who went down to ask him about something had an egg thrown at him; he was fortunate it was not a plate. "I'm sorry to have to tell you," Norah said, "that the president is not coming to dinner."

"Alors ...." Zonda said more than that. It was a dreadful disappointment, and he took out his frustration on his culinary masterpiece, the desserts. He smashed one of them with his hand, shattering the spun-sugar basket and its tricolour ribbon, and he sent another one skittering onto the floor. Norah thought that he was going to smash them all. But the destruction of two of them seemed to relieve his feelings, and Norah slipped quietly out of the kitchen.

Each of the one hundred and twenty guests was notified by telephone that the party was off. The meat course had not been started but the fish was being cooked and it was distributed to the household staff and they had Arctic char that day as only Zonda could prepare it. All was not lost: Mike and Maryon Pearson and Roland and Norah Michener ate the De Gaulle dinner, the full seven courses, in the privacy of the dining room at Rideau Hall. It was Mike and Mitch again. Mike had written out the toast he would have given if De Gaulle had come to Ottawa (Pearson's autobiography, *Mike*, vol. 3), but Mitch said that he didn't think Mike gave it on that occasion. Instead, they toasted each other in the champagne specially selected for the French president. It was a cheerful dinner party, just the four of them, with no attendants, and they talked about the future.

Roland Michener had been Governor General for only three months.

∾ 16 ∾

EXTENDING THEIR
EXCELLENCIES

ON BECOMING GOVERNOR GENERAL, Roland Michener had informed Prime Minister Pearson of the way the Queen had encouraged him to make trips abroad as a Canadian head of state. Mitch and Mike probably discussed this matter at the intimate and convivial post-De-Gaulle dinner party they had in Rideau Hall. If there were any serious conversation at that informal affair, Michener could not remember it. He knew that Pearson was very much in favour of extending the work of Their Excellencies, as Mike would have put it, and was pleased with the suggestions that Her Majesty and Prince Philip made at Windsor Castle. However, they agreed that there was no point in making any travel plans during Centennial Year.

By the end of July, when the crisis over *"Vive le Québec Libre"* had been unhappily resolved by the departure of President De Gaulle, they were not halfway through the list of official visitors; there were still thirty of the fifty-five heads of state or heads of government and special envoys to come, which meant another thirty state dinners or lunches; but there would be a break with formality when the young princesses of Denmark and Sweden arrived toward the end of September. Roland and Norah, who liked dancing, had decided that dinner dances should be given for the princesses, and that there should be a break with protocol and a younger group invited to these two parties.

It was thus obvious that no decisions would be taken on such an unprecedented course as sending the Governor General abroad as head of state until 1968 at the earliest. Then Prime Minister Pearson announced his retirement — he might have warned Michener, during the Centennial celebrations, that he intended to do so, since he made it official that he was quitting at the end of December 1967.

Pierre Trudeau was elected leader at the Liberal Party's convention in Ottawa on April 6, 1968, and almost immediately sought the dissolution of Parliament; a general election was called for June 25, when Trudeau gained the majority (one hundred and fifty-five seats) that had always eluded Pearson. The political exigencies of a new government meant that an initiative such as a state visit abroad by the Governor General would have to be further postponed.

Prime Minister Trudeau was an unknown quantity as far as the Micheners were concerned; they had met him in the mid-fifties during a tour of India and Pakistan sponsored by the CIIA, and had seen little of him since; he had been an infrequent guest at the Centennial celebrations in Rideau Hall. (Norah had got to know him better than most on the tour of India and Pakistan because she was the only one of the Canadian delegation who spoke French.) Nevertheless Trudeau had assured Roland Michener at the earliest opportunity that he would carry out any commitment Mike Pearson might have made, and that he was quite ready to authorize his going on head-of-state visits abroad. But they would have to be careful that the constitutional issue of the Governor General acting as the representative of the Queen should be understood by the countries selected for these visits.

Some time after he had retired from politics, Pierre Trudeau revealed that he was even more enthusiastic than Pearson about strengthening the position of the Governor General. "How do you put real content into a [viceregal] role that is more a facade than a reality?" he asked. He had tried to get certain prerogatives of the Queen so that her representative in Canada could be viewed as Canadian head of state. Then there was Bill C-60, an act to amend the constitution of Canada, which stated that the Governor General should represent the

Queen and "exercise for her the prerogatives, functions and authority belonging to her in respect of Canada," and also asserted that the Governor General must be a Canadian citizen and would "have precedence as the First Canadian"; the bill was given first reading on June 20, 1978, but never passed. Instead, Bill C-60 aroused an impassioned debate and led to renewed charges of Trudeau's being an antimonarchist. "If I were an anti-monarchist," Trudeau said, "I should leave the post alone and let it become obsolescent, let the Governor General do nothing but attend boy scout rallies."

One of those opposed to Bill C-60 was Dr. Eugene Forsey, the popularly regarded constitutional expert. He said that he was "totally against it" and as a Senator — and he had been made a Senator by Prime Minister Trudeau — he fought against the bill in the Liberal caucus. He was very angry about the perception of the Queen as the Queen of Britain when she visited foreign countries and blamed this on a claque of "noisy and mendacious Grits." Although he had passed the retirement age for a Senator, he was considered such an authority on Canadian affairs that he was allowed to continue using an office in the Parliament Buildings. "I want to see the Governor General left alone," Dr. Forsey asserted. Trudeau's attitude was quite the opposite. The former prime minister expressed it forcefully when he said, "It's either the Governor General becoming more and more the head of state or nothing."

As a result of Prime Minister Trudeau's good office, Roland Michener made his first visit abroad as a head of state in February 1969; he toured the Caribbean, visiting Jamaica, Guyana, Trinidad and Tobago, and Barbados. It was felt that these newly independent Commonwealth countries would be a good beginning for such a bold and unprecedented move as this. They understood the viceregal role because they all had governors general, although one of them, Guyana, was on the way to becoming a republic; they accepted Michener as the acting head of state, notwithstanding the fact that the Queen was the legal head of state, as she was as far as their own countries were concerned; and they gave him the full honours due to a head of state, including a twenty-one-gun salute. Furthermore, these first visits, according to Michener, were generally well accepted by the public and the press in Canada, "without any noticeable dissent or discontent."

The student revolt of the late sixties had reached its climax with the occupation and demolition of the computer floor at Sir George Williams University (now part of Concordia University) in

Montreal, and this happened to have occurred just before Governor General Michener set off on his official tour of the Caribbean. The police arrested the leaders of the radical group responsible for the wanton destruction of some two million dollars' worth of university equipment; many of the students were from the countries that Michener was going to visit, and one in particular was the son of Cheddi Jagan, the leftist leader in Guyana who had been briefly premier but had lost in an election to Forbes Burnham, who was premier at the time of the Canadian tour of the Caribbean.

When he was in Guyana, Michener met Cheddi Jagan, who was quietly respectful and merely made a plea for his son, and there was no other reaction. There was still a British governor general in Guyana and he arranged for the Canadian party to visit the interior of the country which was a vast area of lush jungles and great swamps and also, on the higher ground, large cattle ranches. They flew everywhere in small Canadian-built Otters that could land in jungle clearings or on farm fields, and they were told that communications were so bad that produce had to be flown to market. The cattle were slaughtered on the ranches and the best parts of the carcasses sent by aircraft to the coast.

It was in Trinidad that there was trouble. After the twenty-one gun salute and all the formalities of a state reception at the island's international airport, the Micheners were taken in a cavalcade of cars to the University of the West Indies. A crowd of students waited outside the university gates, waving placards and shouting slogans denouncing Canada for racial prejudice and imprisoning Cheddi Jagan's son and others for the Sir George Williams riot. Norah wrote in her copy of the program for the official visit, "We were met by howling mobs of students." The police wanted to drive past the demonstrators at full speed, but Michener insisted on slowing down and stopping in the midst of them.

He got out of the car and said, "What's this all about? Can I join you?" Michener was wearing the shining white uniform that he had designed for himself and was so well suited to taking salutes and inspecting honour guards — but was hardly meant for confronting protestors. A number of placards were stuck in the grassy bank beside the gates and Michener pulled up one that proclaimed NO RACIAL DISCRIMINATION. "This, of course, is what I believe in myself," he said, and raising the placard aloft, joined the students. Esmond Butler, who was an eyewitness, thought that "Roly Michener was so clever," and Don McKinnon said that "he simply diffused the whole thing"; he talked to the students for a few minutes and turned them around from antagonists to protagonists and had them cheering him when he got back into the car for a tour of the campus.

At the University of the West Indies (in Trinidad and Tobago), Michener planted a tree to commemorate his visit; he made a short speech in which he repeated more or less what he had told the student demonstrators: "When I'm in your country, I'm subject to the laws of your country. If I'm arrested, if I do something wrong, I can expect to stand trial. But I don't worry about it, because I have faith in your justice. Now, that's the position of your comrades in Montreal. They've been taken to court for what's alleged that they have done. They'll get justice, and, I think, with sympathy too."

The head-of-state visits to the Caribbean were run on a tight schedule with the Canadian Governor General and his entourage spending five days in each country: this meant that during their official tour of Trinidad and Tobago there was only time for a flying visit to the smaller island. However, they did have the advantage of having the Canadian aircraft carrier, HMCS *Bonaventure*, docked at King's Wharf, Port of Spain, the capital of Trinidad. (This was the same ship that had carried the first Canadian contingent of the United Nations Emergency Force to the Middle East.) Michener gave a state dinner party on board the *Bonaventure*, and the following evening had a reception to which many more could be invited, including some of the student demonstrators, followed by a dance by moonlight on the flight deck.

It was a good beginning for state visits. Nothing went wrong, and Roland Michener had done well. Although, as he said, not much diplomacy was involved, he had been able to mollify the students who were up in arms over the arrest of Cheddi Jagan's son and others involved in the Sir George Williams riot. There were no negotiations, and, aside from the students, no disputes to be resolved; the whole purpose of these exercises was public relations, the ceremonial expression of good will and friendship. The only question was: was it worth the cost? The tour of the Caribbean aroused few hackles, but Paul Martin said that he was against it; he asserted that the Governor General was not the representative of the Queen outside Canada. Michener made the distinction that in these foreign visits he was representing not the Queen but the Crown. Martin's view, and it was the view of External Affairs, was that official visits abroad should be made by the head of the government, by the prime minister rather than the Governor General.

While preparations for the Caribbean tour had not taken an inordinately long time (it had been originally arranged for early 1968 but had to be postponed because of the election), the planning for the head-of-state visits to the Benelux Countries took months, if not years, judging from the fact it did not occur until April 1971, more than two years later. There were all kinds of obstacles in the way of the Micheners' going to the Netherlands, Belgium, and Luxembourg, and officials dragged their feet in the safe knowledge that the new External Affairs minister, Mitchell Sharp, was opposed to this junket and was quite ready to argue with Prime Minister Trudeau about the propriety of having the Governor General act as head of state abroad. In fact, Trudeau said that Sharp was quite "testy" on the matter, but the prime minister was adamant; he insisted that it be carried out and saw it as an important constitutional test. Once the obstacles were overcome, Sharp even agreed to go along with the Micheners in the expectation of having some worthwhile diplomatic discussions.

> We then tried it [head-of-state visit] with the Benelux Countries, who couldn't have been more friendly [Michener said]. Holland was so grateful to Canada for its role in the war that they were still giving us flowers and covering us with thanks. Her Majesty [Queen Juliana] couldn't have been more willing or gracious. She probably enquired of our Queen whether there was any objection to proceeding in this way [and found there was none]. So it was all settled, and each of those three countries accepted me as the head of state *pro tem* and gave me all due honours. We had just the sort of state visit that a president or a monarch from another country would have been given.

The Benelux tour was conducted with much more pomp and circumstance than the Caribbean tour. The viceregal party set off from England in a flotilla of Canadian warships for the Netherlands; the Governor General and Mrs. Michener were aboard HMCS *Preserver*, a naval supply ship, where, Michener said, they had "very excellent quarters." The *Preserver*, with an escort of three destroyers (the External Affairs minister, Mitchell Sharp, was on one of them), sailed across the North Sea into Amsterdam harbour — shades of the *Colbert* and De Gaulle at Quebec City. Queen Juliana, Prince Bernhard, and all members of the Dutch cabinet were on the jetty to welcome them, and there were bands playing the national anthems and the usual inspection of the honour guard to a booming twenty-one-gun salute.

Since the Canadians were going to be put up at the Dam Palace in the main square of Amsterdam, the police had to clear the hippies, many of them drug addicts, from the palace yard where they had been camping. Because of its liberal attitude toward narcotics, Amsterdam had become a centre of the drug culture in Europe and the hippies were drawn from many countries, including Canada. There was some resistance and a good deal of fuss over the action the authorities took in clearing and cleaning up the palace environs, but Roland Michener was not met by any protest demonstrations as he was in Trinidad. This may have been due to the fact that the Dutch police kept the hippies under close surveillance and away from the Canadian visitors.

It was a beautiful old palace, the Dam Palace, and, by all accounts, Queen Juliana's state dinner for the Governor General in the palace's great banqueting hall was a brilliant and memorable affair. Michener returned the hospitality with a state dinner on board the *Preserver*: the ship's hangar, which could accommodate four or five helicopters, was rigged up as a ballroom, and the sailors served at a great U-shaped table.

> The Queen was simply delighted with it, [Michener recalled]. It was such a novelty. So much so that she told the King of the Belgians. Baudoin had said that we didn't have to offer him a return dinner party as we didn't have the facilities in Belgium and it would have been difficult to arrange. But when he heard about this [naval banquet], he decided that he would like to dine aboard ship too. So we had a second dinner party for King Baudoin on the *Preserver* [in Antwerp harbour].

As might be expected, the Micheners were taken to an experimental farm for tulip bulbs, and Norah named a new tulip, but the most important event was the visit to the cemetery at Holten to honour the Canadian war dead. Thorough preparations had been made because this had been on the official program from the beginning. An honour guard from the Canadian maritime forces and a naval band had been brought over on the warships and accompanied the Micheners on the long drive to Holten, which is on the other side of the Ijsselmeer from Amsterdam. It was a moving and poignant ceremony as the fourteen hundred Canadians buried in that cemetery were among the last killed in the Second World War: the Second Canadian Division had suffered heavy casualties around Holten in April 1945 during the drive to free North East Holland. Schoolchildren were standing beside the stone markers that had replaced the wooden crosses, and when the piper played the lament at the end of the ceremony, the children laid flowers on the graves. Princess Margriet, who had been born in Ottawa where her mother, Queen Juliana, lived during most of the war, was with the Micheners on this tour, which included, beside the Holten cemetery, a huge Phillips electronics plant.

Roland Michener celebrated his seventy-first birthday while he was in the Netherlands. At the end of the three days of the official program he spent a couple of days with the Canadian ambassador, A. J. Pick, who had a beautiful residence near The Hague. They were playing tennis on the ambassador's court during the afternoon of April 19, 1971, when Pick said, "I think we'd better go in now and get washed up and changed. There's someone coming for tea." That someone was Queen Juliana, who drove up in her car with only the chauffeur and no escort. "There was a [birthday] cake," Michener said. "I think the Picks had got the cake. I don't think the Queen brought that, but she came to celebrate my birthday and stayed an hour and a half. We had a very friendly and delightful chat. It was an indication of her feeling toward Canada and her very temperament — she was an unassuming and very delightful, hospitable, and friendly person."

After the Netherlands the viceregal party went to Belgium and were put up in the royal palace in Brussels, and, as has been said, returned King Baudoin's hospitality with a state dinner aboard HMCS *Preserver* in Antwerp harbour. The visit to Luxembourg was much less formal: they stayed at the palace but drove from one end to the other of the mountainous little state and were received in villages and towns. Michener was a great hit with the Grand Duke's five children when he presented each of them with an Eskimo parka. Norah, who was very fond of jewellery, spent a happy hour looking at the Grand Duchess's collection. The head-of-state visits, which began in Amsterdam on April 14 and continued in Brussels on April 20 and in Luxembourg on April 26, were over at the end of April, and the Micheners and their entourage flew directly back to Canada.

The official tour of the Benelux countries had been a patriotic exercise and had shown the Canadian flag, which was what Prime Minister Trudeau expected and wanted of such visits. If their purpose was to make countries more conscious of each other, they were entirely successful. There was extensive coverage in the media, par-

ticularly in the countries visited; there was less in Canada, and some
of it negative in character, with a few newspapers questioning the role
of the Governor General as a visiting head of state. Still, good relations
were established with the media in the Netherlands, Belgium, and
Luxembourg, and the journalists there were invited to visit Canada.
As Esmond Butler said, the tour "really heightened Canada's image
in all three of the countries."

It was a personal triumph for Roland Michener, who felt that
Benelux had really established a precedent for head-of-state visits
by the Governor General: there were all the trappings of power, the
transportation by warship, the military presence, the accompaniment
of the External Affairs minister; these had been absent from the
Carribean trip, which had been more of a neighbourly good will
mission. Michener believed that Mitchell Sharp was very pleased with
the visits. The External Affairs minister, he said, "got more attention
by coming with me than if he had gone on his own or with the
prime minister, because [in the case of the latter] he would be together
with the prime minister, whereas with the Governor General, he
could talk to members of the government and negotiate by himself.
And he had the entrée provided by the Governor General's visit."
Sharp evidently spoke to Michener and expressed his satisfaction
at the outcome of the Benelux tour.

Perhaps the External Affairs minister was merely being polite since he was opposed to the head-of-state visits to the Benelux
countries from the beginning and said that he was embarrassed
to have had to take part in the tour. He had made no impression on
Prime Minister Trudeau when he argued against such state visits
and he quoted Trudeau as saying, "I've agreed to these visits, and
you've got to go." Sharp asserted that there was nothing wrong about
visiting Commonwealth countries, which had or had had governors
general, but his contention was that the Governor General's role
would be a puzzle to Europeans because it smacked too much of colonial status, although he did admit that Roland Michener was treated
as a head of state during the visits to the Benelux Countries. There
might have been a personal side to Sharp's objection, since he complained about the number of functions that he had to attend and of
having to wear a morning coat and silk hat and walk a few steps
behind the Micheners.

The External Affairs minister felt so strongly about this whole
question of head-of-state visits abroad by a Canadian Governor
General that he wrote an article about it in 1977, some years after

the Benelux tour. However, he had second thoughts about letting it be published — his bureaucratic background got the better of him, for Sharp, like Pickersgill and Pearson, had graduated from the civil service. Nevertheless, he agreed to the last part of the article being used to illustrate his argument:

> The fact is that the Queen does not and cannot in practice travel abroad as a Canadian head of state to promote good relations between Canada and the country she is visiting. Some years ago, I headed a trade mission to Latin America as Minister of Trade and Commerce at the same time as the Queen was on an official visit to several countries in the same region. She was there promoting British interests. I was there promoting Canadian interests. Since the Queen is not recognized outside Canada as our head of state, who then can travel abroad as the non-political representative of Canada? It may be argued that such visits are not necessary, that the Prime Minister and other Ministers can represent Canada abroad for all practical purposes. My experience does not lead me to this conclusion. Moreover, the Prime Minister has enough to do without burdening him with good-will visits that could better be undertaken by a non-political head of state.
>
> What about the Governor General? He has already represented Canada on official visits abroad, both within and outside the Commonwealth. Within the Commonwealth, there were no problems relating to the constitutional position of the Governor General because viceroyalty is a familiar concept to the governments and citizens of Commonwealth countries.
>
> As Minister of External Affairs, I accompanied Governor General Michener and his gracious wife on an official visit to the Benelux countries — Netherlands, Belgium and Luxembourg — in 1970 (sic). The Excellencies conducted themselves as admirable representatives of Canada. They were received by the sovereigns of those countries with the utmost courtesy and full honours due a head of state were accorded to them. But what did the people of the Netherlands and Belgium think about a visit by the Governor General of Canada? The very title reminded them of their own colonial governors in the Dutch East Indies and the Belgian Congo. Was Canada still a colony of Britain? I heard the chit-chat and it did not make me feel very comfortable as a member of the Government of an independent and proud country.
>
> One comment on that visit by a highly placed personage and a staunch friend of our country still rings in my ears. "It isn't worthy of Canada."

Then there was the party that the Shah of Iran gave in October 1971 for what was said to be the twenty-five hundredth anniversary

of the Persian Empire. Michener counted this as his third head-of-state
visit, and he was given a twenty-one-gun salute when he stepped off
the plane at Shiraz in southern Iran, some twenty-five miles from the
desert area near the ruins of Persepolis, where the whole extraordinary pageant was staged. However, External Affairs Minister Sharp
denied that Michener was there as head of state; he said that it was just
an anniversary party, there were no ministers in attendance, no business was done, and the Governor General was there merely as the
representative of Canada.

It was true that the Iran visit was not in the same category
as the Benelux tour or even the Carribean tour, and the Shah's party
was notable only for the fact that it was the height of conspicuous
luxury, and a folly of megalomaniacal proportions. The Micheners
were put up in a magnificent silk tent that contained a drawing
room with a fireplace, a small kitchen, quarters for the lady-in-
waiting, and, behind doors, two bedrooms and two bathrooms with
gold-plated fittings. There were gifts in the tent, including a finely
woven portrait of His Excellency (later Norah was given a beautiful woven portrait of herself), a wicker basket of sweets, a large
wooden inlaid box with cigarettes and cigars, an Imperial plate of
Persia, one bronze and gold jar with lid, a silver sugar container,
a replica of the Darius stone, a shelf of deluxe-edition books on
Persian history and philosophy. There were fifty such tents, all numbered, and arranged like the spokes of a wheel around a fountain.
The Micheners were in Tent Number 20.

Since it was hot in the daytime and cold at night, the tents
were both air-conditioned and heated. Besides these large bell tents,
there was an enormous marquee where the Shah gave a dinner
party for five hundred people, the guests of honour sitting at a huge
serpentine table. Two bands, one inside and one outside, played
during the seven courses and seven wines served at the banquet. A
desert wind was blowing that night, according to Esmond Butler
who accompanied the Micheners on this trip, and the great tent undu-
lated throughout the dinner. It was a feast worthy of Belshazzar (who
was defeated by the Persian king, Cyrus) but none of the guests saw
a finger writing on the wall, or rather the side of the marquee. They
were there for a good time, and not to report back to their governments as to the effect on the Iranian people of this blatant display
of luxury and wealth. The dinner was followed by a *son-et-lumière*
show at the ruins of Persepolis.

The Shah must have spent a fortune in France, for all the ca-
tering was done by the French, who also put on the *son-et-lumière*
show. However, the French president did not deign to come; the
reason, according to Michener, was that he would not sit below the
Emperor of Ethiopia or any other emperor, but there were few heads
of state from the great powers at the party. France was represented
by the foreign minister, the United States by Vice-President Spiro
Agnew, and the United Kingdom by Prince Philip and Princess Anne.
(Michener was told by the Queen that she was not going to the party,
and "so, with that information, there was no possibility of embarrassment in having two heads of state for Canada on the scene at the
same time — and the government very readily gave consent to my
accepting the Shah's invitation.")

At about four o'clock in the afternoon of the following day,
there was the great parade of thousands (Michener spoke of seven
thousand) replaying the triumphant periods of Persian history up
to the present; they were dressed in authentic uniforms and costumes and armed with the weapons of the times. War elephants and
camel corps were in the lead, followed by squadrons of cavalry and
even quinquarines, the warships of the ancient world of Cyrus and
Darius, which were rolled past by sailors. It was great pageantry,
made all the more spectacular by the setting sun. The Shah and his
guests sat in a comfortable, plush-lined reviewing stand, and were the
only ones to see this four-hour-long show, which must have cost millions of dollars to stage. Very few of the Shah's subjects saw even a
reproduction of it because television was in its infancy in Iran. It was
a monumental ego trip by the Shah that was meant to establish his
credentials as a great leader, a worthy successor of Cyrus and Darius,
and it did for a few years.

Besides the three days at Persepolis, there were a couple of
days of ceremonies in Teheran, and the Micheners spent the last few
days of the ten-day trip at a resort on the Caspian Sea. The Shah's
party was the last time that Roland Michener went abroad as a head
of state, or representative of Canada. He would have liked to have
paid an official visit to Italy because of Norah's interest in that country and the fact that she could speak Italian like a native, and he
wanted to return, as Governor General of Canada, to India. He was
invited to go to Morocco by the King, who was very anxious to establish better relations with Canada. But the government would not
agree. And Michener had to give the usual excuse to the Moroccan

King that he could not come because of an impending federal election
and the possibility that he would have to install a new government.

Prime Minister Trudeau's desire to make the Governor General more a head of state had been worn down by the arguments of Mitchell Sharp and the opposition of the bureaucracy. External Affairs officials, according to Geoffrey Pearson, were always afraid of what the Governor General would say when he was abroad; they need not have worried about Michener, who was always circumspect in any pronouncement that he made. Then it was so much work to set up a head-of-state visit, and civil servants did not like extra work. But the most telling argument of all was the high cost. "You can't afford to do too much of this," Geoffrey Pearson said; he estimated that a recent visit of Queen Beatrix of the Netherlands to Canada would have cost a million dollars, at least, and it was certainly not as elaborate or as lengthy as Governor General Michener's visit to the Benelux Countries. Thus, for the last two years of his extended term of office (he served almost seven years), Roland Michener had to be content with being head of state in Canada, as long as the Queen was not present, and had to confine himself to travelling within the country.

❧ 17 ❧

GOVERNOR
GENERALITIES

THE GOVERNOR GENERAL AND MRS. MICHENER travelled more than two hundred and twenty thousand miles in Canada during their term of office; they visited every province, some of them many times, and almost every community in the Northwest Territories and the Yukon. The number of planned tours, each with its printed program containing a detailed, almost minute-by-minute itinerary and pertinent information about their engagements, finally passed the two-hundred mark. The comptroller of Government House, Colonel Don McKinnon, the naval captain-turned-accountant-and-manager, kept a meticulous record of all their comings and goings. "Sounds rather like perpetual motion," Michener quipped, and there was no doubt that he journeyed farther and made more official visits than any other Canadian Governor General. In part it was because he was so active and gregarious himself and because he and Norah really enjoyed ceremonial functions of all kinds. Michener believed in seeing and being seen, and felt that by doing so he was contributing to national unity.

Much of the travelling was done by rail in the Governor General's private railway cars (there were two of them), which served the dual purpose of transportation and hotel-office accommodation. But the Micheners also went by ship, plane, and other vehicles, such as snowmobiles and dogsleds, all of which the Canadian armed forces provided. In such cases, the private railway cars were often moved ahead to tour sites in order to serve as mobile residences. The Micheners visited lumber camps and paper mills, mining towns and Indian villages in Northern British Columbia on board the Canadian destroyer, *Mackenzie*, and they sailed on HMCS *Assiniboine* to the outports of Newfoundland and the North Shore of the St. Lawrence.

For the latter cruise, the commander of the *Assiniboine* took on board as a pilot a retired merchant seaman called Captain Tom who knew the inlets like the back of his hand. Michener was introduced to him as soon as he and his party went aboard, and he expressed his pleasure that they would all have the benefit of his experience and knowledge of the outports. "I suppose you know where the rocks are?" Michener said. "I can't rightly say I do, sir," Captain Tom replied, "but I know where they ain't."

At the Newfoundland outport of Crowhead, there was a line of seven men with old muzzle loaders who were determined to give the viceregal party a royal salute. When Roland Michener started to go ashore from the *Assiniboine*, they fired the first round. "There was a tremendous explosion and a cloud of black smoke," Esmond Butler recalled, "Mr. Michener was blown back and fell on Mrs. Michener. He picked himself up and started down the gangway to the dock when the second round was fired which almost knocked him back again." Butler said that the Newfoundlanders fired three thunderous rounds from their muzzle loaders: the Governor General was entitled to a twenty-one-gun salute, and there were seven of them and the three rounds meant that they had fired a twenty-one-gun salute.

Of the six special tours of the Arctic, the first one, according to Michener, was "a showing of the flag there which hadn't been done for a while." On that occasion the viceregal party took with them on a great lumbering Hercules aircraft forty members of the media, most of whom had not been much farther north than the Laurentians. As a result, the Arctic was "rediscovered" and thoughtful pieces were written about the Northwest Passage and the question of Canada's sovereignty. The press stayed with the Micheners during the eleven-day tour of seventeen Eskimo communities, starting at Frobisher Bay.

The Mounties provided security in the North and elsewhere. Michener recalled an incident at Medicine Hat where they had arrived by train early in the morning. At seven minutes to six, the RCMP officer in charge roused the Governor General to report that the police had received a telephone warning that a bomb had been placed in the train set to go off at 6 A.M. "We both agreed," Michener said, "that it was probably a prank by someone who would be on hand outside to witness our discomfiture." Still, they could not take chances, and so the whole party was turned out of bed, "the ladies to tour the town in their night robes, and the rest of us to watch for any signs of gloating in the vicinity. There was none. Nor was there any bomb." A pop bottle was found near one of the carriage wheels.

It was a trivial incident, but there were some serious crises during Michener's term of office as Governor General, one or two of which brought visions or nightmares of a place in history beside Lord Byng.* The first occurred less than a year after he had been installed. He was in Quebec City, attending the Winter Carnival, and was actually in the Capitol Theatre at the time, enjoying the antics and songs of the French comedian, Fernandel, when about halfway through the show Esmond Butler leaned over and said that he had just got word that the government had been defeated in Ottawa. Michener rose immediately and with the rest of the members of his party left the theatre and returned to the residence in Quebec, the Citadel.

A call to the Clerk of the Privy Council, Gordon Robertson, confirmed their worst fears that the government had been defeated on a money bill, the classical textbook case, as Michener put it, for a government's resignation. How had it happened? It was a Monday night (Febuary 19, 1968), when attendance was usually low; on top of that, too many ministers were away campaigning for the leadership that Pearson was giving up, and Pearson himself was in the Caribbean. Thus the Conservatives were able to spring a snap vote and defeat an important tax measure. Michener telephoned Eugene Forsey, a friend and a constitutional authority, who advised him to stay put and not return to Ottawa, as had Gordon Robertson. Later that night a jubilant Davie Fulton, an old friend of the Governor General, rang to say that there was going to be an election, and "we're going to take power."

---

*Viscount Byng of Vimy, a British cavalry officer who commanded the Canadian Corps in the attack on Vimy Ridge in April 1917 and was Governor General of Canada, 1921 – 26. In 1926 Lord Byng refused Prime Minister Mackenzie King's request for dissolution of Parliament and precipitated a constitutional crisis.

Michener decided to continue with the carnival festivities until he heard from the prime minister, who was rushing back to Ottawa. For once, Mike Pearson showed himself to be a hard-nosed politician: he was furious that his sojourn in Jamaica, where he had gone for an honourary degree, should have been cut short, and he exerted the greatest pressure on Robert Stanfield, the new Tory leader, and even sent the governor of the Bank of Canada around to warn him that there would be a run on the dollar if he brought down the government on this tax bill. Stanfield, who was unsure of himself but the most honourable of men, decided that the country came before his party, and let Pearson have the time he needed to rally the forces behind his minority government and win a vote of confidence in Parliament. Thus the crisis passed and with a sigh of relief Michener returned to Ottawa.

Next, in chronological order, was the 1970 October crisis and the proclamation of the War Measures Act. This was not equated with the defeat of the minority Pearson government, since it did not, in Michener's mind, involve the Reserve Powers of the Crown. Prime Minister Trudeau had kept the Governor General informed of developments: on October 5 the British Trade Commissioner, James Cross, had been kidnapped by the FLQ (Front de Libération du Québec), and five days later Quebec Labour Minister Pierre Laporte had been seized by members of the same revolutionary separatist organization. Trudeau had spoken of the possibility of asking for the proclamation of the War Measures Act because of the turbulent situation in Montreal, and Michener's reply was that the prime minister would have to be the judge of that. "If you think it's necessary," he said, "I shall, of course, proclaim the act on your advice." There were alarmist reports of two thousand heavily armed FLQ members in Montreal— rumours that were being spread by no less a person than the federal cabinet minister and Trudeau's good friend, Jean Marchand.

On October 16 the Governor General was roused from sleep to give Royal Assent to the War Measures Act; it was four o'clock in the morning, and an official from the Privy Council had brought the proclamation document to Rideau Hall. Michener put on his dressing gown and came down to his study. "I looked it over," he said. "It seemed to be in order, so I signed it." Years later Trudeau acknowledged that it was the police who insisted that the War Measures Act should be proclaimed at 4 A.M. so that they could make early-morning raids on the homes of suspects, but the Governor General was never informed of this. Michener assumed that he had been got up at such an unearthly hour because the situation had become suddenly worse: "it seemed to be rising in a crescendo to the possibility of violence."

By half-past five that morning, when it was announced that the War Measures Act was in force, the police had rounded up one hundred and fifty suspected members of the FLQ (they never picked up any of the real members). Altogether, more than four hundred and fifty people were arrested in Montreal; many of them might have been sympathizers, but eventually, after all the hysteria had died down, it was revealed that the two operating cells of the FLQ had a total of twelve members. In retrospect, Trudeau seemed to want to play down his role in the 1970 October Crisis; he emphasized that the War Measures Act was implemented only because of repeated requests from the Quebec premier, Robert Bourassa, and also from the mayor of Montreal, Jean Drapeau, and Michener also said that the prime minister had told him at the time that he had been under pressure from Bourassa, who was "quite alarmed and was anxious to get more authority and power."

After invoking the War Measures Act the Governor General returned to bed, but left shortly after noon that day (October 16) to fly to Edmonton where, at six o'clock that evening, he opened the new Press Club. On the following day Michener was the guest of honour at the homecoming celebrations of his old alma mater, the University of Alberta, and at the dance that night he heard that Pierre Laporte had been murdered. This was the reaction of the FLQ to the War Measures Act, and meant the crisis had deepened. Later that night Michener received a wire from Trudeau advising him to return to Ottawa.

The next day, which was Sunday, October 18, an armed forces Yukon was diverted to Edmonton to pick him up; besides himself and his staff, which included Esmond Butler, there were eighty troops in full battle dress who were being flown east to put down what was described as an "apprehended insurrection." Michener was back in time for the debate in Parliament, where overwhelming approval was given to the use of the War Measures Act. The next day, October 20, he took part in the national memorial service for Laporte in Ottawa's Roman Catholic basilica; soldiers with automatic weapons at the ready stood guard in the church. Rideau Hall was like an armed camp and Michener was guarded everywhere he went but he said, "So far as I know, there was never any threat in my direction."

The third and final crisis was the election of the minority Trudeau government and this definitely involved the Reserve Powers of the Crown: on October 30, 1972, one hundred and nine Liberals were elected to one hundred and seven Progressive Conservatives, which put Roland Michener in the same dilemma that Lord Byng faced almost half a century before. If the Liberal government was defeated, could he refuse dissolution of Parliament if Prime Minister Trudeau requested it? Shouldn't he let Robert Stanfield try to form a government if the Conservative leader asked to do so? Stanfield never came closer to becoming prime minister than he did following the 1972 federal election. All those ifs and buts. Michener confessed to "have been in a state of jittery indecision ever since the thirtieth of October," and while he said so more or less in jest at the Parliamentary Press Gallery Dinner on February 24, 1973, this constitutional issue was to haunt him for much of the rest of his time as Governor General.

It was Michener's last Press Gallery Dinner, and he devoted much of his speech to "a definitive statement on the Reserve Powers of the Crown," which was what he expected his audience of roistering reporters wanted. He said that he had been "pursuing the Royal Prerogatives in the works of Dicey (who, in spite of what his name now sounds like, is still pretty reliable)" and numerous other British experts. "There are not a few of our own Canadian constitutionalists, and very good ones." Michener went on, "You all know the famous duo, King and Byng, or Byng and King, depending on one's view of proper precedence. These latter deserve special attention. They both had the advantage of being practitioners as well as theorists. The brief works of my predecessor, I almost said preceptor, Lord Byng, set out his views concisely in a couple of pages, to tell posterity, if not the electors of the day, exactly why he did what he did."

However, Michener said that he had come to the conclusion that all this learning might well be ignored. First of all, he had to remember that the Crown, in moments of decision, was a person, and "that I am 'It.'" This was the reason for his "state of jittery indecision." Second, he said, "It is axiomatic that the Crown tries never to act politically unless it has someone to take the blame, and so I keep looking around hopefully for an easy way out of every dilemma." It was a lighthearted exposition, but in a way made the media aware of the perplexities of his office, in this, his last Press Gallery Dinner speech.

As might be expected, Prime Minister Trudeau was in a state of shock over the 1972 election results; only a couple of years before, in the aftermath of the 1970 October Crisis, he was at the height of his popularity, especially in English Canada, where public opinion polls showed him with a phenomenal 80 percent support, and now the majority in English Canada had voted for the Tories. What was mortifying was that he had been sustained by French Canada, which he knew was no endorsement of his policies but largely a tribal vote — fifty-six of the one hundred and nine Liberal members came from Quebec. When he turned up at the Parliament Buildings on the day after the election, Trudeau seemed to be in a daze. He wore a deerskin jacket as if it were a hair shirt, and even showed up at Government House in this Indian garb. When he saw the look on Esmond Butler's face, he said, "I guess I should have a tie on." So Butler had to take off his tie and give it to the prime minister, who put it on and was then shown in to His Excellency.

Pierre Trudeau's appearance in this leather jacket with Butler's hastily knotted tie did not make Roland Michener feel very confident about the future of the Liberal government. Yet Trudeau said that he was determined to hang on, and that he had a couple of months to line up support for his minority government since the House would not be meeting until the beginning of 1973. He reached an agreement with David Lewis and got the backing of the thirty-one NDP members, and, as Michener said, "The Trudeau government managed to keep the support of the Commons long enough to establish a new regime which would entitle them, in due course, to ask for dissolution, which might have been refused in the first months of that Parliament."*

There was a regular weekly meeting of the prime minister and the Governor General; this was not a fixed engagement but a matter of convenience, and, during Roland Michener's term, if both parties were in Ottawa, the meeting was usually at six o'clock on Wednesday evening. With Prime Minister Pearson, it was a very informal affair: Mike would relax in an armchair with a glass of Scotch in his hand and brief his friend on what went on in Cabinet and any appointments that were to be made; he might talk about foreign affairs in which they were both interested. During the spring and summer of 1967 there was no need for any weekly meeting because they saw each other so often at all the receptions and dinners and luncheons for the heads of state and other foreign visitors to Expo.

---

*The minority Trudeau government was defeated on May 9, 1974, which was some months after the Micheners had left Government House. In the election that was held on July 8, 1974, the Liberals were returned with one hundred and forty-one seats and a majority government; not only was the NDP reduced to sixteen members but David Lewis lost his seat.

Pearson was older than Michener and had more experience in gov-
ernment and politics, and, after all, had appointed him Governor
General, and, aside from joshing each other as they had done at
Oxford, Mike tended to be the dominant figure.

   With Prime Minister Trudeau, it was very different. Pierre
came from a different cultural background, and there was not the
same intimacy. He was much younger and a generation gap existed,
with all that implied with regard to understanding. In looking back
on the weekly meeting with the Governor General, Trudeau recalled
that Michener talked to him "like an older friend or professor." The
discussions were always amicable, and he could not remember any
disputes. The prime minister would walk over from his residence
at 24 Sussex Drive and the Governor General would meet him at the
door of Rideau Hall and take him to his study. Michener said that
he offered him a drink or tea or "whatever he wanted." There was
never any agenda, but the talk, while friendly, was much more
formal. There was not much discussion of policy; mainly it was
about appointments: Trudeau would ask him what he thought of
such and such a person, and if Michener knew the man or woman he
would make a comment.

   The Governor General was particularly interested in the appointments of lieutenant-governors because, in the order of representatives of the Crown, which was not established, they were supposed
to come under him. At least Michener said that, according to the BNA
Act, he had the power to dismiss a lieutenant-governor for cause, but
that never happened with him, and he did not think it was ever done
without the involvement of the Council (the federal government).
Sometimes a lieutenant-governor would ask the Governor General for
advice but the junior (provincial) representative of the Crown was
usually told to go through the proper channel of communication,
which was the secretary of state. Whereas the head of state and the
head of government in Canada had regular consultations, the Governor General and the lieutenant-governors never met, and Michener
felt that this was an anomaly and should be corrected.

   In August 1973 he invited all lieutenant-governors to a conference to be held at Rideau Hall during the November 6–9 weekend.
All of them came, except for the Lieutenant-Governor of Alberta who
had commitments elsewhere at the time. They discussed their constitutional responsibilities as well as the way to discharge their unoffi-
cial and ceremonial functions. As an old hand at policy conferences,
Michener saw to it that the necessary papers and documents were

prepared for the meeting; he also arranged for constitutional authorities to come and talk to the group; these experts included Senator Eugene Forsey, whom Michener had consulted more than once, "having confidence in his good Victorian solidarity."

There was an exchange of ideas and the lieutenant-governors learned a lot from each other, as well as from the Governor General and the constitutional authorities, on the conduct of their offices. "It was counted a success," Michener said, "especially by those newly appointed to the office who had very limited instructions and few independent advisers." It was an innovation that was greatly needed, but the meeting with the lieutenant-governors occurred late in Roland Michener's term as Governor General (he was to have retired at the end of November but Norah wanted a last Christmas at Rideau Hall and Trudeau agreed to an extension to mid-January 1974). However, there was pressure on his successors to have further meetings and the conference of lieutenant-governors at Government House in Ottawa became a regular biennial affair.

As he had shown in the past, Michener believed in mixing the social and the instructional (perhaps this was due to Norah's influence; she did not like wives being left out) and he invited the lieutenant-governors and their wives to attend the weekend seminar, which was a party as well, at Rideau Hall. They would have been among the hundred thousand guests of the Micheners at luncheons and dinners, at dances and receptions and garden parties. Roland and Norah Michener were, without doubt, not only the most travelled viceregal couple but the ones who entertained the most, and they had the figures to prove it. Tabulated statistics for the first four years (1967–71) were: luncheon and dinner guests, 11,372; guests at dances, 4,197; guests at receptions and levees, 30,575; guests at garden parties 27,306.

Norah ran Rideau Hall. She would meet with the chef at ten o'clock in the morning and decide on the menus for that day, and the next if there were a luncheon or dinner party. She would talk to the comptroller, Don McKinnon, about the allocation of rooms if guests were expected, and she would check the rooms and make sure that they had flowers and books. She had very strict standards; she expected the footmen and the housemaids to be neat and immaculately clean, and if they were not, she would not hesitate to tell them to their faces that they had to smarten up; she would not leave this to be done by some senior member of the household. She was, in McKinnon's view, "extremely competent, intelligent and sophisticated."

While the comptroller had the greatest respect and admiration for Mrs. Michener, he said that she was very firm in her convictions and that, at times, made her seem like an obstinate and difficult person. However, when her judgment proved wrong, she did accept full responsibility. There was the example of the maître'd whom she insisted on hiring because he had served the Micheners when Roland was Speaker of the House of Commons. She did so over McKinnon's strong objections. A year or so later Norah realized that she had made a grave mistake. She talked to the comptroller about it, and he said, "Well, that's fine, I'll take care of it." "Oh no, you won't," she said. "I hired him over your objections and I'll fire him myself." And she did so. Even though it was a sticky business, since the maître'd lived with his family in a house on the grounds and had to be evicted, she handled the whole problem herself and would not let McKinnon do anything.

Then there was her booklet on etiquette, the *Memorandum for Wives* of MPs. Norah wanted to update it and was anxious that the Governor General's secretary help with the task. But Esmond Butler felt that he had more than he could handle at the time. "It wasn't an area that interested me greatly as to whether women should wear gloves, and whether they should come to the elbow or just to the wrist, and all of this sort of thing," he said. Norah did not take kindly to opposition to her pet project of protocol and Butler was in her bad books for a while. In the end she got the assistance of an official at External Affairs, and the revised edition of her *Memorandum* was brought out and has continued to prove useful to anyone invited to Government House.

It was easy enough to know what to wear at a ball or formal dinner, but what about supper? "Call one of the aides at Government House and ask what will be worn." Always "Sign the book within three days of the function whether you have attended or not." Then there were ways of replying to invitations from the Governor General: "Mr. and Mrs. John Smith have the honour to accept the gracious invitation of His Excellency ..." or "Mr. and Mrs. John Smith regret that, due to unavoidable circumstances, they are unable to accept the gracious invitation ...." The replies should be addressed to "The Aide-de-Camp in Waiting, Government House, Ottawa."

During much of 1967 Norah sat next to Prime Minister Pearson at all the state dinners and luncheons for the foreign visitors to Expo, and Mike often asked her how she was getting on with the "restoration," as he put it, of Government House. A lot had to be done to Rideau Hall since previous governments had not been overly generous in paying for its upkeep. "Now's your chance, Norah, to get everything done," Pearson said, "Because the government doesn't mind expense for our Centennial celebrations."

So Norah went ahead. She had a penchant for chandeliers (there was the one that she got for the Speaker's Chambers which so annoyed Diefenbaker), and she had the finest Austrian crystal chandeliers installed in the Tent Room at Rideau Hall and also in the dining room of the Citadel. She had the upholstery redone in both residences; she replaced the scatter rugs in many of the rooms with wall-to-wall carpeting. The ladies' cloakroom at the entrance to Government House was small and ugly, with naked pipes and peeling paint; Norah had it enlarged and redone with a honeycomb ceiling, soft lights, and carpeting, and on its walls she hung one of the finest collections of Jump cartoons of the Ottawa scene in the 1870s. These changes evoked a lot of favourable comment, and Roland Michener remarked, "You wouldn't think that this aspect of Government House would be so important."

However, changes Norah made to some of the offices and most of the bathrooms at Rideau Hall did not produce the same praise that she received for the alterations to the ladies' cloakroom — at least not from everyone. After deciding that the bathrooms in the royal suite should be redone, she had an old bathtub ripped out and replaced with a modern shower with sliding doors. Prince Philip was quite upset, according to Esmond Butler, because he did not enjoy taking a shower; he preferred the old bathtub with its sloping back in which he could relax and have a good soak.

The restoration work that Norah had done went far to rehabilitate the old building. However, the government would not agree to the major changes that the Micheners wanted when they first moved into Rideau Hall. Roland wanted to have an indoor swimming pool and a separate administration building (which was really badly needed) but neither was approved, although he was able to get funds to rebuild the two tennis courts that were across from the gardens and the conservatory. Norah saw to it that the chapel that the Vaniers had created with their own furnishings — furnishings that Pauline took with her when she left — was reconstituted as a nondenominational place of worship. She also ordered a whole new set of Limoges china, which Don McKinnon said arrived in time for most of the dinner parties for visiting heads of state in 1967. As for glassware, the comptroller said that Norah initiated the purchase of large quantities of the Belgian Val St. Amber glassware, as well as sterling silver cutlery, for both Rideau Hall and the Citadel. While these were major expenses, they were regarded as being made for the Centennial celebrations, and there was no objection.

In the circumstances, it was surprising, as McKinnon said, that some of Michener's successors felt that Rideau Hall had not been kept up. The answer was that a house of its age and structure was always going to have a lot of maintenance costs. "It doesn't matter if you spend a million dollars today," the comptroller went on; "tomorrow you have to spend another million." Parts of Rideau Hall are more than one hundred and fifty years old and while MacKay's villa* is almost lost in all the extensions and additions, most of the building still dates from the 1860s and 1870s. The preservation of an old house, its remodelling and modernization, would always be an expensive business, and even when the government had first taken it over and was fixing it up as a residence for the Governor General, Sir John A. Macdonald was to say, "We have spent more money patching up Rideau Hall than a palace would have cost at Nepean Point."

The constant restoration and reconstruction work was due not to an accumulation of neglect, Don McKinnon said, but to an accumulation of the ills of an old building. The walls, he pointed out, were so thick that a system of central air-conditioning could not be installed: it would have caused condensation that would have led to further trouble. However, summers in Ottawa could be so hot and humid that some method of cooling the public rooms had to be devised. The answer was individual air-conditioning units which were installed in most of the windows of Rideau Hall. They looked like rows of bee-hives and did not improve the appearance of the building; however, the Micheners would have it no other way; they believed in preserving the heritage of the country, no matter the cost, and they thought that Rideau Hall was a fine old house, with some beautiful rooms, particularly the ballroom and the Tent Room. With its fine park of some eighty acres, it was worthy of being a viceregal lodge.

---

*Thomas MacKay, a stone-mason from Perth, Scotland, built Rideau Hall in 1838 out of the money he made as contractor for the Lachine and Rideau canals. Born in 1792, he immigrated to Montreal in 1817 and was a partner of John Redpath, another pioneer builder. Rideau Hall, which Mackay designed himself, was a good example of a Regency villa. It is now "almost lost to view among the additions made piecemeal over the past century." That quote and the Macdonald quote are from R. H. Hubbard's book, *Rideau Hall - An Illustrated History of Government House, Ottawa.*

❧ 18 ❧

THE LAST VICEROY

As GOVERNOR GENERAL MICHENER was to say, a major development during his term of office and one that added greatly to the social and administrative responsibilities of Government House, and "also increased the interest in my work," was the Order of Canada. It was instituted on July 1, 1967, the Centennial anniversary of Confederation. While this was a most appropriate occasion to launch a Canadian system of honours, and while the first investiture saw an extraordinary assemblage of the greatest living Canadians, including the former Prime Minister Louis St. Laurent, former Governor General Vincent Massey, and Madame Vanier, the new Order was not fully accepted, largely because there was really nothing beyond the top grade of Companion. There was a Medal of Service for those who did not make the rank of Companion, but it was a wretched consolation prize; the actual medal was likened to a beer bottle top compared with the brilliant stylized snowflake of the Order of Canada, and many of them were returned with thanks but no thanks by indignant recipients.

The Order of Canada was proposed by Vincent Massey in an informal and confidential report to Prime Minister St. Laurent in 1951. Although a prominent Liberal who served briefly in Mackenzie King's 1925 Cabinet (he failed to win a seat), Massey was an ardent royalist who, when he was Canadian High Commissioner in London, "seemed to know every Duke by his first name," according to Mike Pearson. Massey envisioned the Order of Canada as an Imperialist Order, modelled after the Order of the British Empire, with three classes or grades, those of Companion, Officer, and Member. However, his report was shelved. Prime Minister St. Laurent was not in favour of any Canadian honour system, and Prime Minister Diefenbaker much preferred British civilian awards, which carried no titles, and his greatest triumph, according to his own account (*One Canada*, vol. 3), was to be made a Freeman of the City of London in his last year of power.*

It was Prime Minister Pearson who felt that, along with the new maple leaf flag that he had got Parliament to approve, there should be a distinctive Canadian honours system such as the Order of Canada. (He would have liked to have rounded off his nationalist endeavours with an agreement on "Oh Canada" as the national anthem, but that was not to come until later.) So Pearson dusted off Massey's old report and turned it over to a parliamentary committee, the only stipulation being that its deliberations be ended in good time so that the first awards could be presented on July 1, 1967. There was a consensus on the need for such an honours system as the Order of Canada but opposition to the proposed three grades; they were felt to be elitist, anti-democratic, and redolent of the class system in the United Kingdom. When the matter finally came before the Cabinet, it was decided that there should be only one level of awards, that of Companion.

At the time Prime Minister Pearson felt that this was a mistake, that it would restrict the Order to too small a group — there were to be only one hundred and fifty living Companions — which was not what he had expected or wanted. The newly approved honours system included the Medal of Service, which was poorly designed and was not to be compared with the beautiful badge of the Order of Canada and, in any case, had really nothing to do with the Order. It was an unsatisfactory compromise that led to much anguish and

---

*John Diefenbaker was made a Companion of Honour in January 1976; it was a recognition of "conspicuous national service," and was one of the highest awards, at the designation of the Sovereign, that conferred no title.

discontent; Michener realized this from the beginning and urged the government to reconsider the whole honours system. In 1970, some three years after it was instituted, a committee was set up to review the Order of Canada; it was chaired by a senior diplomat, Jules Léger, who was to succeed Roland Michener as Governor General.

Finally, in 1972, as a result of the recommendations of the Léger Committee, Prime Minister Trudeau's government approved the three grades of the Order of Canada that Massey had originally proposed. Those who had received the much-scorned Medal of Service, whether they had returned them or not, were made Officers of the Order of Canada. Furthermore, a military side to the Canadian honours system, if not to the Order of Canada itself, was instituted with the Order of Military Merit, which also had three grades, those of Commander, Officer, and Member. The badge of the Order of Military Merit was a dark-blue enamel cross with a red maple leaf in a roundel in the centre and a crown above it.

At the same time, awards for bravery were established which also came in three grades: the Cross of Valour, the Star of Courage, and the Medal of Bravery. The highest award, the Cross of Valour, which was given in only exceptional circumstances, was to take the place of the Victoria Cross and the George Cross, and the initials, cv, were just the reverse of the vc. The bravery awards filled out the Canadian honours system and meant that, in peace and war, Canadians would no longer have to rely on British decorations as they had done in the past.

The awards were in the hands of an advisory council consisting of the chief justice of the supreme court of Canada; three civil servants, the chairman of the Canada Council, the clerk of the privy council, and the under secretary of state; and the presidents of three learned societies. The advisory council had an office in Government House and Esmond Butler looked after it and was named Secretary for Honours. Roland Michener was the first Chancellor of the Order of Canada and, as such, was automatically a Companion "so I didn't need to be invested." He decided not to appoint anybody that the council had not named, although he reserved the right not to appoint everybody on the honours list — and "there were one or two that I held up on my own responsibility." The self-limiting rule that Michener established was praised by Gordon Robertson who, as clerk of the privy council, was a member of the first advisory council, especially as it came to be accepted by his successors as Governor General.

However, Michener did not agree with the council's own rule that no politician should be given the Order of Canada while still actively engaged in politics. The rule was adopted, Robertson said, because of the difficulty of distributing the awards equally among the parties. "I didn't complain so much about that," Michener said, "but it did deprive a man like Pierre Trudeau, who went abroad with no decoration of any kind. He should have had it. So should any Prime Minister [or Premier], I think, automatically have it." Judges were also on the forbidden list and Michener did not believe in that either, but he acknowledged that the rule "did avoid any log-rolling for decorations." Both Mike Pearson and Pierre Trudeau were made Companions of the Order of Canada after they retired, so were a number of provincial premiers, but John Diefenbaker never received the award because he died while still a member of Parliament.

That did not worry the old Chief since he was contemptuous of the Order of Canada and regarded it as a "Liberal bauble to go with the Liberal flag." Furthermore, he would have abhorred attending an investiture and receiving the award from Roland Michener. Diefenbaker did his best to ignore Michener as Governor General; he only went to Government House when it was unavoidable and, according to Don McKinnon, would only stay at a reception the shortest possible time. Michener described Diefenbaker's attitude toward him as being "a little cool." "I think he was not happy to find himself below me in rank," but Michener did not like to dwell on Diefenbaker's antipathy toward him: it was his genial nature to always try to see the best in anyone. The Chief, he said, "was decently polite throughout — and we got along quite well."

There were two investitures a year and, in the mind of R.H. Hubbard, the historian of Rideau Hall, they increased the prestige of the Governor General "immensely." Michener insisted that "white tie" should be worn at the investitures and while "white tie" would be on the invitation card and most men did wear white tie and tails, there were some who did not have such clothes and others who would not wear them on principle. Esmond Butler recalled a backwoods man from British Columbia who was one of the first appointees to the Order of Canada, a "marvellous man with a great white beard." He was wearing an ordinary dark suit, and after the ceremony, he came up to Butler and said, "I saw on your invitation that we were supposed to wear a white tie. He lifted up his beard and underneath he had a white tie on."

Michener believed in dressing up: for him it was an integral part of the pageantry of monarchy, and, as the surrogate of the Crown, it was up to him to maintain the regal standards of wearing apparel. So, "white tie and decorations" were on invitations to a ball or a dinner party at Government House. Norah shared her husband's regard for uniforms and formal attire, and she herself had written about the subject in her *Memorandum* to wives on etiquette, how long white gloves reaching to the elbow should be worn with an evening dress. As vicereine, she took a large wardrobe of dresses with her when she went on tour and changed two and three times a day.

Both Roland and Norah fitted well into their viceregal roles; they were not quite as grand as their predecessors, General and Madame Vanier, but they followed them in the seigneural tradition. Roland had "class," according to the anti-royalist journalist, Walter Stewart; he had "flair, dignity, that indefinable something called presence." He looked good in formal attire and the uniforms that he had designed for himself; he looked the part of a Governor General. He had the right temperament and was never bored with the endless receptions and addresses of welcome; he always had a good word to say to anyone and everyone. In fact, he genuinely enjoyed ceremonies, which could be achingly dull, the salutes and the playing of the national anthem, and felt they helped to make the country aware of its government and its heritage. Norah played the part of the consort so well that Olive Diefenbaker complained that she was behaving like the Queen, and Maryon Pearson was a little jealous of the attention she was getting abroad. Her booklet on etiquette reflected her great appreciation of protocol — and clearly this was an asset to anyone in the position of Governor General. It was because of her rather old-fashioned view of what constituted the right behaviour that she resented the curtsy being abandoned.

Judy La Marsh told a poignant story about Norah Michener, whom she did not really like, in her book *Memoirs of a Bird in a Gilded Cage*. She said that when Roland Michener was appointed Governor General in 1967, there were two private rehearsals of the installation ceremony in the Senate Chamber and at both Norah curtsied to her husband despite the recent agreement to dispense with this custom. She was reminded of this and told not to do so, and Norah, who was close to tears, argued that "she wished to curtsy, that this was her husband and she wanted to pay him homage no less than had been paid to his predecessors." When the real ceremony occurred, Judy

said that she and Under Secretary of State Ernie Steele watched as
Norah, who was the first woman to pass in front of the Governor
General after he was sworn in, "hesitated for a moment, then slowly
bowed from the waist, and went back to her seat." They "breathed a
sigh of relief that the curtsy had at last passed into disuse in Canada."

Not everyone liked to dress up and wear white tie and tails,
and Prime Minister Pearson decreed that a tuxedo or "black tie"
would be the height of evening formality during the heat of the Centennial summer. Prime Minister Trudeau tended to be even more
casual, "but," Michener said, "he always came in the appropriate
garments [white tie and tails] for our dinners and for our investitures
of the Order of Canada." However, dress uniforms and other formal
attire were on a knife's edge. Ambassadors used to have a splendid
uniform, similar to the Governor General's uniform, but when the
rank was democratized after the war and all heads of foreign missions
were recognized as ambassadors, the uniform disappeared, and diplomats wore civilian clothes. Times change and costumes change.

Jules Léger never wore the silver-embroidered viceregal uniform; as a diplomat he had been used to a morning coat and he wore
that on formal occasions, such as the opening of Parliament. But the
morning coat was also on the way out, as were the white tie and
tails. Trudeau said that people didn't like wearing them and asserted
that Edward Schreyer, the former NDP premier of Manitoba who succeeded Jules Léger, never owned a morning coat. Even Michener did
not favour a morning coat and replaced it on formal occasions with
a short black coat and striped trousers. Perhaps Trudeau's choice of
the socialist Schreyer as Governor General was a revolt against the
formal wear demanded by the royalist Michener. At any rate, Schreyer
wore mainly dark business suits and gave Government House a
prairie populist atmosphere and even served egg rolls at receptions,
much to the astonishment of the social set in Ottawa.

The role of the Governor General changed, and Roland
Michener, although a traditionalist, gladly made the first visits abroad
as a head of state. His successors also made such junkets: Jules
Léger visited Spain after the restoration of the monarchy and was the
guest of King Juan Carlos; Ed Schreyer made two head-of-state trips
abroad, to the Scandinavian countries and to Greece and Romania;
and Madame Jeanne Sauvé went on an official visit to France. But
none of these was on the scale of Michener's triumphal tour of the
Netherlands, Belgium, and Luxembourg; after all, a fleet was involved, probably the largest assemblage of Canadian warships in

peacetime: the naval supply ship HMCS *Preserver*, on which he sailed, and the destroyers *Assiniboine, Margaree,* and *Ottawa*. The military component of this trip was very large and included a Canadian honour guard and a naval band for the memorial service at the Holten Canadian war cemetery in the Netherlands. The head-of-state visits abroad by Michener's successors did not attract anything like the attention that the Benelux tour did; they were kept on a low key, and perhaps deliberately so.

When Roland Michener was installed in the early spring of 1967, there was a debate as to the future role of the Governor General. The Centennial Year was a logical time for pundits to look backward and forward; but it was also a time of student revolt and nationalist unrest in Quebec. The *Toronto Daily Star*, which had the largest circulation of any newspaper in the country, called for the replacement of the Governor General by a president, and said: "We hope that when English and French speaking Canadians have thought more about what they want to change and what they want to keep in the present political system, they will sit down together and write a constitution for the Republic of Canada."

The *Star Weekly* Magazine was even more specific: it declared that "Roly Michener could make an ideal Governor-General — but we should make him Canada's first president instead." Walter Stewart, a *Star Weekly* staff writer at the time, wrote: "The archaic title [of Governor General], with its sonorous clang of empire, royalty and the British connection, has become out of place in a nation no longer imperialist, royalist or even particularly British." The 1961 census showed Canada's ethnic makeup to be 44 percent British, 30 percent French, and 26 percent "others," with the trend toward the "others," and Stewart went on: "... common sense and the national interest both urge us to stop kidding ourselves that we are still England's baby brother, loyal, timid and Anglo Saxon." Furthermore, he said, most of the jobs performed by a governor general could be taken on by a president, the only major exception being his role as representative of the Crown and symbol of British tradition, "and it is this role that should be abolished."

In its July 1967 issue, *Saturday Night* agonized about the role of Governor General; the magazine's editor, Arnold Edinborough, described the constitutional division of the Crown as being "Alice-in-Wonderland type of fiction" and asked: "What can we do to bring some reality into the situation while still maintaining our tradition of monarchical government?" He denied that there would have to be a republic, and went on, "There is no reason why we should not have our own governor general as the actual head of our own monarchical system," and seemed to imply that all that had to be done was to declare sovereignty and have the governor general appointed by the Canadian government without any reference to the Queen. This would cut the last colonial bonds and "bring Canada out of the fairyland of legal fiction into the world of real men and women."

However, Edinborough did not say what the new Canadian head of state would be called. It would be "a new kind of monarchy" but would the title be King or Queen, or Regent — there was the prewar case of Admiral Horthy who was Regent of Hungary, a monarchy without a monarch? Then how was this person to be appointed and for what duration? Edinborough seemed to be calling for a "nominated monarchy," as opposed to that ardent royalist Sir Robert Borden's description of the Governor General as a "nominated president."

There was so much criticism of the monarch at the time that the Duke of Edinburgh got into the debate. While the Queen was constitutionally and by title the Queen of Canada, she was recognized everywhere else, and by many even in Canada, as the Queen of Great Britain. Her dual or multiple role, since she was Queen of other parts of the Commonwealth, could result in a conflict of interest, as others beside Mitchell Sharp had pointed out, but this was always resolved, as it had to be, in favour of her primary role as the British Queen. Britain's entry into the European Common Market was an issue; it was expected to affect Canadian and Commonwealth trade, but the Queen would have to ratify a move that could be harmful to other parts of her realm. So the argument went, and at a press conference in Ottawa on October 18, 1969, Prince Philip said that, if Canadians felt that the monarchy had no further role to play in Canada, "then, for goodness sake, let's end the thing on amicable terms without having a row about it." But it would not be as easy as that: there would be an angry outcry from British elements and those who wanted to keep the British connection, and, as Roland Michener said, "it would cause a lot more trouble than it would be worth."

Yet there was the dilemma over the title "Governor General," with its imperialist connotations, and Michener admitted that "its colonial significance has never quite disapppeared." Traditionally, the governor was sent out by an imperial power to govern, although, in reality, the present Governor General has much less authority than the past colonial governor. "No one has found a suitable substitute name for it [the Governor General]," Michener said. "We all thought about it and talked about it, but you can't call a Governor General a president, or a Pooh-Bah, or some other [name]. You can't invent a name very well.

"The real question about the role of Governor General is: what would be a better system?" Michener asked and answered with another question: "How would we get along with a president?" In reply, he said that if the president were elected, he would inevitably become a competitor to the prime minister. India was an example of a leading member of the Commonwealth, headed by the Queen, which had a president, and Michener was Canadian High Commissioner in India for two and a half years. He spoke of possible difficulties, but said that, as long as the Congress Party was dominant, not only at the centre but in the provinces, the government was assured of having a supporter in the president's office. There was an ingenious system of election in India whereby the thirty-four hundred members of the state legislatures and the members of both federal Houses constituted an electoral college which voted for the president. If the same were to apply in Canada, the electoral college would be composed of the members of the provincial legislatures and of the House of Commons, probably not the appointed Senate. In order to change the role of the Governor General to president with the least trouble, "you could invite the Queen to be head of the Commonwealth only," Michener said, but added, "I have never advocated that."

In fact, Michener accepted the status quo "without trying to divine the future," although he recognized that "our institutions change, and ought to change, with the circumstances and with the times; if they don't, they don't fulfill their usefulness." Therefore he expected change, although he felt that, in some respects, it was "downgrading the office by taking away part of the pageantry of royalty." And so he wore the traditional and distinctive silver-embroidered uniform of the Governor General for the opening of Parliament; he visited every base in Canada and wore uniforms that he had had specially adapted for inspection of the armed forces; and he carried on the traditional pageantry of viceregal salutes by the military.

"I looked on myself as the actual presence of the Crown in Canada, when the Queen wasn't here, which was most of the time," Michener said, "and therefore the symbol of our unity and our integrity as one country. In that capacity I considered it my duty and useful occupation to visit all parts of Canada and show the flag, so to speak, represent the Crown, and be received and respond and visit schools and go to city halls and factories and universities and travel in the North. I went to the Arctic six times in the course of my seven years [in office], and covered pretty well the whole of Canada with very few exceptions. I extended the patronage of my office," Michener went on, "to all national organizations that were making some useful contribution to Canadian life in every field and encouraged volunteer organizations everywhere."

Actually, when he was Governor General, Roland Michener was official patron to one hundred and twenty-three national associations, and jointly with Mrs. Michener to another nineteen, with honourary office or membership in one hundred and fifty others. When their national meetings were held in Ottawa, the Micheners would try to receive their representatives at Rideau Hall. Many of the Governor General's five hundred prepared speeches were given at these association meetings.

While his official visits abroad had moved the Governor General's role forward to that of a *de facto* head of state, Michener maintained that he never attempted to change his constitutional duties. However, it was disclosed late in 1972 that Prime Minister Trudeau had approached Buckingham Palace with regard to shifting certain external affairs functions from the Queen to the Governor General; this was done, it was said, simply "to lighten the paperwork load of Her Majesty." Apparently the Queen raised no serious objections to four of the proposals — or suggestions, as the prime minister's office preferred to call them — which dealt with the appointment of foreign ambassadors, the recall of foreign ambassadors, the appointment and recall of Canadian envoys, and the establishing or severing of diplomatic relations; but she demurred on the fifth proposal, which would have had her hand over to the Governor General the signing of the letters of credence of Canadian diplomats. As a result, the whole matter was dropped, and a spokesman for Trudeau said, "nothing has changed."

This was not sufficient assurance for those suspicious of the government's so-called republican tendencies, and led to a renewal of the debate. The *Edmonton Journal* alleged that it was Trudeau's settled policy to turn the Governor General into a *de facto* head of state, and said: "This would be a major and fundamental change in our constitution — achieved by means of a few obscure procedural moves, without the electorate being aware of what was happening. For a Governor General exercising in his own right the prerogatives of the monarch would in reality be a president, appointed by the prime minister. Canada would stealthily have been turned into a republic, instead of a constitutional monarchy — and a republic lacking most of the safeguards about the appointment of a president that are usually found in republican constitutions."

Michener was not involved in these negotiations with Buckingham Palace, or "sounding out," as the prime minister's office liked to describe them, and did not really approve of them, although he said, "I was quite prepared to sign [the letters of credence] if the government felt that was the best way to do it." The reason that the Queen did not want to give up signing the credentials of Canadian envoys was that it would cause confusion in foreign countries as to who the head of state in Canada was. It was, nevertheless, an anomalous situation, as Her Majesty did not sign the letters of credence as the Queen of Canada, but simply "Elizabeth R." Still, the transfer of this prerogative to the Governor General would mean a diminution in the role of the monarchy, and Michener would not want that to happen. (Trudeau finally got his way, and the execution of credentials and the administration of diplomatic changes were all moved to Ottawa in 1977, when Léger was Governor General) "I always considered," Michener said, "that, as long as we are a monarchy, the office [of Governor General] has significance by reason of the monarchy. Some of that rubs off on the incumbent. And the fact that he is appointed by the Queen gives a direct connection with the rest of the monarchy."

Although Roland Michener was a stickler for protocol and liked all the ceremony and trappings of the viceregal office, he could relax and be part of the family at Rideau Hall on the odd evening when he did not have to do any official entertaining. R.H. Hubbard, an honourary member of the household, remembered the "wonderful, jolly times" they had, especially at Christmas, when Roly would play the piano in the drawing room, and they would all gather around and have a sing-song. Sometimes Norah, who was more of a classical pianist, would join in, and they would play duets. The young aides-de-camp would have their own parties, and Bob Hubbard was reminded of one that was given in the Tent Room, which was called "Discotheque in the Tentotech," and, of course, he said, the Micheners attended and danced the night away.

As a close observer of the governors general, both British and Canadian, Hubbard did not like to make comparisons, but he agreed that the Micheners and the Vaniers, and Vincent Massey, the first Canadian to hold the viceregal office, were more in the mould of the

Bessboroughs and the Willingdons as viceroys than their successors. However, Hubbard would not agree that the Légers and the Schreyers, and Madame Sauvé, had more of a presidential approach; "the trappings don't really matter," he said, it was a different attitude, perhaps, a more modern outlook. There was a generation gap, certainly as far as the Schreyers were concerned, and then the Micheners, the Vaniers, and Massey came from older and more established and aristocratic families. Of the British governors general, Lord Tweedsmuir (novelist John Buchan) was the informal kind, and Hubbard thought that he could be compared with Jules Léger; they were also both intellectuals.

On the main wall of the Reception Hall of Government House there are, or were in the summer of 1989, three full-length, life-sized, portraits of the first three Canadian-born governors general, and they were all painted in the traditional viceregal uniform, splendid with silver and plumes: General Vanier is in the centre, full-faced, looking across the hall at the panel displaying the coats of arms of all the governors and governors general of Canada since Champlain; on either side of him and looking at him are Vincent Massey and Roland Michener. In a speech to the 1975 annual meeting of the Canadian Historical Association, Michener said that his viceregal uniform "now reposes in the Museum of Man in Ottawa."

In his article on the appointment of Roland Michener as Governor General, Walter Stewart posed the question as to whether he would be the Last Governor General — it was the title of his 1967 *Star Weekly* Magazine piece. Michener was not the last Governor General, but he could be said to have been the Last Viceroy.

❧ 19 ❧

LIFE
AFTER

As GOVERNOR GENERAL, Roland Michener saw much more of his friend Mike Pearson than he did when he was Speaker. At both times they were together in Ottawa and not separated by hundreds of miles, as was the case when Michener was a lawyer and provincial minister in Toronto and Pearson was with External Affairs in Ottawa or serving as a diplomat abroad. But, as Speaker, Michener was inhibited in his social contacts, and although he did see Mike on occasion at a private party, it was not as often as he could have wished for. There were no such restraints in the viceregal office, and during the Centennial Year, when so many heads of state or their representatives descended on the nation's capital, Michener and Pearson met more than twice a week at official functions. They kept in close touch after Pearson retired as prime minister; "I saw him regularly as a friend," Roland said. In fact, they saw more of each other at this time than at any period since the early days of their friendship when they were just Mitch and Mike.

In 1970, while on a visit to Europe, Pearson had an operation in which one of his eyes was removed; he returned with a glass eye, which he joked about and said that he should be photographed from that side as it was better-looking than his real eye. But Michener was, as he put it, "frightened": he knew that the reason for the operation was cancer and was afraid that it would recur. Mike was cheerful and hopeful, but Michener said, "I don't really believe that he accepted the doctors' view that they had got everything out because he made every effort to get on with his memoirs." In his retirement Pearson was one of the "three wise men" who were making a study of international aid for the World Bank, and he worked very hard to get this out of the way so that he could concentrate on his autobiography. However, precious time was lost — he could not very well give up this undertaking — and he was able to complete only the first volume of his memoirs, although he left enough notes and memoranda and first drafts of chapters so that the editors could complete the second and third volumes of *Mike, The Memoirs of Lester B. Pearson*.

The end came very quickly. Michener kept in close touch with Pearson during the last month of his life, and was surprised when he decided, at this late stage in his illness, to spend Christmas of 1972 with friends in Florida. However, his son Geoffrey pointed out that he was still able to get around on his own and did not have to be carried onto the aircraft. "I think," Michener said, "he realized that he wasn't going to survive, and he dreaded going back to hospital. He went down there for another week of sunshine, hopefully free of pain, but he suffered a sudden relapse, and had to be brought back." Michener helped make arrangements for him to be flown back to Ottawa in a government plane on December 24, and sent his limousine out to the airport to drive him to the Pearsons' home in Rockcliffe, not far from Rideau Hall. Pearson had insisted that he not be taken to the hospital. "He didn't want to die there, but to go home. And he only lasted a couple of days."

Roly Michener saw Mike Pearson on the night before he died, and it was a heart-wrenching experience. "He was really far gone then," Michener said. "He was just expiring. He couldn't speak and I don't think he could see. He was certainly alive but not conscious but if he were conscious, he couldn't do anything about it. So, mercifully, he didn't last much longer." He died the following day, December 27.

Shortly before Christmas, when Mike knew that he was dying, he had prepared a present for Roly that was touching evidence of their great friendship. He had come across one of the postcard photographs of the old Oxford ice hockey team that had been taken at the Hotel des Alps in Switzerland, at the time of the game with Cambridge some fifty years before. The half-dozen members of the team in their uniforms were sitting on a bench with their sticks in front of them and a snowbank behind, and Pearson had had everybody cut out except for himself and Michener. There they were, Mitch and Mike, sitting side by side, and he had had the picture enlarged and framed and gave it to the Governor General just before Christmas.

In his tribute to the former diplomat, the only Canadian to win the Nobel Peace Prize, the former prime minister, and his good friend, Roland Michener said: "There is a happier side to our present sorrow, as we think, in the spirit of Ecclesiasticus 44, of our debt to this `famous man,' and of how much he has given to us. We thank God for a life which has been of such profound benefit to his times, and a blessing to such a countless number of friends. He will be remembered by so many for so much."

Michener helped in the funeral arrangements and Geoffrey Pearson found him to be "always a great comfort, a man with whom one could discuss anything—no formality, no protocol, really." The state funeral was held on December 30, 1972, just three days after Pearson's death; there was unusually inclement weather for Ottawa at that time of the year, and Michener marched in the procession in a downpour of rain.

"One of the reasons that my father and Michener were so close was that they were both very informal people," Geoffrey Pearson said. "They were people who preferred to let out their energies and frustrations in sports and play, and otherwise to conduct themselves in a civilized, humane, pleasant way. They were very similar, although I think Michener was more optimistic. My father often had bouts of depression about the future of the world and where it was going. He was quite `Cassandra-like.' Michener has never been like that, as far as I can remember. He's always been a great optimist."

There was a year to go in the Governor General's term of office — less than that really, as Prime Minister Trudeau was to agree to a short extension so that the Micheners could enjoy another Christmas at Rideau Hall. The last few months were spent in preparations for a return to civilian life, and the most important matter was the question of the pension. At the time it was not very generous, a third of the viceregal salary of ten thousand pounds sterling (which was converted as $48,666.63), or $16,222.21. (It should be pointed out that

this statutory stipend, which dated back to Confederation, if not earlier, was tax-free and had come to represent little more than pocket
money or, as Michener said, "my own money to do what I liked with":
it was a very small amount compared with the substantial sums,
amounting to millions of dollars, now needed to run Government
House, which were provided by the federal government and were in
the Estimates and part of the nation's budget.)

Norah was indignant at such a paltry pay-off. She said that
President Richard Nixon, who had been the Micheners' guest at
Rideau Hall when he was on an official visit to Ottawa, had retired
in disgrace but received a pension and allowances of six million
dollars a year. "And they're going to push us out on the street with
nothing but a pittance," she said. Roland would probably have accepted the original pension; he considered that being Governor
General was sufficient recompense and that he could not expect to
be kept in luxury after he left office, but because of Norah's protests,
he got Don McKinnon to make a study of the viceregal pensions.
As a result, the prime minister agreed to a formula that gave
Michener a taxable income of twenty-five thousand dollars annu-
ally, which would go up and down with the cost of living. Somewhat
later, in Governor General Léger's time, the government made
provision for annual expense allowances somewhat similar to
those that MPS were enjoying. This authorized the Treasury Board
to cover for the Governor General the cost of an office, a secretary,
and a messenger-driver, plus provision for necessary expense to
cover obligations due to the office.

It was three months short of seven years that the Micheners
were at Rideau Hall, and Roland would have stayed longer, and so
would Norah. "I guess rotation is more important than anything else,
from English to French Governors General, in deciding when the
change should be made," Michener said. There were discussions in
early 1973, "and the Prime Minister wasn't interested in making a
change, and I was enjoying it and was in good health, and so was my
wife, and we were quite prepared to go on." However, an election was
coming up in Quebec, and it was the right time politically to announce
the nomination of a new French-speaking Governor General.

At first the Micheners thought of staying in Ottawa and
bought a house in Rockcliffe, not far from Government House, and
then, to save everyone embarrassment and to be nearer their family and old friends, they decided it would be better to return to
Toronto. A flagpole was erected by the Governor General's Horse

Guards at their old house, 5 Rosedale Road, and at eleven o'clock in the morning of January 14, 1974, when Jules Léger's official flag was being raised in Ottawa, Roland Michener's was coming down ceremoniously in Toronto.

However, 5 Rosedale Road was but a temporary retirement home; for Roland turned over the house that he had acquired in the thirties to his daughter, Diana Schatz, and her family. The Micheners soon found suitable accommodation in a charming Regency-style house at 24 Thornwood Road, just a short walk from their old home.

"I enjoyed Rideau Hall," Michener said, "I enjoyed the opportunities that come to a Governor General to meet people. I'm an extrovert. But I didn't regret leaving and settling down quietly again."

Still, it was not just going back to private life. There were certain things that a former Governor General does not do: he does not engage in partisan politics, but that was a self-denying ordinance that Michener had adopted as Speaker. And as a professional lawyer he could not go to court or even practise. His old law firm, Lang Michener, gave him an office and made him an associate counsel but "I had no clients and if I had any, I'd turn them over quickly to the practising lawyers."

Michener did accept the chancellorship of Queen's University which, as he said, was a very interesting and pleasant responsibility suitable for a former Governor General. He returned to the board of four companies with which he had been associated before going to India. He became chairman of the Metropolitan Trust Company and honourary chairman of its successor, Victoria and Grey Trust Company; he was chairman and then honourary chairman of the Teck Corporation. He became president again of the Canadian Institute of International Affairs and held that office for five years, only retiring from that position in 1980 but remaining an active member of the CIIA. There were so many calls on him to be sponsor of this and patron of that and to head such and such an organization here and another one there that he had to say no to many of them. "The way I express it," Michener said, "is that if you become Governor General, you become a sort of public property and that lasts the rest of your life."

His greatest interest in retirement, and one that, he said, took up more of his time than anything else, was the promotion of fitness and health. It was a continuing interest of his — the reason he had wanted to have the swimming pool at Rideau Hall was because he considered swimming to be the best exercise — and his jogging while he was Governor General got a lot of publicity in the press and on television. In fact, when he was initiated into the honourary Kanai chieftainship of the Blood Indians at a ceremony in Standoff, Alberta in the summer of 1970, he was given the highly appropriate name of "Chief Running Antelope." Michener would jog every day and everywhere, at a country railway stop or in the centre of a great metropolis, as Esmond Butler knew only too well. He, or an aide de camp, was expected to accompany Michener on his runs: and Butler found himself padding around the snowbound recesses of the Arctic in bitterly cold weather and puffing along in the sweltering heat of an Ottawa summer.

One day, he recalled, when they had just checked into the Savoy Hotel in London — the Governor General was on a private visit — Michener said, "We're going jogging tomorrow morning." "But I haven't brought any running shoes," Butler said, but that was no excuse and he was told to get a pair. At six o'clock the next morning they were off jogging down the Thames Embankment. They ran as far as the Billingsgate Fish Market, and Michener wanted to take a look inside, so they jogged around the stalls, to the amazement and applause of the costermongers, but the Governor General of Canada (incognito in his sweatsuit) slipped on the greasy floor and, if it had not been for the prompt action of his secretary, might have fallen and hurt himself, which would have made for a great story in the more sensational British newspapers.

Even when he was Governor General, Michener would take part in charity runs. "I played up my jogging," he said, "because I realized that Canadians as a whole were not up to the standards they ought to maintain in fitness and in health." He continued with this after he left Rideau Hall. "I've been an advocate," Michener went on, "of carrying on whatever program of exercises you adopt into your mature and senior life, as long as you can do it. That's been my policy, and I've been glad to appear here and there and everywhere, either as an exhibit or an exponent." Michener was a good "exhibit": he drank moderately and only socially, and he did not smoke; he had given up cigarettes early on when he discovered that, after a party, they gave him a hangover; he enjoyed smoking cigars and, as Governor General, he had the best, but when he left Government House, he gave away his boxes of Cuban cigars and stopped smoking altogether. As a result, in his retirements he became involved in all kinds of sports activities, from starting marathon races to awarding prizes and attending banquets for athletes. He never stopped playing tennis; he played at the Toronto Lawn Tennis Club, which he had joined in 1926, the Badminton and Racquet Club, and at the exclusive Queen's Club with its two indoor courts.

Life after Rideau Hall was a busy round of speeches and of meetings, of jogging and of tennis, and of receiving and giving awards (he always participated at the presentation of the Michener Awards for Journalism), almost as busy as it had been when he was Governor General, and Roland Michener was enjoying himself until one summer night when they were staying on their island in Georgian Bay and Norah wandered off into the dark and had to be rescued. She had Altzheimer's disease, and it grew gradually worse and finally in 1984 she had to be hospitalized. On his own in their retirement home, 24 Thornwood Road, Roland felt lost and lonely. He visited her every day, and, even though she did not recognize him, "her eyes would light up," Michener said, "I knew it meant something to her." On January 12, 1987, Norah Evangeline Willis Michener died; she was eighty-five years old. Roland was distraught; his health suffered, but, with a conscious effort, he overcame his grief and, as he said, "lifted my sights to another decade and the prospect of tennis at ninety."

At a memorial service in Toronto on January 21, 1987, Diana Schatz said of Norah Michener: "Though her upbringing appeared to us distinctly Victorian, Mother was actually a woman ahead of her time. She had an appreciation of the value of each individual and of the obligation to develop fully one's talent. At the same time she understood the importance of the family and the responsibility of each to other family members. She ensured that we three daughters had a broadly based formal education with the opportunity to develop our particular interests—Wendy in languages, writing, and theatre arts, Joan in sculpture and painting, and I in mathematics and science."

Norah was not really a feminist; she might have believed in the equality of women but she was too much of a traditionalist to do much about supporting or promoting such an issue. She did believe in continuing education for women. In *A Personal Message*, which she wrote when she was Vicereine, she said: "I think it is extremely important for women especially to continue to develop their abilities and tastes. At the age of about twelve, I startled my music teacher, Frederick Chubb of Vancouver, by announcing to him that I was a person in my own right and that after I married I intended to go on studying. He laughed heartily at me and said, `Well, my dear, I venture to suggest that you will do pretty much as other women before you have done. You will stay home and look after your husband and your children.' I replied that of course I should do so, but that in addition I would do something to develop my own abilities, and that in this way I would not only become a better person, but also enrich the lives of my husband and my children ...." Years later, after marriage and motherhood, she finally finished her Ph.D. in philosophy, and sent a copy of her book, which was her doctoral thesis, on the French philosopher Jacques Maritain to Frederick Chubb; in it, she wrote, "In payment of an old wager."

To Roland Michener, Norah was the "perfect wife and companion." Although she was a scholar and a keen student of religion and philosophy, there was a practical side to her that was revealed in the magazine articles and book she wrote on cooking and in her concern about position and pensions. She was a driving force, of that there was no doubt, and she was ambitious not so much for herself as for her husband. Roland could not have done without her. Norah was his strong right arm. They complemented each other; they made a great team. As Diana said, at the memorial service for her mother, "To us our parents were one."

Yet they were different. Roland was much more easygoing, much more accommodating, than Norah, who did not suffer fools gladly. Like many successful women, she got along much better with men than with women — and, in this, she was like Fiorenza Drew, the wife of Roland's friend and former leader, George Drew. She kept voluminous diaries when she was in New Delhi and at Government House (they were referred to in the citation for the honourary degree that she received from York University in 1970: the citation expressed the hope that these diaries would "someday constitute an important public account of the substance of life at high levels of public responsibility"),* whereas her husband was the soul of discretion and did not even keep notes. Bob Hubbard thought of Roland Michener as the "happy warrior," which was a good description of his cheerful, outgoing nature, while Norah was introspective and less sanguine. Others described him as an "Edwardian gentle-

---

*In her will, Norah Michener decreed that her diaries should not be made public until thirty years after her death (she died in 1987). Although her husband had "glanced" at them, he did not and would not read them. As he said, he would like to know what she really thought of him, but acknowledged sadly that it was most unlikely that he would ever find out.

man." He liked the Edwardian style of clothes, and was proud of a lounge suit that he had had his tailor make for him with a four-button single-breasted jacket. Norman Keevil, Michener's mining friend, said that he had never heard Roland say an unkind word about anyone, but his wife did not forgive or forget easily, and never hid her antipathy for John Diefenbaker.

It was Norah who sat in the Speaker's Gallery in the House of Commons and kept such a watchful eye on proceedings that she earned the somewhat derisory soubriquet of "Madame Speaker"; Erik Spicer was rather surprised to find her sitting beside her husband in the Speaker's Chambers when he went for his first interview after being appointed parliamentary librarian. She recognized the importance of the chairman's role in a parliamentary democracy and did much to raise its status in the order of precedence. When Roland Michener was asked which, of all the careers that he had had, had he enjoyed the most, he replied, without hesitation, "Being Speaker." There was a great sense of power, sitting in the high Chair above the tumult of the debates, keeping order and controlling the opposing forces so that the country could be ruled by the will of the people. Michener tried "to see that the debates were kept on track and arrived at conclusions, the business of the day thereby being done." He considered the Speaker's role to be "one of the most important functions in our whole system of government, becoming more important as time went on."

At first it was not taken too seriously, Michener said, and was often looked on as little more than a consolation prize for not getting into the Cabinet. As noted earlier, the Speaker ranked rather low on the totem pole, below all the ministers of the government who sat in front of him and obeyed his orders. But that changed, and Michener gave credit to "my wife's propaganda" for elevating the office so that now the Speaker came after the Governor General, the Prime Minister, and the Chief Justice and before all other ministers. Another change that occurred after his time in the Chair, although it had been abandoned in practice before he left, was that there should be no appeal against a Speaker's ruling; that gave him absolute control over the interpretation and application of the rules of procedure. Michener considered this "the basis of orderly debate and decision on legislation."

"It is clear," he said, "that the effectiveness of the House of Commons, in its most important role of providing legislation on all subjects of federal jurisdiction, is dependent on the Speaker's influence and capacity to keep the members to their task. [This means the Chair] is perhaps as important as any power of government." His successor, Marcel Lambert (who was also a Rhode Scholar for Alberta and was also at Hertford College) spoke of the Speakership as "a derailment of his political career," and Roland Michener recognized that it was probably not the ideal role for a younger person. A Speaker had to have common sense and some understanding of human nature and a certain amount of wit, and especially, Michener said, "the ability to calm and mollify the Members of Parliament"; these were the attributes of an older person like himself with some knowledge as to how the legislature and the government worked.

The Speaker had to have the confidence of both sides of the House of Commons if he was going to sit in any comfort in the Chair. Michener's role model was the British Speaker: "when he takes the Chair he leaves party prejudices and interests and does his job as one of the Members of the House of Commons, giving his rulings with the utmost impartiality and indifference to party interests." All four of his deputy Speakers were taken from the Chair and given portfolios in the government as ministers of the Crown, but Michener said that he would not have accepted such an appointment because it might reflect on his impartiality as Speaker; the same principle applied after he was defeated and was the reason he did not run again. He was very much in favour of a permanent or continuing Speaker, and once again he would follow the British system whereby a Speaker who had earned the respect of both sides of the House and the right to stay in the Chair would not be opposed (at least not by any party candidates) at the next election.

Roland Michener was greatly influenced by Oxford University and his years there as a Rhodes Scholar, and much of his style and manners were derived from that seminal experience; the same was true of Mike Pearson, although perhaps to a lesser degree. Both of them preferred understatement and eschewed bravado and exaggeration, and both liked the quips and rags of the college common rooms and dining halls. An example of Pearson's self-deprecating humour was at a time when his government was stumbling around and teetering on the brink of disaster: he dismissed an earnest young aide who warned him of an upcoming problem by saying, "We'll fall off that bridge when we come to it." In the same sense, Michener, after presenting (to the 1975 annual meeting of the Canadian Historical Association) a long and detailed account of all that he had done as Governor General, of all the innovations that he had made, ended with the line, "Posterity will doubtless conclude that mine was a 'reign' in which nothing much happened." Bob Hubbard felt that he must have had "his characteristic twinkle in his eye" when he made that remark.

As to his performance as Governor General, it was not the great events, such as the first head-of-state visits abroad, that Michener wanted to recall, but his pleasure in being able to present "a focal point for Canadian interests," and his assessment that he was "the only person above the political struggles of the parties and therefore a potential representative of the whole country politically." Just as he had harped on "impartiality" as being the main qualification for Speaker, so Michener emphasized political "neutrality" as an essential element for a governor general. He travelled extensively throughout Canada and visited as many Canadians as possible. He was sometimes disappointed at the lack of public interest in his official tours, although, when he showed the flag in the Arctic, the press made much of the occasion as an assertion of sovereignty: this was at a time when the United States was challenging Canada's claims in the Arctic and the American supertanker, *Manhattan*, navigated the North West Passage.

In retrospect, Michener was to marvel at the way that "two of the most important roles in our constitutional setup could fall into one man's lap, not by choice but by chance." He could have been made a minister in the Conservative government but by some quirk John Diefenbaker picked him for Speaker, although, as an Opposition member, he had paid very little attention to the rules of procedure in the House. His defeat in the 1962 election and Diefenbaker's refusal to appoint him to the Senate, which he wanted, opened the way for Mike Pearson to send him as Canadian High Commissioner to India in preparation for making him Governor General. But there was so much that could have prevented his being installed in the viceregal office. Pearson had a minority government. "His cabinet might have protested against appointing a man who had been a Conservative when there were plenty of good Liberals or ex-Liberals available," Michener said. Then there was General Vanier: if he had recovered his strength, he would have been a great Governor General during Centennial Year and that would probably have been the end of Michener's expectations. It was fate that was responsible for his career, and the *Toronto Star* put it best when it described Michener as "always one of fortune's favourites."

Yet he did not drift aimlessly on the sea of life. His boyhood ambition to follow his father into politics and the public service made him decide, as a young man, to reach his goal by becoming a lawyer. He was highly regarded in the legal profession, but there was nothing spectacular about him, no claims to be a whiz kid. It was a slow and stolid advance to the nation's capital, which had always been his objective, but he was in the right place and at the right time when the lightning struck. A good player, they say, makes the breaks, and if anyone could be said to be the architect of his own fortune, it would be Roly Michener.

A mountain in the Rockies was named for Michener; this was a signal honour because mountains are not usually named for living persons. However, the Province of Alberta made an exception as far as one of its most illustrious native sons was concerned. Premier Peter Lougheed named a prominent feature and a landmark in the upper valley of the North Saskatchewan River, Mount Michener at a ceremony on the lower slopes of this 8,350-foot peak. The date was August 26, 1979, and, although he was almost eighty years old, Roland Michener insisted on climbing to the top of "his mountain" and having his picture taken on the summit, thereby setting a record as the only person after whom a mountain was named who ever reached its peak.

At the last count, there were five schools that bore Roland Michener's name; they are in such places as Kanata, a suburb of Ottawa; South Porcupine in Northern Ontario; Saskatoon; Calgary; and Great Slave Lake in the Northwest Territories. Two parks were called after the former Governor General, one in his birthplace of Lacombe, Alberta, and the other on the campus of the University of Alberta in Edmonton.

Michener was the first Chancellor and Principal Companion of the Order of Canada, the first Commander of the Order of Military Merit, Prior for Canada and Knight of Justice of the Most Venerable Order of the Hospital of St. John of Jerusalem, and he has some twenty honourary doctorates of law and a half-dozen honourary fellowships. Of all the honours bestowed on him, the one that he prized the most was the Royal Victorian Chain, which was given by the Sovereign as a mark of esteem and affection. Michener was one of only two Canadians to be so honoured (the other was his predecessor as Governor General, Vincent Massey), and, as Michener pointed out, the latest list (1987) of holders of the chain showed that "all the deceased appear to have been heads of state, but at present we are more or less royal."

As he himself said, Roland Michener had an "open mind" on most questions, which made him a nonpartisan politician and a nonsectarian Christian. He had been born in a Methodist parsonage; his mother was a Presbyterian and his Michener ancestors were Quakers. He became an Anglican largely because of Norah, but found being an Anglican made little difference to his outlook on religion or life. He spoke of the doctrine of "as if," and said that to be a good Christian and observe the church's teachings, one could accept the probability of Almighty God, the Creator, and accept the possibility of the Father, the Son, and the Holy Spirit, the Virgin Birth, the Resurrection, and other parts of the Creed; "then in effect you don't have the comfort of absolute faith but you have the guidance of the past and an open mind for what we cannot fully understand or settle in this life, if you know what I mean."

Norah Michener's ashes rest in a niche in St. Bartholomew's Church across from Rideau Hall in Ottawa, and Roland Michener has willed that his should be put beside hers in that little Anglican church.

❧ INDEX ❧

Abbott, Douglas, 107
Abrahams, H.M., 9
Adeane, Sir Michael, 165
Agnew, Spiro, 193
Air Canada, 77
Alan, Carlton, 40
Albany Club, 54–56, 59–60, 64, 83, 102
Alberta, 2, 19–20, 19fn, 25–27, 30, 32, 37–41,
    47, 65, 91, 109, 112, 202, 228
Alberta House (Alberta Legislature), 22,
    24–26, 29, 31
Alberta and Great Waterways Railway
    Scandal, 24, 28
Algoma East by-election, 86
Amory, Lord, 106
Amsterdam, 187–188
Anaconda (mining company), 97–98
Anglican Church, 50, 231
Antwerp, 188
Arab, 117, 119
Archery Club, 4
Arctic, 196, 216, 229
Armistice, 38
Armstrong, Major James, 76
Art Gallery of Ontario, 50
Assiniboine, HMCS, 196
Atlantic provinces, 104
Atomic bomb, 70–71
Australia, 149, 178
Ayub Khan, General, 151

Bacon, Mac, 6
Baden-Powell, Robert, 34
Banff, Alberta, 15–16
Barker, Billy, 36
Beamsville, Ontario, 37–38
Beaudoin, René, 112–113, 126, 137
Beddoe, Alan, 170
Belgium, 187–191, 212
Bell, R.A. "Dick," 59, 120
Benelux, 187, 189–191, 192, 213
Bennett, R.B., 22, 24–25, 30, 54, 57
Bessborough, Lady, 168–169, 218
Bessborough, Lord, 168, 218
Bickle, Ed, 62
Bilingual, 92–93, 95, 155
Bishop, Billy, 36
Blackwell, Leslie, 55
Boissevan, Manitoba, 93
Bombay, 153
Bonaventure, HMCS, 119, 186
Bonnycastle, Richard "Dick," 6, 8–10
Borden, Sir Robert, 25, 27, 30 32, 36, 54, 214
Boucher, Russel, 86
Bourassa, Robert, 199

Boy Scouts, 34–35
Bracken, John, 59–60, 80, 82–83, 88
Brecher, Michael, 150
Britain, 40, 42, 77, 105, 117–120, 125, 150
British Columbia, 196, 210
British Commonwealth, 60, 89, 105, 125,
    157, 159, 164, 184, 214–215
British Empire, 29, 31, 159
British immigrants, 76-78
Broulan (mining company), 47
Brunt, William R., 139
Brussels, 189
Buckingham Palace, 165, 169, 216–217
Buffalo, New York, 75, 77
Burnham, Forbes, 185
Burns, General E.L.M., 117
Burwash Hall. See University of Toronto
Butler, Esmond, 161, 163, 165, 175–176,
    178–179, 185–186, 190, 192, 196–197,
    199, 201, 204–205, 209–210, 224
Byng, Lord, 197, 197fn, 200

CCF, 54, 57, 63, 66–69, 74, 81–82, 89, 100, 104,
    113, 123, 126, 132
CIDA (Canadian International Development
    Agency), 154
Cadina Tea Rooms, 3, 4
Calgary, 20, 22, 25, 28, 34–35, 47, 120, 230
Calgary Eye Opener, 30, 30fn
California, 25–26, 42
Callendar, Ontario, 53
Cambridge University, 7, 9, 221
Cameron, Colin, 113
Campney, Ralph, 119
Canada, 10, 37, 42–43, 71, 77–79, 93, 106,
    110–112, 118, 120, 134, 151, 153, 158,
    164, 179–180, 184, 186, 189–192,
    213–217, 229
    Order of Canada, 175, 207–210, 212
Canada Council, 170
Canadian dollar, 145
Canadian Encyclopedic Digest, 46
Canadian Institute of International Affairs
    (CIIA), 48, 105–106, 124, 223
Canadian Northern, 22
Canadian Pacific Railway, 109–110
Canadian Press, 55
Canmore, Alberta, 16
Caribbean, 184–187, 190, 192
Carleton by-election, 86
Carscallen, Allen, 17
Carscallen, S.N., 17
Carson, Sir Edward, 42
Carter, Kenneth, 148
Castonguay, Nelson, 123

Centennial, 160, 163, 165, 172, 176–177, 179–180, 182–183, 205, 207, 213, 219, 229
Chalmers, Floyd, 58
Chaudhuri, General Muchu, 151
Cherrier, A.G., 163, 165
Chevrier, Lionel, 122
Chief Running Antelope, 224
China, 150
Chou En-lai, 150
Christie, Mabel, 37, 49–51
Christmas, 26, 39, 73, 96, 203, 217, 220–221
Chubb, Frederick, 225–226
Churchill, Winston Spencer, 75
Citadel, 179, 197, 205–206
Clarke, H.G., 56
Closure, 111–112
Clovis, California, 41
Cochrane, Ontario, 75
Cockeram, Lieutenant-Colonel Alan, 57
Cody, Canon H.J., 51
Coldwell, M.J., 132
Colonial Club, 3, 4
Comfort, Charles, 6fn
Commonwealth. See British Common-wealth
Commonwealth Parliamentary Association (CPA), 142–143
Commonwealth Petroleum, 41
Communist Party, 63, 66, 69, 82, 84, 118
Congress, 143
Congress Party 150–151, 215
Conant, Gordon, 61
Conservative Party, 22, 24–25, 27–32, 36, 51, 54–63, 66–69, 72–74, 78, 81–82, 84–92, 99–101, 104, 107–109, 111, 113–116, 118, 120–125, 135, 137–138, 144–147, 197, 200, 229
Conscription, 30, 32, 36, 57
Co-operative Commonwealth Federation. See CCF
Cranston, Robert, 97
Cross, James, 198
Crown, 186, 198, 200, 202, 213, 215, 228
Crutwell, Dean C.R.M.F., 5–6

Das, Arup, 158
Davos, Switzerland, 7,
Day, Harold, 48–49
De Gaulle, Charles, 178–182
De Gaulle, Madame, 179
Dennison, William, 63, 65, 67, 81
Desta, Iskander, 174, 174fn
Dickens, Punch, 36
Diefenbaker, Edna, 139
Diefenbaker, John, 60, 71, 83–85, 90, 92, 103, 105, 109–110, 114, 116–118, 120–126, 129, 131–133, 135–137, 139–140, 143–148, 148fn, 150, 205, 208, 208fn, 210, 227, 229

Diefenbaker, Olive, 139–140, 147, 211
Dionne Quintuplets, 53
Disher, Anna Margaret, 15
Douglas, T.C. "Tommy," 147
Doukhobors, 39
Doylestown, Pennsylvania, 14
Drapeau, Jean, 173, 180, 199
Drew, George, 60–63, 65–68, 70–73, 75–78, 80–93, 102–103, 105, 108–109, 111, 113–117, 120, 122, 125, 226
Drew, Fiorenza, 93, 93fn, 114–115, 226
Drouin, Mark, 131, 143,
Duplessis, Maurice, 70–71, 84, 87, 90

Eberts, Chris, 179
Edinborough, Arnold, 213–214
Edmonton, 20–21, 24, 26–27, 33, 35–36, 199
Edmonton Journal, 216
Edwards, Bob, 30fn
Egypt, 117, 119–120
Eisenhower, Dwight D., 143
Eldon, Donald, 114
Elections
    Alberta, 21, 24, 28–32
    Federal, 56–57, 85, 88, 90, 97, 99–100, 102, 121–123, 132–133, 145–146, 183, 187, 199–200, 229
    Ontario, 61–63, 65–67, 80, 83, 146
Emery, Howard T., 37, 39
Emperor Haile Selassie, 173–176, 174fn, 193
Ethiopia, 174–175
Europe, 118
Expo 67, 160, 172–173, 176, 178, 204

FLQ (Front de Liberation du Québec), 198–199
Farthing, Jack, 6
Finlayson, Rod, 57–59
Fleming, Donald, 55, 58–59, 83, 85, 102, 108, 112, 117, 120–121, 129, 145
Fort McMurray, 24
France, 118–119
French, 9–10, 27, 35, 91–97, 128–129, 155, 167, 170, 172, 183
Forsey, Eugene, 184, 197, 203
Frost, Cecil, 59, 59fn, 62
Frost, Leslie, 59fn
Fulton, Davie, 111, 117, 120–121, 197

Gandhi, Indira, 151–153, 157
Gandhi, Mahatma M.K., 152
Gardiner, Fred, 55, 57, 59, 83
Gardiner, James G., 132
Geneva Conference, 150, 153
George, David Lloyd, 72
Germany, 8–10
Gestapo charge, 68–69
Gilson, Etienne, 94
Glasson, Edward and Minnie, 24
Globe and Mail, The, 85, 101, 123

Goudie, Miss, 27
Government House. *See* Rideau Hall
Governor General, 133–134, 172, 178,
     183–184, 186–187, 190–192, 194, 200,
     202–204, 212–215, 221–223, 229
Grand Trunk Pacific, 22
Graves, Robert, 4
Gray's Inn, 48
Green, Howard, 60, 111, 118, 140, 144
Gregory, Goldwyn, 45–46
Gregory, Colonel Phillips, 14
Gregory, W.R., 45–46
Gregory and Gregory, 45–47
Grits. *See* Liberal Party
Grosart, Allister, 116
Guyana, 184–185

Halifax, 119
Hamilton, Alvin, 135, 144
Hamilton, John, 130
Hamilton, W. McL. "Bill," 126
Hamilton, Ontario, 38
Hansard, 108, 121, 129, 138
Hanson, R.B., 57
Harris, Walter, 107–108, 112–113
Harvey, Alan Burnside, 37, 39, 44–45
Heeney, Arnold, 72, 123
Hees, George, 102
Heidelberg, 8
Heighington, Wilfrid, 62
Hepburn, Mitchell, 53, 55–56, 61, 66-67, 69,
     69fn, 72, 76
Herridge, H.W., 143
Hertford College, 2–3, 6, 8, 40, 43, 170, 228
Hicks, Douglas, 159
Hindi, 154–155, 157
Hiroshima, 70
Hoadley, George, 22, 25
Holdsworth, Sir William, 4, 5
Holland. *See* the Netherlands
Holmes, John, 124
Holten (war cemetery), 188–189, 213
Hopper, Harry, 58
House of Commons, 36, 57, 70, 75, 83, 92,
     97, 102, 105–110, 112–114, 118, 121,
     125–128, 131–134, 136–138, 140–145,
     170–171, 215, 227–229
Howard, Frank, 137
Howe, C.D., 70, 77, 108–112
Hubbard, R.H. "Bob," 206fn, 210, 217–218,
     229
Huguenots, 12, 14

Ice hockey, 6, 7, 43, 221
Ilsley, J.L., 70–71
Imperial Oil, 39
India, 105–106, 149–150, 153–159, 162–163,
     172, 183, 193, 215, 229
Indo-China Commissions, 150, 153

Israel, 119
Italy, 193

Jackman, H.R., 56, 158–159
Jagan, Cheddi, 185–186
Jamaica, 184
Jogging, 224–225
Johnson, Daniel, 173, 179
Johnson, Madame Reine, 173, 179
Johnson, Edward, 93fn
Johnson, Lyndon B., 118, 179
Jolliffe, E.B. "Ted," 48–49, 48fn, 52, 54–55,
     63, 66–69, 82, 99–100
Jonasson, Jonas, 34

Kane, Edward William Scott "Ted," 27, 37
Kashmir, 151
Keevil, Dr. Norman B., 97–99, 227
Keevil, Dr. Norman B. Jr., 99
Kennedy, Major General Howard, 74
Kennedy, Tom, 72
Kilbourn, William, 110, 110fn, 113
Kimberley Clark, 48
King Baudoin, 188–189
King Edward VII, 158–159
King Juan Carlos, 212
King, W.L. Mackenzie, 54fn, 56–57, 61, 70,
     72, 75–76, 85–87, 197fn, 200, 208
Kingsmere, 130
Knowles, Stanley, 126, 132, 143
Kosygin, Alexei, 151
Kota, Maharao of, 150

Labour Progressive Party. *See* Communist
     Party
Lacombe, Alberta, 16, 230
Lady Margaret Hall, Oxford, 2
Lambert, Marcel, 147, 228
La Marsh, Judy, 166, 177, 211–212
Lamport, Allan, 63
Lang, Daniel Webster, 46–49, 53, 55
Lang, Michener, 47–50, 53–55, 97, 223
Langford, George, 36
Laporte, Pierre, 198–199
Laurier, Sir Wilfrid, 18fn, 20, 25, 29, 36, 56,
     103
Laval University, 95–96
Law, Richard "Dick," 4
Law Society of Upper Canada. *See* Ontario
     Bar
Lawrence, Leslie, 96
Lawrence, Wendy. *See* Michener, Wendy
Le Devoir, 96
Leger, Jules, 160fn, 209, 212, 217–218, 222
Leger, Gabrielle Carmel, 160fn, 218
Lesage, Jean, 173
Lett, Sherwood, 8
Lewis, David, 54, 201, 201fn
Liberal Party, 20–22, 24–25, 28–29, 31–32,
     36, 40, 51, 53, 57, 61, 63, 66–69, 72, 74,

85–86, 88–90, 99–101, 104, 108–113, 117, 120, 122–124, 131, 136–138, 143–145, 147, 162, 183–184, 200–201, 229
Lieutenant-Governor, 202–203
Livingstone, David, 15
Lochnan, Carl, 164–165
Lok Sabha, 154–155
London, 5, 40, 77, 149–150, 163–165, 168, 224
Long Beach, California, 26
Lord's Day Alliance, 18, 18fn
Lougheed, Senator James, 25
Lougheed, Peter, 230
Love, G.A., 17, 32
Luxembourg, 187, 189–191, 212

MacAdams, Roberta, 31fn
Macdonald, Sir John A., 56, 110, 206
Macdonald, Lorne, 72
MacDonald Malcolm, 4
Macdonnell, James M., 55, 56–58, 102, 115
Macdowell, John, 84
MacKay, Thomas, 206, 206fn
Mackenzie, HMCS, 196
Mackenzie, Alex, 62
Mackenzie, N.A.M. "Larry," 50
MacLeod, Alex A., 66, 69
Macmillan, Harold, 107
MacPherson, Murdoch, 59, 61
Madras, 153, 155
Magdalen College, 44
Maheux, Abbé Arthur, 94–95
Manion, Robert, 56, 59
Manitoba, 19, 41, 44, 51, 59, 148
Manitoba Commission on Finance, 148
Marchand, Jean, 198
Margaree, HMCS, 213
Maritain, Jacques, 94, 226
Martin, Paul, 106, 131, 137, 143–144, 156, 159, 161–162, 175, 179, 186
Massey, Vincent, 132, 165, 167, 169, 171–172, 177, 177fn, 207–208, 218, 230
Massey Foundation Fellowship, 3, 44
Matthews, Beverly, 55
Maxwell automobile, 29
McCann, James J., 75
McCaul, Ronnie, 6
McClung, Nellie, 30
McCullagh, George, 85
McKinney, Louise, 31, 31fn
McKinnon, Don, 165, 167, 186, 195, 203–206, 210, 222
McNaughton, General A.G.L., 102
McQuesten, Thomas Baker, 76
McRuer, James, 123
Medicine Hat, Alberta, 197
Meighen, Arthur, 57, 59
Memorandum for Wives of Members, 133–135, 204, 211

Mennonites, 12–14
Michener, Anna Marie, 16, 17fn, 18, 27, 54fn
Michener, Charles Edward, 17, 17fn, 23
Michener, Daniel Roland, 41–42, 47, 49–52, 54, 57, 91–97, 99, 116, 148–149, 160–161, 205, 220, 223–231
  birth, 16
  childhood, 19–27, 29, 35
  education, 1–10, 26–27, 33–40
  Governor General, 11, 34–35, 52, 162–203, 207, 209–219, 221–222
  High Commissioner, 11, 97, 149–159, 162
  law, 11, 42, 44–49 ,52–53, 97, 104–105, 125
  Member of Parliament, 102–109, 111–114, 117, 120–121
  Ontario government, 70–80, 146
  party politics, 22, 28, 31–32, 55–56, 58–69, 81–89, 99–101, 120–124, 147
  Rhodes scholarship, 1–10, 27, 39–45, 48–49, 99, 106, 156–157, 164, 228
  Speaker, 11, 92, 126–133, 135–147, 219
Michener, Diana, 94–96, 100, 223, 225–226
Michener, Edward, 9, 11, 15–18, 26, 36, 39–42, 44, 47, 54fn, 122
  Mayor of Red Deer, 19, 21, 24
  provincial politics, 21, 24–33
  Senator, 20, 32–33, 38, 41–42, 47, 53–54, 92
Michener, Grace Eileen, 17fn
Michener, Jacob, 14–15
Michener, James A., 14
Michener, Joan, 51–52, 94–96, 225
Michener, John, 12, 13
Michener, John Victor, 17fn, 18, 23
Michener, Joseph, 13, 14
Michener, Joseph Stanley, 17fn, 31, 38
Michener, Margaret Ruth, 17fn, 21, 23
Michener, Marion Louise, 17fn, 23, 47
Michener, Mary Edith, 15, 18–19, 22–23, 26–27, 30–33, 36–39, 41, 47
Michener, Norah, 49–52, 93–95, 99–100, 105–106, 114, 130, 133–135, 139–141, 144, 147–149, 152, 157–158, 162–167, 170, 177–181, 183, 185, 188–189, 191–193, 195–196, 203–204, 211, 216–218, 222, 225–227, 226fn, 231,
Michener, Olive Rose, 17fn, 26
Michener, Sarah, 13
Michener, Wendy, 94–95, 225
Michener, William, 13
Michener Hill, 18, 22–23, 32–34, 37, 39, 41
Middle East, 119, 186
Middle Temple, 5, 40, 42–44
Montreal, 87, 91–92, 104, 166, 176, 178, 180, 198–199
Montreal Star, 25
Moody, Maryon. See Pearson, Maryon
Moore, John T., 22, 22fn

Moot Club, 42
Morocco, 193
Mount Michener, 230
Murchison, Clint, 111
Murray, W.E. Gladstone, 66, 68
Murren, Switzerland, 7

Nasser, Colonel Gamal Abdel, 117–120
NDP, 137, 143, 147, 201, 201fn
NORAD (North American Air Defence
    Agreement), 143
Nehru, Jawarharlal, 106, 149–150, 152,
    152fn, 154, 157
Nepal, 163
Netherlands, the, 187–189, 191, 194,
    212–213
New Delhi, 97, 149–152, 155–157, 159,
    162–163, 166, 172, 226
New Democratic Party. see NDP
New York State, 75
New Zealand, 164
Newfoundland, 196
Niagara (Falls) 14–15, 75–76
Nicholson, J.R. "Jack," 151
Nicholson, Patrick, 144
Nicolet-Yamaska by-election, 87
Nixon, Harry, 61, 63, 66
Nixon, Richard, 222
Nobel Peace Prize, 117, 131, 221
North Atlantic Alliance, 105
North Atlantic Treaty Organization (NATO),
    118–119
North Bay, Ontario, 53
North West Territories, 19, 26, 195, 230,
Northern Ontario, 46–47, 75, 86, 92, 97, 104,
    110, 230
Northern Ontario Pipe Line Corporation,
    111
Noseworthy, J.W., 57

Okanagan, British Columbia, 26
O'Leary, Grattan, 115
Ontario, 25–26, 40–41, 46, 49, 58, 60–61, 69,
    71, 74, 75, 77–80, 88–89, 92, 108, 146
Ontario Bar, 42, 44–47, 49
Ontario College of Art, 95
Ontario House, London, 76
Ontario Hydro-electric Power Commission,
    73, 79–80
Ontario Legislature, 45, 55–56, 61, 66,
    68–69, 81, 83, 92, 158, 160
Ontario Northland Railway, 73
Ontario Public Service Commission, 73
Ontario Research Commission, 74
Ontario, California, 26
Osgoode Hall, 45
Ottawa, 11, 19–21, 32, 42, 47, 52, 70–71, 77,
    85, 88, 100, 104–105, 108, 113–114, 120,
    123, 125, 130, 140, 148–149, 151–152,
    157, 161–163, 165–166, 170, 178–180,
    189, 197–199, 201, 203, 205, 216,
    219–222, 231
Ottawa Progressive Conservative Conven-
    tion, 83–85, 120
Ottawa, HMCS, 213
Oxford (University), 1–11, 35, 40, 42–44, 49,
    63, 91, 100, 167, 221, 228
Oxford "Blue," "Half-blue," 9, 34, 43, 47,
    106

Pakistan, 105, 151, 157, 183
Pandit, Vijayalakshmi, 152
Pallett, John Cameron, 138
Paris, 91, 118, 140
Parliament, 91, 102, 104–105, 110, 114,
    116–117, 119, 121–122, 124–126,
    128–130, 132–133, 135, 137, 140,
    143–144, 146, 161, 167, 169, 171, 174,
    176, 198–200, 208, 215, 227–228
Parliamentary Press Gallery, 129–130
    Press Gallery Dinner, 171–172, 200
Patterson, Eliza Catherine, 14
Pearson, Geoffrey, 51, 158, 194, 220–221
Pearson, Lester Bowles "Mike," 2–11, 44,
    50–52, 77, 85–86, 102, 106, 117–119,
    131–133, 137–138, 143–144, 146–147,
    149, 152, 156–157, 160–162, 165–167,
    173, 175–176, 178, 181–183, 197–198,
    201, 204–205, 208, 210, 212, 219–221,
    228–229
Pearson, Maryon, 51–52, 106, 166–167, 173,
    178, 181, 211
Pearson, Vaughan, 11
Penn, William, 12, 13
Pennsylvania, 12–14
Persepolis, 192–193
Peters, Janet. See Michener, Norah
Philadelphia, 13, 14
Pick, A.J., 189
Pickersgill, J.W., 191
Pilly, Kannim, 159
Pincher Creek, Alberta, 39
Pipeline Debate, 102, 104, 109, 110fn,
    111–114, 121–122
Pitblado, E.B., 6
Pitfield, Grace, 166
Pitfield, Michael, 166
Poland, 153
Pontifical Institute of Mediaeval Studies,
    94–95
Porritt, Arthur E., 164
Port Hope (Conference), 57–59, 61–62, 83,
    102
Port of Spain, Trinidad, 186
Porter, Dana, 55, 77
Potter, Robert S., 47
Prairies, 19
Presbyterian Church, 231
Preserver, HMCS, 187–189, 213
Prince Bernhard, 172, 187

Prince Philip, 164, 177–178, 182, 193, 205, 214
Princess Anne, 193
Princess Margriet, 189
Progressives, 59–60
Progressive Conservative (PC) Party. *See* Conservative Party

Quaker, 12–14, 45–47, 170, 231
Quebec, 9, 25, 41, 58, 70, 83–89, 92, 94, 104, 143, 147, 170, 173, 178–180, 198–199, 201, 222
Quebec City, 94–95, 132, 161, 178, 187, 197
Queen Beatrix, 194
Queen Elizabeth, 126–127, 162–164, 167, 172–173, 177–179, 182–184, 186–187, 191, 193, 214–216
Queen Juliana, 172, 177, 187, 189
Queen Mary, 99
Queen Victoria, 159
Queen's Own Rifles, 119–120
Queen's Park. *See* Ontario Legislature
Queen's University, 223
Question Period, 135–137

Rea, Charles, 87
Reciprocity, 25
Red Deer, Alberta, 16–17, 20–22, 25–27, 29, 31–35, 37, 40–42, 170
Redpath, John, 206fn
Regina, 19
Reid, Escott, 156
Rhadhakrishnan, S., 158
Rhodes scholarship. *See* Michener, Daniel Roland
Richler, Mordechai, 169–170
Rickets, Charles Moore, 49
Rideau Club, 52
Rideau Hall, 133–134, 163, 165–166, 168–170, 172, 174–178, 180–183, 198–199, 201–207, 206fn, 211–212, 216–218, 220–226, 231
Robarts, John, 173
Robertson, Gordon, 166, 197, 209–210
Roblin, Duff, 148
Rockies, 15–16, 19, 39, 230
Rocky Mountain House, 31–32
Rohr, Joan. *See* Joan Michener
Rohr, Professor Donald, 95–96
Roland, Anna Margaret, 14, 16
Roland, Daniel C., 14, 16
Roman Catholic Church, 20, 94–95
Ronning, Chester, 150, 156
Rooney, James, 88, 99–100, 102, 123
Roosevelt, Franklin Delano, 75
Ross, Lieutenant-Colonel A.J., 84
Ross, Douglas, 87
Rowe, Earl, 115, 117, 120
Rowell, Newton Wesley, 44–45
Royal Air Force (RAF), 35–37, 36fn

Royal Canadian Mounted Police (RCMP), 123
Royal Victorian Chain, 230
Rutherford, Alex, 21, 24

Sabourin, Ivan, 85
St. Bartholomew's Church, 231
St. David's, Toronto (provincial riding), 62–63, 65, 67, 69, 81
St. Hilda's, Oxford, 2
St. John's College, Oxford, 4
St. Laurent, Louis, 70, 85–88, 99–100, 106, 109–110, 112, 118, 122–123, 126, 129–130, 207–208
St. Mary Magdalene Church, 50–51
St. Moritz, 7
St. Paul's Church, 50–51
St. Paul's riding, Toronto, 87–88, 99–101, 103, 122–123, 145–146, 148
Salsberg, J.B., 66, 69
San Joaquim Valley, California, 41–42
Saskatchewan, 19, 59, 230
Saturday Night, 213–214
Saunders, Robert, 79–80
Sauvé, Jeanne, 212, 218
Schatz, Diana. *See* Michener, Diana
Schatz, Roy E., 96
Schreyer, Edward Richard "Ed," 172, 212, 218
Schreyer, Lily, 218
Senate, 127, 130–131, 141, 143, 146–147, 161, 169, 184, 211, 215, 229
Shaddinger, Anna, 13, 14
Shah of Iran, 191–193
Sharp, Mitchell, 187, 190–192, 194, 214
Shastri, Lal Bahadur, 150–152, 157
Shastri Institute, 158
Shaw, Robert F., 173
Sheard, Terry, 44
Shepherd, Mr., 39
Shiraz, Iran, 192
Sifton, Arthur, 24–25, 28, 31
Sifton, Sir Clifford, 24
Simultaneous interpretation, 128–130
Singh, Hookam, 154
Singh, Swaran, 153
Sir George Williams University, 184–185
Sisters of Jesus Mary, 94
Smith, Arnold, 157
Smith, Sidney, 58, 120, 124, 142
Social Credit Party, 100, 104, 132, 147
Socialists. *See* CCF
Sorbonne, 91
Soviet Union, 117–118, 151
Spanish flu epidemic, 2, 2fn, 37–38
Speaker, 112–113, 126, 129–130, 135–137, 139–147, 170–171, 227–229
Spicer, Erik, 137, 227
Stanfield, Robert, 198, 200
Star Weekly, 213, 218

Starr, Mike, 116, 126
Steele, G.G.E. "Ernie," 163–164, 166, 212
Stevenson, Sir William, 106
Stewart, Walter, 211, 213, 218
Stornoway, 114
Strong, Maurice, 154
Suez Crisis, 117–122, 131
Sunday School, 34
Sussex Drive, 24, 147–148, 202
Sylvan Lake, Alberta, 35
Symington, H.J., 77

Tamil, 155
Tashkent, 151
Taxation, Royal Commission, 148
Teck Corporation, 98–99, 148, 223
Teck Hughes, 98–99
Teheran, 193
Television, 127
Temagami, 97–98
Temagami (mining company), 97
Temiskaming, Ontario, 75
Tennis, 11, 34, 85, 105, 225
Thomas, Margaret, 50
Thompson, Robert N., 147, 174–175, 174fn
Thorson, J.T., 138
Thorvaldson, G.S., 84
Tilley, W.N., 49, 52
Timmins, Ontario, 47
Tories. See Conservative Party
Toronto, 11, 37, 42–45, 48, 50, 56, 59, 69, 77,
    80–81, 85, 91, 96, 100, 104–105, 114,
    122–123, 138, 158–159, 219, 222, 225
Toronto Board of Trade, 48
Toronto Conservatory of Music, 51, 93
Toronto Institute of Medical Technology,
    96
Toronto Lawyers' Club, 48
Toronto Star, 68, 213, 229
Trades and Labour Council, 58
Trans-Canada Airlines. See Air Canada
Trans-Canada PipeLine, 102, 109–112
Trans-Ocean Airways, 76–77
Trinidad and Tobago, 184–186
Trudeau, Pierre Elliott, 93, 106, 183–184,
    187, 189–190, 194, 198–199, 200–202,
    209–210, 212, 216–217, 221–222
Turner Valley, 41
Tweedsmuir, Lord, 168

Union Government, 32, 36
Union Nationale, 84–85, 87
United Empire Loyalists, 2, 14
United Nations, 106, 117–119, 152
United Nations Emergency Force (UNEF),
    117–121, 131, 186
United States, 25, 60, 80, 108, 112, 118, 126,
    145, 230

University of Alberta, 2, 33–35, 39–40, 63,
    199, 230
University of British Columbia, 93
University of Calgary, 158
University of Manitoba, 58
University of Toronto, 11, 36, 38, 44, 50–52,
    93, 96–97, 120, 124
University of the West Indies, 185–186

Vancouver, 51, 93, 105, 123, 225
Vanier, Georges Philias, 160–161, 165,
    167–169, 211, 217, 229
Vanier, Jean, 166
Vanier, Pauline, 160, 160fn, 165–167, 205,
    207, 211, 217
Verigin, Peter, 39
Vietnam War, 153

Wahn, Ian, 144, 146
Walker, David, 55, 60
Walwyn, Arthur, 124
Wanless, Mrs., 27
War Measures Act, 198–199
Washington, 77, 108, 143, 149
Waskasoo Creek, 23, 34
Waugh, Evelyn, 65fn
Welland, Ontario, 15
Welliver, Robert, 28, 31
West (Western provinces), 19–20, 23, 29–30,
    38, 44, 93, 104, 147
Westminster, 72
White, Dr. Paul Dudley, 161
Whitton, Charlotte, 58
Willan, Healy, 51
Willingdon, Lord, 218
Willis, Eric, 51
Willis, Norah Evangeline. See Michener,
    Norah
Willis, Robert, 51, 93
Willis, Sarah Jane, 51, 93,
Wilson, Ernest, 41
Wilson, Melville "Mivvie," 42
Windsor Castle, 163–165, 182
Winnipeg, 149
Winnipeg Convention, 58–61, 120
World Bank, 220
World War One, 29–30, 36, 38, 41, 54
World WarTwo, 57, 68–71, 75, 80, 165, 188
Wrong, Professor G.M., 44

York South by-election, 57
York University, 226
Young Conservative Association, 64
Yukon, 195

Zonda, M., 177, 177fn, 180–181